Narrative Parallels to the New Testament

SOCIETY OF BIBLICAL LITERATURE
Resources for Biblical Study

Edited by
Bernard Brandon Scott

Number 22
Narrative Parallels to the New Testament

Compiled and Edited by
FRANCIS MARTIN

NARRATIVE PARALLELS TO THE NEW TESTAMENT

Compiled and Edited by
Francis Martin

Scholars Press
Atlanta, Georgia

Narrative Parallels to the New Testament

© 1988
The Society of Biblical Literature

LIBRARY OF CONGRESS
Library of Congress Cataloging-in-Publication Data
Martin, Francis, 1930-
  Narrative parallels to the New Testament.

  (Resources for Biblical study/Society of Biblical
Literature ; no. 22)
    Bibliography: p.
    Includes index.
    1. Bible. N.T.--Relation to the Old Testament.
2. Rabbinical literature--Relation to the New Testament.
3. Greek literature--Relation to the New Testament.
4. Narration in the Bible. 5. Narration (Rhetoric)
I. Title. II. Series: Resources for Biblical ; no. 22.
BS2387.M37   1988   225.6   88-38010
ISBN 1-55540-285-5
ISBN 1-55540-259-3 (pbk.)

Printed in the United States of America
on acid-free paper

DEDICATION

This book is dedicated to the Faculty and Students of the Ecole Biblique et Archéologique Française in Jerusalem with whom I spent five fruitful years learning and teaching.

ACKNOWLEDGMENTS

I thank the following publishers for their permission in using excerpted material for this book. In each instance of use, I attribute the appropriate source:

Harvard University Press for the Loeb Classical Library (full acknowledgment is listed at the end of this book); Soncino Press for *Talmud Babli, Derek Ereṣ/Rabbah*, and various *Midrashim*; Johns Hopkins University Press for Edelstein, E. and L., *Asclepius: A Collection and Interpretation of the Testimonies*, 1945; Yale University Press for Braude, W. (ed.), *Midrash on the Psalms*, Vol. 13 (1959) and *Pesikta Rabbati*, Vol. 28 (1968); Doubleday for Charlesworth, J.H. (ed.), *The Old Testament Pseudepigrapha*, Vol. 2, 1985; Scholars Press for Tiede, D., *The Charismatic Figure as Miracle Worker* (SBL Diss. Ser., 1), 1972; Magnes Press, Hebrew University, for Fraenkel, J., "Bible Verses Quoted in Tales of the Sages," and Safrai, S., "Tales of the Sages in the Palestinian Tradition and the Babylonian Talmud," in J. Heinemann, D. Noy (eds.), *Studies in Aggadah and Folk-Literature* (Scripta Hierosolymitana, 22), 1971; Oxford Center for Postgraduate Studies for Vermes, G., "Ḥanina ben Dosa," *JJS* I, 23 (1972); Pontifical Biblical Institute for Fitzmyer, J., *The Genesis Apocryphon of Qumran Cave 1* (2nd ed., Biblica et Orientalia, 18A), 1971; Consejo Superior de Investigaciones Cientificas for Díez-Macho, A., *MS Neophyti I*, 1968-79; Routledge and Kegan Paul, Ltd., for Hadas, M. and Smith M., *Heroes and Gods* (Religious Perspectives, 13), 1965; Oxford University Press for Danby, H., *The Mishnah*, 1933; SPCK for Danby, H., *Tractate Sanhedrin, Mishnah and Tosefta*, 1919; Penguin, Ltd., for Scott-Kilvert, I. (tr.), *Plutarch, The Age of Alexander*, 1986.

CONTENTS

PREFACE

This collection of narratives and anecdotes has been assembled to provide scholars and students of the New Testament with a handy resource in consulting comparative narrative material often referred to but seldom given *in extenso*. Rather than give only those texts which are most frequently alleged, I have made a wide selection so that the reader may experience for him/herself the literary atmosphere which produced the texts. The material has been restricted to that which is geographically and chronologically closest to the NT milieu.

The four indices provide various possibilities for consultation. The first index gives a list of subjects contained in the stories or treated in the Introduction. The second lists NT texts that are referred to in one or another story. Another index, by author and work, usually giving a date for the author, allows for easy access to literature referred to in the commentaries, etc. A fourth index gives the proper names appearing in the stories.

The accent has been placed on short narrative material comparable to the pericopes in the Synoptics and Acts and, where they exist, to those in the Fourth Gospel. Extension of the collection's scope to include, for instance, voyage narratives or material usually adduced in a study of Wisdom Christology would have made the collection unwieldy.

I began work on this collection during the years 1973-1978 while teaching and doing research at the Ecole Biblique et Archéologique Française in Jerusalem. I decided to gather the actual texts of the stories together as the result of a casual suggestion made by my friend John Strugnell of Harvard, who was living at the Ecole and working on the Qumran material. Since then, many colleagues and friends have asked that the collection be published. I am glad that I am finally able to make the material available. In work of this sort, there are bound to be shortcomings; either something is overlooked, or the importance of something was not appreciated when it was omitted. I would welcome suggestions which would make any future edition of this collection more useful and efficient. In the words of the novelist Laurence Sterne, but with a different nuance, I, too, would invite the reader to "halve this matter amicably."

In a long list of friends who have encouraged this work, three stand out for particularly grateful mention. First, William Kurz, S.J., of Marquette University, checked the Hellenistic material, brought the research up to date, and made many valuable suggestions. Secondly, Mrs. Cathleen MacDougall, Ph.D., typed and retyped the material into the computer and helped with the indices. Thirdly, Miss Laura D. Millman, J.D., checked the whole work over carefully, making it a more accurate research tool for which I am, and I am sure the reader will be, grateful.

Mother of God Community
P.O. Box 2206
Gaithersburg, MD 20879

Dominican House of Studies
487 Michigan Avenue, N.E.
Washington, D.C. 20017

OLD TESTAMENT STORIES

RABBINIC STORIES

THE EARLIEST SAGES

A Series of Stories about R Hillel and R Shammai

THE FIRST GENERATION OF TANNAIM
APPROXIMATELY 1-90 C.E.

A Catena of Stories Concerning R Ḥanina

THE SECOND GENERATION OF TANNAIM
APPROXIMATELY 90-130 C.E.

THE THIRD GENERATION OF TANNAIM
APPROXIMATELY 130-160 C.E.

THE FOURTH GENERATION OF TANNAIM
APPROXIMATELY 160-200 C.E.

A Series of Stories About R Judah the Prince and the Emperor Antoninus

HELLENISTIC STORIES

WONDER STORIES TOLD IN CONNECTION WITH EMPERORS AND NOTABLES

ANECDOTES TOLD IN CONNECTION WITH EMPERORS AND NOTABLES

WONDER STORIES ABOUT PHILOSOPHERS AND OTHER WISE MEN

*Three Collections of Wonderful Things Reported About
Pythagoras*

ANECDOTES RECOUNTING SAYINGS OF PHILOSOPHERS AND WISE MEN

Examples of Apollonius' Wisdom

STORIES ABOUT WONDERS WORKED BY
GODS AND HEROES

Various Testimonies to the Healing Power of Asclepius

INTRODUCTION

The Collection

There are three classes of material in this collection: "Old Testament," "Rabbinic," and "Hellenistic." The Old Testament section contains various short pericopes which recount the activity of some heroes of Israel's past: Abraham, Moses, Elias and others. These were selected because of their aptitude for literary comparison with NT stories about Jesus. Though the selection is limited, it serves to corroborate the widely held view that the closest literary resemblance to the Gospel stories is to be found in the Elijah-Elisha cycle. The OT narratives are presented along with other narratives of the same event in the Jewish tradition in order to illustrate the ancient practice of interpreting an event by retelling it.[1] The presentation allows the reader to trace the manner in which successive generations actualized the text by bringing it into their own context. It also permits comparison between various ways of retelling and reinterpreting a narrative. For instance, we can see that the narratives which reflect Semitic literary conventions differ, in ways that I will discuss, from those which are more indebted to a Hellenistic mode of narration. Though language is not the primary factor which makes for these differences, it is often significant. For that reason, I have indicated the language of some of the works not likely to be known by beginners in the field. When two languages are listed, the first indicates the original language and the second, the language of the version when the original text is lost or fragmentary.

The next part of the collection, entitled "Rabbinic," contains anecdotes told of various religious leaders in Israel. The stories are classified according to the probable date of the protagonist named in the account using the designations, "Early Sages,"

---

[1] See, I. Heinemann, *Darkê ha Aggada*, 3rd ed. (Jerusalem: Masada, 1970). In his study of Rabbinic exegesis, Heinemann distinguishes between "creative history" and "creative philology." By the former, he means an interpretive retelling of the event; by the latter, the process by which a meaning is drawn out by "etymology," association, etc.

"First Generation," etc., proposed by H. Strack.[2] It is not rare to
find the same story, saying, or trait attributed to different
Rabbinic figures. To take but two examples, the reader may
compare R 88 and R 159 or R 167 and R 168. Of course, this
makes dating the material very difficult. I have opted for a middle road, trying to avoid the extremes of thoroughgoing skepti-
cism and naive optimism, while leaving the question of more
exact dating open to further study.[3] When we have a number of
stories about one person which contribute to a consistent image
of that person, we may be moderately optimistic in accepting
the attribution of tradition. In other cases, we must apply more
general norms. Actually, from a literary point of view, it suffices
to establish a *terminus a quo* for a story by tracing its earliest
attribution and paying attention to its stylistic features. The tendency over the centuries, verifiable in the material presented, is
toward the imaginative, symbolic and fantastic. Some of these
later stories are retained to give the student examples of this
tendency. A few random instances would be: R 74; R 83; R 94;
R 97; R 104.

In general, we may say that the Gospel pericopes bear a
closer stylistic resemblance to the Rabbinic stories than to any
other body of literature. In addition, we have a "synoptic problem" in that multiple narratives of the same event use very similar wording and proceed by way of "movable blocks" present in
one narrative and not in another. Some of these "synoptic" narratives are given in parallel columns to facilitate study, for example, R 72 and R 73; R 75 and R 76. In contrast to the Gospel
narratives, the Rabbinic stories, whether they exist singly or in
catenae or cycles, are not told primarily for the sake of portray-
ing the protagonist. They serve rather to illustrate or embellish
a particular haggadic or halakic point.[4]

The third part of the collection is termed "Hellenistic" and

---

[2] See his *Introduction to the Talmud and Midrash* (New York: Meridian Books, 1963).

[3] This aspect of Rabbinic studies is one that is receiving a good deal of scholarly attention today. See, for instance: A. Saldarini, " 'Form Criticism' of Rabbinic Literature," *JBL* 96 (1977) 257-74; D. Ben-Amos, *Narrative Form in the Haggadah. Structural Analysis* (Unpublished Dissertation, Indiana University, 1967) (Ann Arbor: University Microfilms Inc.); and the extensive work of Jacob Neusner.

[4] Thus, E. Urbach, *The Sages. Their Concepts and Beliefs* (ET Jerusalem: Hebrew University, 1975) 116-17, can make the following observation: "An outstanding feature of the miracle stories in Rabbinic literature is the fact that the personality of the miracle-worker is not emphasized . . . . This point established a difference of principle between stories and the tales about the miracles of Jesus, whose entire purpose is to accentuate his might and power."

deals with stories about emperors, gods, heroes, and sages. This material allows the reader to compare an important literary and cultural milieu into which the Gospel was brought and from which Jewish culture had already borrowed. On the level of literary discourse, the resemblances between these narratives and those of the Gospels are not very great. There are, however, other considerations, such as structure, motif, and certain forms of literary convention, which must taken into account in determining possible contact and influence.[5] Only in Hellenistic culture do we find Biography of a type that can be compared with the Gospels. The dating of this material is easier because of the individualistic manner in which it is transmitted. In a Hellenistic milieu, each writer tends to leave his or her personal stamp on the literary production.

There is a fourth category of material which deserves consideration, namely the NT apocryphal literature. I did not include the narratives from this literature for two reasons. First, in order to save space and, secondly, because much of the relevant materials is readily available in the collection of Edgar Hennecke.[6] The most useful comparisons are with the apocryphal Infancy Gospels, which I suspect may all derive from one original cycle. A handy collection of this material with a Spanish translation can be found in the work of Aurelio de Santos.[7] It is interesting to observe that Paul Achtemeier has established the fact that no miracles are attributed to the adult Jesus in the apocryphal material before the 5/6th century *Acts of Matthias and Andrew*.[8] This seriously weakens the proposal that the Gospel material developed in a traceable "trajectory."

Format

The stories are numbered consecutively with a designation to indicate in what part of the collection they are found. Thus,

[5] These features are considered by V. Robbins in his work, *Jesus the Teacher* (Philadelphia: Fortress Press, 1984).

[6] *New Testament Apocrypha*, re-ed. W. Schneemelcher (ET Philadelphia: Westminster Press, 1959/64).

[7] *Los Evangelios Apócrifos* (Biblioteca de los Autores Cristianos, 148) (Madrid: 3rd edition, 1975). See also: S. Grebaut, *Les Miracles de Jésus. Texte éthiopien publié et traduit* (Patriologia Orientalia, 12/4) (Paris: Firmin-Didot, 1917); P. Peeters, *Evangiles Apocryphes*. Vol. II, *L'Evangile de l'enfance* (Paris: Picard, 1914). See also R. Funk, *New Gospel Parallels* (Philadelphia: Fortress Press, 1985).

[8] P. Achtemeier, "Jesus and Disciples as Miracle Workers in the Apocryphal New Testament," in E. Schüssler Fiorenza (ed.), *Aspects of Religious Propaganda in Judaism and Early Christianity* (University of Notre Dame Center for the Study of Judaism and Christianity, 2) (Notre Dame University, 1976) 149-86, esp. p. 161.

the Old Testament stories, numbered 1-55, are preceded by
"OT"; the Rabbinic stories, numbered 56-173 are preceded by
"R"; and the Hellenistic stories, numbered 174-294, are preceded by "H". Each story is given a title, and its source is indicated, accompanied by a reference to an original language
edition except when it is a question of the text of the OT and the
targums. When a translation is used, that is also noted. Sometimes I have slightly modified these translations in order to high-
light a feature of structure or vocabulary in the original text
which is important for comparison with the NT. I have provided a very literal translation of the OT texts in order to help
those students who do not read Hebrew to have a sense of some
of the stylistic features of Hebrew necessarily omitted in more
fluent translations.

When a title is preceded by a "(1)", "(2)", etc., this indicates
that the narrative is found in a series of stories part of which at
least is being presented in the collection itself. Some examples
would be: R 120-R 123; R 159-R 166. An "A)", "B)", etc. before
a title indicates that the narrative is one instance of a multiple
narrative transmission of the same event, and that other instances are being consecutively given in the collection. Thus, H
177-H 181; H 208-H 211, etc. A lower case "a)", "b)" etc. is used
in a series of anecdotes found together. These merely facilitate
reading and reference. Examples would be H 199-H 201; H
233; H 234.

Four expressions frequently occur in the notes appended to
many of the stories. *Same Narrative* means that the same story
in nearly identical terms is found in the place(s) listed. This occurs almost exclusively in the "synoptic" narratives of the
Rabbinic literature. A striking example of this feature can be
found in the note to R 137. *Story* indicates that a story of the
same type but with different protagonists can be found in the
place referred to, usually the NT. Thus, the healing at a distance of a boy with a fever is found in R 75-R 76 and with many
of the same features in John 4:46-54. This is a comparison on the
level of plot. *Comparable Narrative* serves to indicate that the
narrative(s) referred to is similar but does not bear as close a
resemblance as in the two previous categories. Thus, R 129
records a conversation at the deathbed of R Eliezer which turns
upon the notion of "precious chastenings." R 167-R 169 are also
deathbed conversations on the same theme, although these latter result in a healing. *Motif* calls attention to the presence in
other places of an identical or similar feature of a narrative. A
motif is the smallest unit of meaning that can function signifi-

cantly in a series of different contexts. It may be an image, a phrase, or a word or formula. In the literature we are comparing, it is usually a significant gesture or theme word.

Comparing Narratives

Some general principles from the theory of narrative are necessary for a correct comparison of narratives. The enthusiasm with which the early proponents of the History of Religions School undertook their comparative work led at times to a certain "parallelomania."[9] Because the actual texts were not widely available for control, conclusions were then accepted which needed substantial correction in the light of subsequent investigation. The previous conclusions were often the result of a reductive tendency in the research which led people to compare smaller units of meaning without understanding their role in dissimilar contexts.[10] Comparison must be made on the level of discourse and cannot be limited to that of structure, vocabulary or motif. The dynamic unity of the literary work must be studied so that its component parts are grasped in their proper and formal function within the work. When this principle is neglected, there is a tendency to postulate a close similarity between two narratives and the world views they represent merely on the basis of a commonly held motif or turn of phrase.[11] In order to avoid this kind of comparison, we must

[9] This term was made famous by S. Sandmel in his presidential address to the SBL in December, 1961. He defines parallelomania as "that extravagance among scholars which first overdoes the supposed similarity in passages and then proceeds to describe source and derivation as if implying literary connection flowing in an inevitable or predetermined direction." "Parellelomania," *JBL* 81 (1962) 1-13; citation is from p. 1.

[10] The positivist bias in much of the early work done in the social sciences, and this would include comparative religion, has been discussed by R. Bernstein in, *Beyond Objectivism and Relativism. Science, Hermeneutics, and Praxis* (Philadelphia: University of Pennsylvania Press, 1985). I disagree with Bernstein, however, in his rejection of moderate realism.

[11] One can read a similar plea for care that contexts and not merely components be compared in the remark of E. P. Sanders. Speaking of efforts to compare Paul and Palestinian Judaism, Sanders begins his criticism of the studies of Buchanan and Flusser by saying: "Motif research is so common in New Testament research, and the supposition that identity of motifs indicates identity or similarity of viewpoint is so widespread, that we shall pause to give two examples of how false conclusions can readily be drawn on the basis of similarity of themes." *Paul and Palestinian Judaism* (London: SCM, 1977) 13. For a wider and more philosophical treatment of the issues involved in an, work of comparison, see R. Bernstein, *Op. cit.* (note 10) "Incommensurability and the Social Disciplines," 93-108.

appreciate more clearly the nature of narrative and the principles governing the work of comparison.

Narrative is the literary presentation of a complete action.[12] Neither lyric, description nor chronicle presents an action. Lyric expresses interior experience; description moves in the time of pure (as opposed to sequential) duration; and chronicle lists events but does not link them so as to present an action, which is a change that takes place in and through temporal sequence. The current philosophical debate concerning the narrative's mode of reference, *i.e.*, whether the telos of the action is in reality or in the mind of the narrator, does not affect what is said here. It is important, however, to understand that the unity of the action as it informs the text is due to the teleological perspective of the author. An author's capacity to coordinate and inform all the elements of a narrative by a grasp of this one action is what makes for success in mediating an event. This holds true whether we are discussing the over-arching unity of a novel or the narrow confines of a pericope.

That process by which event becomes word precisely by being interpreted through the judgment of the narrator is a work of emplotment.[13] When what is being mediated is something that took place in the realm of human activity, then it is up to the narrator to discover a principle of continuity in a myriad of minor happenings and transmit them in the light of a unified action. An author "configures" an event (the term is Paul Ricoeur's)[14] by shaping it according to what he has perceived to be its most salient unifying dynamic principle, its action. The articulation of that action is called the plot. Perhaps the most complete definition of plot is that of Tzvetan Todorov:

> The minimal complete plot consists in the passage from one equilibrium to another. An "ideal" narrative begins with a stable situation which is disturbed by some power or force. There results a state of disequilibrium; by the action of a force directed in the opposite direction, the equilibrium is re-established; the second equilibrium is similar to the first, but the two are never identical.[15]

[12] The following description of narrative is an adaptation of the opening pages of: F. Martin, *Encounter Story. A Characteristic Gospel Narrative Form* (Washington, D.C.: The Word Among Us Press, 1979).

[13] For a more ample discussion of this process, I refer the reader to my study, "Literary Theory, Philosophy of History and Exegesis," *The Thomist* 52 (1988) 575-604.

[14] See: *Time and Narrative*, tr. K. McLaughlin and D. Pellauer, Vol. I (University of Chicago Press, 1984) 64-70.

[15] T. Todorov, *The Poetics of Prose* (ET Oxford: Blackwell, 1977) 111. The same

Narrative, then, presents an action; plot is the articulation of the action; and structure is the primary manifestation of plot, not plot itself, but rather the skeleton of the narrative. In order to "flesh out" narrative, we must consider its various levels.[16]

The Levels of Narrative

Comparison between narratives must be made on the same level of literary existence.[17] It is legitimate to compare the component parts of narratives on the various levels of their existence. We must, however, return to the formal dynamic unity constituted by each text in order to determine whether the perceived resemblance is still present when this is taken into account. The level at which most comparisons are actually made is that which we will call "organization." Similarity at this level is a valuable indication but, of itself, it does not determine what degree or type of relation exists between the literary works being compared.

There are five levels or aspects to narrative. *Event* is the action itself, the content of the story. The *narrative* is the actually existing verbal texture through which the event is mediated; it is the text. The *account* is the basic verbal expression in which the plot may be resumed. *Narration* is the act of narrating, the process by which event becomes word. This extremely complex activity involves the creative choice of possibilities that give to the narrative its unique existence. The level of a narrative just below the surface, at which all the possibilities available to a narrator are selected and given shape, may be termed *organization*. Organization is to narrative what tone of voice is to speech. It is instinctively selected prior to the "performance" of

accent on the transition from tension to resolution can be found in the study by C. Westermann, "Arten der Erzählung in der Genesis," in, *Forschung am Alten Testament* (Theologische Bucherei, 24) (Munich: Kaiser, 1964). Article is on pp. 9-91. When the accent is placed on the sequential and temporal dimension through which the action is mediated, plot may be defined as: "The chain of events in a story and the principle which knits it together." E. Muir, *The Structure of the Novel* (London: Hogarth, 1938) 16. Or, "the dynamic sequential element in narrative literature," R. Scholes, R. Kellog, *The Nature of Narrative* (Oxford University Press, 1966) 207.

16 In what follows, I am indebted mostly to the work of G. Genette, especially *Figures III* (Paris: Seuil, 1972) (part of which has been translated by J. Lewin as, *Narrative Discourse* (Cornell University Press, 1980)), and A. Greimas, *Du sens. Essais sémiotiques* (Paris: Seuil, 1970), though my approach is not quite the same.

17 See: R. Wellek, A. Warren, *Theory of Literature*, 3rd ed. (Penguin Books, 1963), Chapter 12, "The Mode of Existence of a Literary Work of Art," 142-57, esp. pp. 142-46.

the utterance, and it determines what kinds of words will be used, what polyvalence will be exploited, what motifs will be invoked or alluded to, what narrative stance or point of view will be operative, how the inner time of the narrative will be conveyed, how the audience will be solicited to enter into the text, and so forth.[18] Not all of the above choices take place with the same degree of reflexive consciousness; some of them pertain to the realm of artistic intuition. Organization is more inclusive than account, and less particular than the actually existing verbal texture of the narrative.[19]

Some examples will help illustrate this description and show its relevance to the work of comparing and situating NT narratives. Matt 8:1-4, Mark 1:40-45, Luke 5:12-16 and Papyrus Egerton 2 state, in effect, that "Jesus healed a leper." The words in quotation marks express the *event*. An *account* would run something like: "A leper came asking Jesus to heal him; Jesus healed him and sent him away to the priest." We have four *narratives* of this event composed by giving to the linguistic possibilities and narrative grammar available to the authors a certain *organization*. We have only these four texts; the previous levels are abstractions. A study of these narratives shows us the actual work of *narration* and from this, we can see how each author actually interprets the event as he narrates it. The work of shaping a narrative to mediate the author's interpretation is what Ricoeur calls "configuration." Differing narratives help us to become alert to the possibilities available to the individual authors and to understand more deeply their individual interpretation. The question of their mutual literary dependence, or their dependence upon previous oral or written tradition, is an important one, but it is secondary to the understanding of the actual textual expressions themselves. Each narrative is an interpretation of the event for which the author takes responsibility with the expectation that the text is to be understood on its own

---

[18] P. Ricoeur, in his very valuable study of narrative already referred to, does not distinguish sufficiently between emplotment and what I am calling here organization. Most of his discussion is to be found in the first volume of his study, but the reader should also consult: *Time and Narrative*, Vol. 2 (University of Chicago Press, 1985). The third volume *Temps et Récit* (Paris: Seuil, 1985) will appear in English shortly.

[19] Another perspective on the way in which the intermediate levels between event and narrative are grouped together is that of Greimas, who speaks of an "immanent level" which constitutes some sort of common stock where the narrativity is located and organized prior to its manifestation. The narrative itself is described as the "obvious level" where the representation of what is to be conveyed exists as subject to the specific demands of a linguistic system. *Du sens*, p. 158 (see note 16).

terms. The principle of responsibility is an important one. It means that, regardless of what material is used, an author takes responsibility for the meaning function it fulfills in the text as it actually exists.

In the Hellenistic world, multiple narratives of the same event seldom yield a "synoptic problem" because there is less adherence to a tradition on the level of narration/organization. The authors are more intrusively individualistic in their story telling. Something close to a synoptic presentation in Hellenistic literature may be found in the successive list of Pythagoras' feats given by Apollonius the Paradoxographer (H 199), Iamblichus (H 200) and Porphyry (H 201).[20] All the ancients, no matter what their literary milieu, considered that the basic function of narrative was that of interpretation. Events, especially those which were commonly current within a tradition, were treated in much the same way that Cézanne treated the scenes he painted: using purposeful distortion in order to make a statement about something well-known. We have, for instance, five narratives of Alexander's crossing of the Pamphylian Sea (H 177- H 181). Two of these are explicit appeals to the miraculous (Arrian [H 177], Ps.-Callisthenes [H 180]), one is an explicit rejection of the miraculous (Plutarch [H 178]), another, a sarcastic allusion to Alexander's lack of care for his soldiers (Strabo [H 179]), while Josephus makes a cautious disclaimer that allows everyone to judge as he sees fit (H 181). The well-known story of how the great physician Asclepiades discerned life in a man being carried out to burial is narrated four times (H 208-H 211), and motifs of this story are transposed by Philostratus to adorn an incident in the life of his subject, Apollonius of Tyana (H 215). In the same way, tradition has preserved for us the threefold narration of Vespasian's healing of two men as part of the numinous atmosphere that surrounded his accession to the throne (H 187-H 189).

Comparison of these stories illustrates once again that the fact of identity of event and even similarity on the level of configuration must still yield to the meaning given by each individual author's responsible use of tradition.

---

[20] Other similar examples, particularly in the various *Lives* of Pythagoras, can be found in, S.A. Tuck, *The Form and Function of Sayings-Material in Hellenistic Biographies of Philosophers* (Unpublished Dissertation, Harvard, 1985) (Ann Arbor: University Microfilms Int., 1985). See also: V. Robbins, *Jesus the Teacher* (see note 5).

Three Important Components of Narration

There are three factors on the organization level of the act of narrating that are particularly significant when comparing material to the NT: point of view, economy of expression, and allusive use of motifs.

1) Point of view

Point of view refers to the relation between narrator, story, and audience. The basic distinction, and the one most relevant to our material, is between a "showing" and a "telling" point of view.[21] In a showing point of view, the narrator stands to one side, as it were, and shows us the action. We are not conscious of a narrator's presence. In a telling point of view, the narrator stands between us and the story. We are more conscious of our dependence upon the narrator for what is being told us. In empirical narrative, that is, narrative purporting to present events of the past, the most characteristic Greek mode of narration is that of direct address, or a telling point of view, while the common Semitic mode is that of dramatic presentation or a showing point of view. Thus, in the story of Moses at the waters of Marah (OT 17-OT 21), the Masoretic text (OT 17) and *Tg. Yer. I* (OT 18) are cast in a showing point of view; the mention in the *Biblical Antiquities* (OT 19) is not a true narrative, while the narratives of Philo (OT 20) and Josephus (OT 21) are clearly organized according to a telling point of view. This difference may be observed wherever in the OT collection there are several narratives of the same event, some of which are composed in a Semitic language and others in Greek.

Point of view pertains to the level of organization and is influenced more by the tone given to the work by its author than by the inherent properties of a given language. For example, though the NT narratives are written in Greek, most of them employ the showing point of view characteristic of Semitic story telling. The same may be said of some other narratives concerning Jesus now found in the apocrypha and other literature.[22]

We have a striking example, in Judg 3:12-20, of the potential

[21] For those who may wish a more complete study of the many aspects of this question of point of view, there are the studies of: F. Van Rossum-Guyon, "Point de vue ou perspective narrative," *Poétique* 4 (1970) 467-97; Scholes-Kellog, *Narrative*, Chapter 7 (see note 15); B. Uspensky, *A Poetics of Composition* (ET Berkeley: University of California, 1973).

[22] See, for instance, K. Aland (ed.), *Synopsis Quattuor Evangeliorum* (Stuttgart: Württembergische Bibelanstalt, 1964). Some examples would be: numbers 42, 150, 302 (Pap. Eg. 2: though the fragment may be too short to judge), 257, etc.

of a showing point of view to transpose an event to the level of word while allowing the event to appear as though it were before our eyes. Judg 2:11-19 presents us first with an abstract summary or overall view of Israelite history. Judg 3:7-11, on the other hand, is a concretization of these same principles which govern the rises and falls on the chart of the people's life. The report given there concerning the activity of Othniel is a sort of telling narrative briefly describing his role in bringing peace back to Israel.

Judg 3:12-30 then narrates Ehud's exploit. After an introduction giving the repeated rhythm of infidelity and oppression and the description of Ehud's handicap, we are presented with a drama containing a number of scenes. At this point, we watch and listen. Our narrator disappears completely from the moment when Ehud enters Eglon's private chambers until the end of the battle. The events transpire before our eyes with an action all their own; there is no commentator present explaining what we behold. At times, the lens "zooms" and we catch a detail, as when we read: "and the hilt went in after the blade and the fat closed over the blade. . ." (v. 22). At another time, we are alongside Eglon's servants, and though we know what they are going to find, we share their surprise: "and they took the key and opened, and behold! Their lord lying on the ground dead!" (v. 25).

It is not difficult to see the power of this type of narrative. In our example, we participate in an act of God with no one to distract us with a telling stance or interjected remarks. The story "speaks for itself." The Synoptic narratives in particular have this same characteristic. They are not so much instances of literature that cannot transcend cultural limitations as they are examples of the exploitation of limitation in order to achieve a particular result. We can see something similar in the choice of icon painters to restrict themselves to two dimensions or the decision of film makers to employ only black and white as in Alain Cavalier's *Thérèse*. Hellenistic narrative, on the other hand, shows a marked preference for the scope allowed an author through the use of a telling point of view.

2) Economy of Expression

A derivative feature of a showing point of view is that of economy of expression. If an author uses many words and striking turns of phrase, and interjects a number of personal reflections, we cannot help but be aware of someone between ourselves and the story. Three symptoms of a showing point of view are: an absence of descriptive detail, the use of formulaic expressions, and the reporting of dialogue in what is almost "play-script" style. The first of these qualities is remarkable in such Synoptic narratives as the healing of Peter's mother-in-law (Matt 8:14-15 par.), and the calls of Peter and Andrew, James and John (Matt 4:21-22 par.) where, in less than fifty words, an action is presented that has been the subject of many artistic representations in literature, film, and painting.

Economy of expression is characterized by the use of formulae held by a narrative tradition as a sort of reservoir of stereotyped expressions.[23] Their redundant use places the story within the tradition in such a way that the audience's assent, based on familiarity, is more easily elicited.[24] TV sports fans can see this dynamic at work in the Miller's High Life Ads where the audience is ready to "connive" in the unfolding of some humorous "plot" involving famous sports figures. In this case, economy of expression and the use of stereotypes eliminate the "static" of distraction. The Synoptic Gospels achieve the same goal in much the same way. Writing which employs formulae is more closely linked to the techniques that characterize orality in contrast to textuality. This does not signify an underdeveloped form of expression,[25] but rather that the force of this type of textual expression relies more on what is held in common than on the verbal ingenuity of the communicator. The phenomenon of "synoptic" texts in whatever culture they may be found is explained in this way: they are organs of tradition, subtly modified by each textual performance. An understanding of this literary procedure, which may or may not include actual textual dependence, is important in grasping the theological function of the Synoptic Gospels.

A final manifestation of economy of expression is to be found in the presentation of dialogue. We can gain an appreciation of how, on the one hand, "play-script" narrative dialogues and a

---

23 When these become a stable part of a literary tradition, they are referred to as topoi. See, E. R. Curtius, *European Literature and the Latin Middle Ages* (New York: Harper and Row, 1963).

24 For a study of the various roles of allusion, see: F. Martin, "The Image of Shepherd in the Gospel of St. Matthew," *ScEsp* 27 (1965) 261-302. The manner in which "redundancy" and formulaic expression provide a certain connivance between author and audience is described by S. Wittig in her study, "Formulaic Style and the Problem of Redundancy," *Centrum* I (1973) 123-36.

25 See, for instance, the study of W. Ong, "Oral Residue in Tudor Prose Style," *Publications of the Modern Language Association of America* 80 (1965) 145-54. This is further developed in the work by the same author, *Orality and Literacy: The Technologizing of the Word* (Methuen, NY: New Accents, 1982).

showing point of view evoke one another while, on the other hand, more elaborate expressions are connected with a telling point of view by comparing the story in the Book of Kings concerning God's care for Elijah (OT 45) with Josephus' narrative of the same event (OT 46). The same can be said in regard to Elijah's call of Elisha (OT 49) and Josephus' indirect style in OT 50 and several other instances in which the Masoretic text and Josephus or Philo present the same event in different narratives. Nearly all Rabbinic dialogues are narrated with this play-script format, so much so that we often find the abbreviation " '*l*" ('*amar lô*/"he said to him") used to indicate the change of speaker, and even this is often omitted (See R 165). The same procedure is noticeable in the Gospel text,[26] while something similar occurs in certain types of anecdotes and *chreiai* in the Hellenistic world (*e.g.*, H 233).

3) Motif

Motif often forms the basis for comparison since it is the element of meaning which travels most easily from one literary or traditional context to another. This quality makes motif a particularly apt means of establishing a connection through the use of literary allusion. We can readily appreciate that there is a great difference between the allusive application of a motif and the narrative re-interpretation of an event. The latter represents an action, while the former establishes a relation between two actions and, most commonly, between two actors. When borrowing a motif, an author indicates a decision to insert the narrative into a tradition and to attribute characteristics from one or more personalities in that tradition to a person in the present narrative. We must establish, of course, that a particular unit of meaning is being treated as a motif and that its reoccurrence is not a coincidence or an instance of a "floating" formula or plot. "Floating" elements appear in several contexts for their meaning function rather than for their potential to establish an allusive relationship. For example, the phrase, "Rise,

---

[26] Once this is pointed out, it is easy to detect "play-script" procedures in the Gospel texts. Here is but one example, from Mark 10:35-39.

And James and John . . . came up to him

saying	Teacher we want you. . .
He said:	What do you want. . .
They said:	Grant us that we sit. . .
Jesus said to them:	You do not know. . .
They said:	We can.
Jesus said to them:	The cup that I drink. . .

let us go from here," found in Mark 14:42; Matt 26:46 and John
14:31, is used in the Gospel tradition as a way of expressing
Jesus' commitment to the Passion and, as such, it is found in different contexts. The question, "Are you a prophet?" with its af-
firmative answer based on an allusion to Amos 7:14 is found in
both R 75 and R 78/R 79. Sometimes a story line or plot is
"floating" in the sense that the same account is repeated with
different actors. An example of this is to be found in R 167-R
169.[27]

In order to assert the presence of allusion by way of motif,
there must be some indication of real borrowing. Then, according to the principle of responsibility, we must see how an author
is employing the borrowed motif.

Generally speaking, there are four ways in which a motif is
pressed into service. First is *embellishment*, a process by which
an author ornaments a text through an allusive reference to
something identifiable by those in the audience who are "in the
know." Examples of this would be Philostratus' mention of Hercules and Alcestis in H 215, the description of Ḥanina's prayer
gesture in R 77 and, in modern literature, the multiple allusions
by Pope in "The Rape of the Lock."[28] The second type of allusion may be termed *use*. This way of narrating includes certain
images and vocabulary found in other stories of the same type.
Examples would be the presence of Jonah motifs in Mark 4:35-
41 par. and R 173, and the patristic use of "sacred language"
when discussing sacred events and themes.[29] Thirdly, *attribution* is a process by which the quality of one person in tradition
is allusively attributed to another. Thus, Moses' making bitter
waters sweet in OT 17 is echoed in OT 51; Pythagoras' feat in H
199e, etc. is attributed to Apollonius in *Life* 4, 10; while the skill
of Asclepiades (H 208-H 211) is also attributed to Apollonius in
H 215. Again, Pythagoras' golden thigh links him to the god

[27] The use of floating formulae has been studied in regard to oral literature by A.
Lord, *The Singer of Tales* (Cambridge: Harvard University Press, 1960), Ch. 3,
"The Formula." The presence of floating formulae and movable or changeable
plots in folk ballads was studied much earlier by F. J. Child in his, *English and
Scottish Popular Ballads* (New York: Houghton Mifflin and Co., 1882-94; repub-
lished, New York: Dover Publications, 1965). See particularly, Vol. I, Ch. 4, "Lady
Isabel and the Elf Knight."

[28] See: E. Wasserman, "The Limits of Allusion in the Rape of the Lock," in G.
Rousseau (ed.), *Twentieth Century Interpretations of the Rape of the Lock* (Engle-
wood Cliffs, NJ: Prentice-Hall Press, 1969) 69-84.

[29] For an excellent study of this last point, see: J. Leclerq, "Ecriture Sainte et Vie
Spirituelle; 3 St. Bernard et le 12e siècle monastique," in *Dict. de Spiritualité* 4,
187ff.

Apollo worshipped by the legendary Hyperboreans (H 200d, H 201c).

Lastly, there is an allusion which is really the *transposition* of a motif into another setting. This last device profoundly changes a motif by placing it in a diverse context. We may look at three clear examples of transposition to be found in Luke/Acts.

The first example is to be found in Luke's use of *koina* in Acts 2:44 and 4:32. In such a context, this term immediately evokes in the mind of the audience the Aristotelian ideal of friendship as practiced by the neo-Pythagorean communities.[30] In Acts 4:34, this allusion is joined to a similar OT theme in Deut 15:4. This combined allusion is a Lukan means of asserting that the ideal of the Greeks has now been realized by the early Christian community as it experiences the fulfillment of the promise made to Israel.[31]

Another example can be seen in Luke 2:10-11 where *euaggelizesthai*, *sōtēr*, and *Kyrios* are placed in the same context as *Christos*. The presence of this key Christian term, derived from Jewish expectations, serves to transpose the three other terms, redolent of the emperor cult, into the context of the newborn Messiah.

A third example is to be found in Luke 7:11-17. There, the motif of Jesus' stopping the bier of a dead man on the way to burial (v. 14) would bring to mind the story of Asclepiades, which was well known and frequently repeated (H 208-H 211). The following verse combines this with a clear allusion to Elijah's gesture in returning the revived boy to his mother (OT 47). Once again, we see how Luke transposes motifs to show that Jesus is the fulfillment of the great works and expectations of both Greeks and Jews. In their new context, these motifs function in a very specific and transposed manner.[32]

The NT allusions to themes and motifs from the Servant

---

[30] Josephus is probably making a similar allusion in his description of the Essenes in *J.W.* 2,8,3.

[31] See: F. Martin, "Monastic Community and the Summary Statements in Acts," in B. Pennington (ed.), *Contemplative Community: An Interdisciplinary Symposium* (Cistercian Studies, 21) (Washington: Cistercian Publications, 1972) 13-46.

[32] In order to grasp what happens in the process of transposition, the reader will find the following philosophical definition helpful. It is given by Bernard Lonergan in his discussion of "sublation" in which, as he states, he is following Karl Rahner and not Hegel: "What sublates [in our case the text of Luke] goes beyond what is sublated [the borrowed motifs], introduces something new and distinct, yet so far from interfering with the sublated or destroying it, on the contrary needs it, includes it, preserves all its proper features and properties, and carries them forward

Songs provide other illustrations of the way in which a new context gives a transposed meaning to a pre-existing literary piece by alluding to some of its motifs. An excellent example of transposition as a more general procedure would be the manner in which John of the Cross takes up "*a lo divino*," a pastoral poem, "El Pastorcico," so that it now speaks of Christ.[33] In the same way, a statue of Hercules drawing up Cerberus from the underworld becomes, in a Christian setting, Christ drawing up Adam.[34] In comparing attributive motifs, we must be particularly aware of the role played by context in determining meaning.

To establish a link between narrative motifs, we must clearly show that we are dealing with the true borrowing of a motif and not merely a coincidence. Secondly, we must determine what type of allusion is being employed on the basis of what the author seems to intend by the allusion. If the text is truly an instance of intersubjective communication, then it is not merely the net result of previously existing material and influences. The author is responsible for the meaning effect of the text produced whether or not the material used is derived from other sources.

The Parameters of Narrative

Abstractedly considered, all that is required for the literary presentation of an action can be compressed into one sentence. Normally, however, a narrative must be long enough to mediate a sense of the sequential duration of time through and in which the action moves. The short narratives of the NT and those in this collection represent the approximate minimal size necessary for this to be realized.

In discussing the parameters of narrative, we must consider three aspects: 1) the difference between a setting and a true narrative; 2) the manner in which one action relates to others presented in the overall narrative; and 3) the formal dynamic unity of the narrative whole.

1) Setting and Narrative

An action may be described or presented, but only the latter

to a fuller realization within a richer context." *Method in Theology* (New York: Herder and Herder, 1972) 241.

[33] For a discussion of this, see: L. Alonso Schökel, *The Inspired Word* (ET New York: Herder and Herder, 1965) 200-02.

[34] For a discussion of this image and of transposition in general, see: E. Panovsky, *Studies in Iconology* (New York: Harper Torch Books, 1962).

is narrative. A story can also be merely the setting for a description of an action or, more commonly, for a saying. In order to grasp this more completely, we must distinguish between a transeunt action, one that goes from an agent to a recipient,[35] and an immanent action, one that produces no external result.

Normally, when we speak of narrative action, we mean transeunt action. An agent acts and produces a result. In a healing narrative, we instinctively await a statement like, "and the fever left her," or "At that exact hour he requested food." In a narrative that presents an intellectual confrontation, the action is "immanent." The result takes place in the reader; there is no necessity for a notice such as "they were amazed at him" (Mark 12:17) in order to know that the action was completed. The cogency of the response brings about conviction in the audience. This is an intellectual narrative because a movement of thought is presented in story form. There is an illation which resolves an intellectual process and thus there is true narrative: a movement from rest through disequilibrium to a new equilibrium.

Stories which present a genuine though immanent action must be distinguished from those which merely supply the setting for a "punch line." This distinction is important when comparing what are called "pronouncement stories." The debate between the elders and the philosophers in Rome (R 111) is an intellectual narrative. The same is true of Matt 22:15-22 par. (taxes to Caesar), but it is not true, for instance, of the three stories in Luke 9:57-62 (conditions for following Jesus), or of the material in H 233-235.[36] Generally, it may be said that Hellenistic pronouncement stories are settings with a punch line, and that this literary form is not used for serious expressions of thought.

2) Incident, Episode, Pericope

The manner in which the actions making up a narrative are presented and related to one another can be classified as: incident, episode, and pericope. An *incident* is an event narrated in such a way that it is clearly seen to be part of a larger complex of events; it is never self-enclosed. Most novels, short stories, and

---

[35] Webster's *New Collegiate Dictionary* (Springfield, MA: Merriam, 1956) defines transeunt as "Passing from one to another; operating, or efficient in producing results, beyond itself; as a *transeunt* cause; — opposed to immanent."

[36] A good initial treatment of pronouncement stories is to be found in: R. Tannehill (ed.), *Pronouncement Stories, Semeia* 20 (1981). See also, S. Tuck, *The Form and Function of Sayings-Material in Hellenistic Biographies of Philosophers* (see note 20).

narrated history present a series of incidents as parts of one
overall action. Some portions of the Acts of the Apostles are
composed in the same way and this is a common feature of the
apocryphal material. An *episode* is the literary presentation of
an action in such a way that, though there is a unity to the presentation, it must function as part of a larger whole to achieve its
meaning. Some examples of episodic narrative in biblical literature would be: the Joseph story in Gen 37-50, the story of Saul
and David in 1 Sam 9-2 Sam 1 (though the story line continues),
and the Gospel Passion narratives. Philostratus' *Lives* of the
Sophists, and his *Life* of Apollonius of Tyana are also episodic.[37]
A *pericope*, as the term is being used here, is a short, free-stand-
ing, self-enclosed narrative unit that functions independently of
any particular context. Other short units, such as non-narrative
pronouncement stories, apothegmata, and so forth, can be
termed *anecdotes*. Pericopes stand in relation to episodes in
much the same way that framed pictures are related to a series
of panelled scenes in a mural. The pictures may be organized in
any number of ways, as in the thematic or chronological showing of an artist. They may thus serve a higher organizing principle, but they maintain their independence.

For the purposes of comparison, it is important to note the
mediate position occupied by pericopes. They are narratives in
their own right but they may also be organized into a larger narrative action. The Gospels, particularly the Synoptics, are characterized by the fact that they respect the pericopic nature of
their material while integrating them into an overall narrative
statement. They achieve this by joining the pericopes together
without tightening the bond between them in such a way that
the pericopes becomes episodes.

The mode of procedure just described is called juxtaposition.
It consists in placing units of meaning, in this case, short narratives, side by side so that while each unit sounds its own note, it
also contributes to an overall "meaning effect." Because of the
shared nature of the traditional material, each pericope also

---

[37] Plutarch hints at the episodic character of his *Lives* when he describes his
method at the beginning of his *Life* of Alexander (1,2): "For I am writing biography, not history, and the truth is that the most brilliant exploits often tell us nothing
of the virtues or vices of the men who performed them. . . . When a portrait
painter sets out to create a likeness, he relies above all upon the face and the expression of the eyes and pays less attention to the other parts of the body: in the
same way it is my task to dwell upon those actions which illuminate the workings of
the soul, and by this means to create a portrait of each man's life." Translation by I.
Scott-Kilvert, *Plutarch, The Age of Alexander* (New York: Penguin Books, 1986)
252.

brings with it a particular set of associations. In juxtaposition, the pericopes are not integrated or blended into a higher synthesis, but are rather left to tell their own story even while they contribute to an overall theological context which gives to each of them a further or enhanced meaning. It is the task of each reader to grasp the total vision of the written work called a Gospel through an understanding of the entropy function conferred on the text by its author who has made a whole from independent yet now mutually modifying parts.

When comparing the Gospels with other material, we must strive to balance the two aspects of pericopes we have just discussed: their independence as narratives, and their function as parts of a larger whole. Possessing as they do their own narrative unity, pericopes gather and organize units of meaning as well as literary procedures into the overall action of a plot. The parts of which a pericope is made are not allowed much independence; their meaning is only as parts of the narrative, though they may retain the power to allude to other contexts. At the same time, because they are parts of the larger work they construct, pericopes are subordinate to its action. This means that the work of comparison must respect the fashion in which the units of meaning function within the dynamic sequential unity of the pericope and at the same time consider the present mediate position of the pericope itself as part of a Gospel which adds a further function to the units of meaning. To take this second aspect into account involves some understanding of the Gospels as literary units.

The Gospels as Literary Units

One of the characteristics of the Gospel literature, as redaction criticism has shown us, is the remarkable manner in which pericopes are accorded an independence while still intimately contributing to the theological purpose of the authors. This leads us to the question: "To what may we compare the Gospels?" As we have seen, stylistically, that is, on the level of organization and narrative, the pericopes themselves compare most closely to the short narratives in the Rabbinic material. This is as true of the miracle stories as it is of the discourse material, and it casts doubt on the accuracy of assigning the origin of miracle stories to the milieu of Hellenistic religious propaganda.

The Rabbinic world, however, provides no parallel for the overall work we call Gospel. In order to try to situate the Gospels, we have recourse to Hellenistic popular Biographies.[38] Examples from this type of literature can be found by consulting the indices under the names of Philostratus, Porphyry, Lucian, Diogenes Laertius, Xenophon, and others. This is not the place to enter into a full scale treatment of how Hellenistic Biographies relate to the Gospels. However, a few words concerning comparative narratology at this level may be useful.

1) Comparison at the First Two Levels of Narrative

Comparing works of literature as global narratives involves the same three levels we applied to pericope. The first level is that of the event. Comparison at this level is a simple affair involving two questions: Is the same event being retold? Is an event being treated as a motif and transferred to another actor or are we dealing with a "floating story?" The second level is that of organization,[39] that is, all that occurs in the act of narration by which the event becomes word. This is, as has been shown, the level at which comparison is possible and most often made.

2) Comparison at the Third Level of Narrative

The third level is that of the actually existing text, the narrative. Each narrative is a unique literary performance and, thus, at this level, comparison becomes classification, the establishing of *genres*.[40] Generic classification is an effort to arrive at some understanding of a work by identifying the type of literature to which it belongs. A work is best classified through a reciprocal process which consists in determining two things, the goal of the author (what the ancients called the *skopos*) and the reaction of the audience. In regard to the Gospels, C. F. Evans invites us to

[38] Much of the recent work done in this regard can be found in the study by C. H. Talbert, *What is a Gospel?* (Philadelphia: Fortress Press, 1977). The reader will find useful information and further bibliography in: D. L. Barr and J. L. Wentling, "The Conventions of Classical Biography and the Genre of Luke-Acts: A Preliminary Study," in, C. H. Talbert (ed.), *Luke-Acts. New Perspectives from the Society of Biblical Literature Seminar* (New York: Crossroads, 1984) 63-87; and P. Cox, *Biography in Late Antiquity* (University of California Press, 1983). For a more theological perspective, see: D. Dormeyer, "Die Kompositionsmetapher 'Evangelium Jesu Christi, des Sohnes Gottes,' Mk 1,1. Ihre Thelogische und Literarische Aufgabe in der Jesus-Biographie des Markus," *NTS* 33 (1987) 452-68.
[39] In using the term "organization," I am purposely avoiding Ricoeur's term "configuration." Configuration refers more to the act of judgment, whereas organization refers more to the actual literary performance.
[40] For a wider discussion of the question of genre, one may consult the still valuable work of R. Wellek and A. Warren, *Theory of Literature* (see note 17).

consider the aspect of audience reaction by imagining how a second century librarian in Alexandria would classify a Gospel if a manuscript were to come into his hands.[41] The possibilities he lists fall under the general category of Biography.[42] However, attempts to fit the Gospels more narrowly within either the ancient or modern subcategories of Greco-Roman Biography have not been completely successful.[43] The reason for this lies in the distinctive nature of the goal the Gospel writers set for themselves.

In determining the intention of a writer of a Biography, or any literary work, we must first attend to what may be said within the work itself concerning its purpose and then to indications within and around the work that shed light on this. Thus, Philostratus tells us that in composing his *Life* of Apollonius of Tyana, he wishes to "write a true account of the man," detailing those "habits of wisdom by which he came to be considered a supernatural and divine being [*daimonios te ka theios nomisthēnai*]."[44] A close reading of the text itself, coupled with a knowledge of its background, helps us to understand that Philostratus is accenting Apollonius' "habits of wisdom" rather than the magical skill attributed to him by his opponent Euphrates. This in turn explains many details of Philostratus' text that would otherwise be difficult to understand.[45] In addition to this expression of intention, we may glean from the many features of the work that resemble a popular Romance that Philostratus wished to win over his audience, including his patroness, to his point of view. His efforts to make his Biography palatable result in sort of a hybrid cross between science fiction and soap opera.

In a successful work of literary Biography, the intention of the author informs the whole work of organization and narra-

[41] C.F. Evans, *et al.*, *The New Testament Gospels* (London: British Broadcasting Corp., 1965), "What Kind of a Book is a Gospel?" 7-21, esp. pp. 7-8.

[42] Evans himself, however, seems to distance unduly the Gospels from this type of literature.

[43] D. Barr and J. Wentling classify Luke-Acts as belonging generally to "a certain type of biography in which stories about the true disciples appear within a biography of the founder." *Op. cit.* (see note 38) p. 73.

[44] *Life* 1,2.

[45] See the discussion by D. Tiede, *The Charismatic Figure as Wonder Worker* (SBL Dissertation Series, 1) (Missoula, MT: Scholars Press, 1972) 23-29. Elsewhere, Philostratus does not evince so high an opinion of Apollonius. In his *Lives of the Sophists*, 1,7, he says of Dio of Prusa that he "lived at a time when Apollonius of Tyana and Euphrates of Tyre were teaching their philosophy, and he was intimate with both men, though in their quarrel with one another they went to extremes that are alien to the philosophic temper (*diapheromenois pros allēlous exō tou philosophias ēthous*). Translation, W.C. Wright in Loeb, p. 19.

tion, thus setting the esthetic tone of the narrative and giving it its particular form of existence. This is expressed in regard to literature in general by René Wellek and Austin Warren in their Chapter 18 on "Evaluation:"

> Instead of dichotomizing "form-content," we should think of matter and then of "form," that which aesthetically organizes its "matter." In a successful work of art, the materials are completely assimilated into the form: what was "world" has become "language." The "materials" of a literary work of art are, on one level, words, on another level, human behaviour experience, and on another, human ideas and attitudes. All of these, including language, exist outside the work of art, in other modes; but in a successful poem or novel they are pulled into polyphonic relations by the dynamics of aesthetic purpose.[46]

The pulling together of pre-existing material of whatever sort by the "dynamics of aesthetic purpose" takes place on the level I have termed "organization." It is the reason why the purpose or *skopos* of the author can be said to inform the work and receive linguistic embodiment in and through the work. Similar purposes, understood through the author's expressed intention and discerned in the organization of the work, give rise to similar works that may be classified as a genre.[47]

It is here that we touch upon what is distinctive in regard to the Gospels. If we consider the expressed purpose of the Gospels, we see that they are addressed to Christians in order to minister to their faith. The notion that the Gospels were written, not as a means of religious propaganda or merely to praise or defend a revered teacher, shifts the focus from what C. F. D. Moule calls "primary evangelism" or the initial preaching of the Gospel to what he calls "explanatory evangelism."[48] This latter function consists in that literary activity by which the life, deeds, sayings, death and resurrection of Jesus are given written narrative existence so that Christians might assimilate more deeply what they had already begun to believe.

Two of the canonical Gospels contain expressions of their au-

---

[46] *Op. cit.* (see note 17) p. 241.
[47] For a more extended discussion of the relation between what informs a work and literary forms, I refer the reader to my study on *Encounter Story* (see note 12).
[48] *The Birth of the New Testament*, revised ed. (New York: Harper and Row, 1982) 9.   Also helpful is the remark on p. 4: "But if the evangelists' main purpose was explanation rather than 'preaching', it gives a different perspective to one's estimate of the liberties taken with traditions."

thor's intention which tend to confirm the view that they are examples of "explanatory evangelism." The Prologue of Luke's Gospel states that it was written so that Theophilus would have "assurance regarding the things in which you were instructed" (Luke 1:4). Joseph Fitzmyer comments: "Luke writes for Theophilus, a catechumen or neophyte, in order to give him assurance about the initial instruction that he has received."[49] While this expression of intention does not preclude additional purposes of an apologetic or propagandizing nature, it must be taken seriously. Luke was well aware of the Hellenistic milieu of his audience as his double allusions to Jewish and to Hellenistic motifs, discussed above, have shown us. We may legitimately infer from this sensitivity to the motifs and aspirations of the Hellenistic world of his day that he knew and was influenced by the type of Biographies known and esteemed in his milieu. Yet his expressed purpose remains distinctive. He writes to provide assurance concerning the fundamentals of the Christian faith.[50]

We find a similar expression of intention in the Fourth Gospel: "I have written these things that you may believe that Jesus is the Messiah, the Son of God, and that, believing, you may have life in his name" (John 20:31). While these words no longer conclude the Gospel, they remain the clearest expression of its fundamental purpose. John's Gospel was written "to deepen the faith of those who were already Christians so that they would appreciate Jesus' unique relation to the Father."[51] Once again we see that the author of a Gospel has a distinctive *skopos*.

Neither Mark nor Matthew contains any such clear statement of purpose. It is significant, however, that the Gospel of Mark opens with the term *euaggelion* which, in this context, would only make sense to someone familiar with Christianity.[52] We must also take into account that the suspended ending at

---

[49] *The Gospel According to Luke. I-IX* (Anchor Bible) (New York: Doubleday, 1981) 310. This opinion would still be valid if Theophilus were an "ideal" reader rather than an actual person: he would be, in that case, the average educated neophyte.

[50] For an extended discussion of the Christian audience of Luke-Acts see, R. Maddox, *The Purpose of Luke-Acts* (FRLANT, 126) (Göttingen: Vandenhoeck und Ruprecht, 1982).

[51] R. Brown, *The Gospel According to John. XIII-XXI* (Anchor Bible, 29A) (New York: Doubleday, 1970) 1060. The same type of remark can be found in R. Schnackenburg, *The Gospel According to St. John*, Vol. 3 (New York: Crossroad, 1982) 338: "So with the majority of exegetes, it is to be maintained that 20:31 is formulated for those who already believe." I refer the reader to these commentaries for a discussion of the textual and philological problems in John 20:31.

[52] See the study of Dormeyer referred to in note 38.

Mark 16:8 requires a knowledge of the whole story in order to make its impact.[53] Matthew does not yield an indication of purpose so easily, but in the judgment of Philip L. Shuler,

> In the encomium biography, Matthew either consciously or unconsciously appropriated a ubiquitous literary type sufficiently flexible to carry out his designs of faith and emulation and to project his kerygmatic assertions within the cult (church) to be used for worship and didactic functions.[54]

I believe that this distinctive purpose of the Gospel writers accounts for the special nature of their literary work. They were not enshrining, protecting or promoting the memory of a dead master; they were explaining the universal significance of the life and death of someone whom they proclaim to be still alive and knowable. They were evangelizing. The fact that their explanatory evangelism was done by way of a narrative of Jesus' life accounts for the fact that, on the literary level, the Gospels may be classified as instances of Greco-Roman Biography. The pericopic nature of most of the narratives, their showing point of view, the fact that multiple narratives of the same event bear such close verbal resemblance, all indicate the attachment of the Gospel authors to the tradition preceding them as well as to the Semitic matrix of their material. When we ask the further question of exactly *why* the Gospels are narrative, we are asking why this form of literary configuration was judged apt first for leading Christians to a deeper understanding of what had been preached to them and, also, for presenting to others an account of the Christian claim. The answer to this question lies in understanding the theological vision which presided over and found embodiment in the text of the NT narratives. In making this collection of parallels to the NT narratives, I wish to lay some of the groundwork necessary for this further theological task.

---

[53] "With a background of interest in Jesus and of instruction regarding his resurrection and subsequent appearances, most readers knew the general contents of the omitted scenes and supplied an ending appropriate to their faith or general knowledge." J. L. Magness, *Sense and Absence. Structure and Suspension in the Ending of Mark's Gospel* (SBL Semeia Studies) (Atlanta: Scholars Press, 1986) 123.

[54] *A Genre for the Gospels. The Biographical Character of Matthew* (Philadelphia: Fortress Press, 1982) 109.

ABBREVIATIONS

(The usual system for abbreviations used is that found in the *Journal of Biblical Literature*.)

'Abot R. Nat.: *'Abot of Rabbi Nathan*. Versions A and B (ed. Schechter; Vienna, 1887; reprinted New York, 1945).

Allen: T.W. Allen, *Homeri Opera*, vol. 5 (Oxford: Clarendon, 1912).

b.: *Talmud Babli*. Cited according to folio and side in the Venice 1548 edition. The tractates are abbreviated in the customary manner.

Bergson: L. Bergson, *Der Griechische Alexanderroman Rezension B* (Acta Universitatis Stockholmiensis, Studia Graeca Stockholmiensia III, Stockholm: Almquist & Wiksell, 1965).

Blake: W.E. Blake, *Chariton's Chaereas and Callirhoe* (Ann Arbor: University of Michigan Press, 1939).

Braude: W.G. Braude, *The Midrash on Psalms*, English tr. from Hebrew and Aramaic, Yale Judaica Series, Vol. 13 (1 and 2) (New Haven: Yale University Press, 1959).

Braude: W.G. Braude, *Pesikta Rabbati*, English tr. from Hebrew, Yale Judaica Series, Vol 18 (1 and 2) (New Haven: Yale University Press, 1968).

Charlesworth: J.H. Charlesworth (ed.), *The Old Testament Pseudepigrapha*, Vol. 1 (1983) and Vol. 2 (1985) (Garden City, NY: Doubleday & Company, Inc.).

Dalmeyda: G. Dalmeyda (ed.), Xénophon D'Ephèse, *Les Ephésiaques ou Le Roman d'Habrocomès et D'Anthia* (Collection des Universités de France sous Assn. G. Budé) (Paris: Société D'Edition "Les Belles Lettres," 1926).

Danby: H. Danby, *The Mishnah* (Oxford: University Press, 1933).

Danby Tr.: H. Danby, *Tractate Sanhedrin, Mishnah and Tosefta* (London: SPCK, 1919).

Díez-Macho: A. Díez-Macho, *MS. Neophyti I* (Madrid: Consejo Superior de Investigaciones Científicas, 1968-79).

Edelstein: E. and L. Edelstein, *Asclepius: A Collection and Interpretation of the Testimonies* (Publications of the Institute of the History of Medicine: The Johns Hopkins University. Second Series, 2) (Baltimore: The Johns Hopkins Press, 1945; New York: Arno Press, 1975). The *Testimonies* are cited according to Edelstein's numeration (whose text is given in Greek and English). Edelstein's numbering of the healings on the Epidaurus inscription follows that of W. Dittenberger, *Sylloge Inscriptionum Graecarum* (3rd ed.; Weinrich, Leipzig, 1931), Vol. III, numbers 1168 and 1169.

Fitzmyer, *The Genesis Apocryphon of Qumran Cave 1* (2d ed.; Biblica et Orientalia, 18A) (Rome: Biblical Institute Press, 1971).

Fraenkel: J. Fraenkel, "Bible Verses Quoted in Tales of the Sages," in J. Heinemann, D. Noy (eds.), *Studies in Aggadah and Folk-Literature* (Scripta Hierosolymitana, 22) (Jerusalem: Magnes Press, Hebrew University, 1971) 80-99.

Gen. Rab. (Exod. Rab., etc.): *Midrash Rabbah Genesis* (Exodus, etc.). Vilna ed.

Ginzberg: L. Ginzberg, *The Legends of the Jews* (seven vols.) (Philadelphia: Jewish Publication Society of America, 1909-38).

Goldin: J. Goldin, *The Fathers According to Rabbi Nathan*, English tr. of Version A, Vol. 10 of the Yale Judaica Series (New Haven: Yale University Press, 1955).

Hadas-Smith: M. Hadas, M. Smith, *Heroes and Gods*. Spiritual Biographies in Antiquity (Religious Perspectives, 13) (London: Routledge and Kegan Paul, 1965).

Herr: M.D. Herr, "The Historical Significance of Dialogues between Jewish Sages and Roman Dignitaries," in J. Heinemann, D. Noy (eds.), *Studies in Aggadah and Folk-Literature* (Scripta Hierosolymitana, 22) (Jerusalem: Magnes Press, Hebrew University, 1971) 123-50.

IG: *Inscriptiones Graecae* (Berlin: Reimerus, 1883ff). The volume which most concerns us is Vol. IV. The Epidaurus material was first edited by M. Fränkel in 1902: the two most useful stelae are numbers 951 and 952. In the second edition, by F. Hiller von Gaertringen in 1929, these become numbers 121 and 122.

Inscr. Creticae: *Inscriptiones Creticae* (opera et consilio Friderici Halbherr collectae), ed. M. Guarducci (Roma: Libreria dello Stato, 1935-42).

JE: *Jewish Encyclopedia* (New York: Funk & Wagnalls, 1925).

Kock: Th. Kock, *Comicorum Atticorum Fragmenta*, 3 vols. (Leipzig: B.G. Teubner, 1880-88; republished, Utrecht: HES Pubs., 1976).

Lauterbach: J.Z. Lauterbach, *Mekilta de-Rabbi Ishmael* (Philadelphia: The Jewish Publication Society of America, 1935, 1961; paperback ed., 1976).

Loeb: *The Loeb Classical Library* (Cambridge, MA: Harvard University Press). When an author's works occupy more than one volume, the Loeb volume number precedes the page number.

m.: *Mishna*, ed. Albeck (Jerusalem, 1957). The tractates are abbreviated in the customary manner.

McNamara: M. McNamara, the English tr. of *Tg. Neof.* in Díez-Macho's edition.

Mek.: *Mekilta of R Ishmael*, ed. H.S. Horowitz (Frankfurt, 1931).

Mekilta Simeon: *Mekilta of R Simeon b Yoḥai*, ed. Epstein-Melamed (Jerusalem, 1955).

Midr. Pss: *Midrash on the Psalms*. Vilna edition.

Nauck: A. Nauck (ed.), *Porphyrii Philosophi Platonici. Opuscula Selecta* (Leipzig: B.G. Teubner, 1886).

Pap. Oxyr.: B.P. Grenfell, A.S. Hunt (eds.), *The Oxyrhynchus Papyri* (London: Egypt Exploration Fund, 1898 and ff.). Cited according to volume number and number of the papyrus. Attribution of the English tr. is according to page number.

Pesiq. R.: *Pesiqta Rabbati*, ed. Friedman (Vienna, 1890). Cited according to folio and side.

Pesiq. Rab Kah.: *Pesikta of Rabbi Kahana*, ed. B. Mandelbaum (New York: Jewish Theological Seminary, 1962).

Reitzenstein: R. Reitzenstein, *Hellenistische Wunder-erzählungen* (repr. Stuttgart: B.G. Teubner, 1963).

Safrai: S. Safrai, "Tales of the Sages in the Palestinian tradition and the Babylonian Talmud," in J. Heinemann, D. Noy (eds.), *Studies in Aggadah and Folk-Literature* (Scripta Hierosolymitana, 22) (Jerusalem: Magnes Press, Hebrew University, 1971) 209-32.

Soncino: *The Babylonian Talmud*, ed. I. Epstein, 34 vols. Page numbers refer to the pages of the tracts (London: Soncino Press, 1935-48).

Soncino: *Midrash Rabbah*, eds. H. Freedman and M. Simon, 13 vols. (London: Soncino Press, 1939; Third Impression, 1961).

Soncino MT: *The Minor Tractates of the Talmud*, ed. A. Cohen, 2 vols. (London: Soncino Press, 1965).

t.: *Tosephta*, ed. S. Lieberman (New York: 1955, 1962, 1967).

Tanḥuma: *Midrash of Rabbi Tanḥuma* (Eshkol: Jerusalem, 1972).

Taylor: T. Taylor, *Iamblichus' Life of Pythagoras* (London: J.M. Watkins, 1926; reprinted, 1965).

Tg. Neof.; *Tg. Yer. I*; etc.: The abbreviations of the targumim are those proposed by the *Newsletter for Targumic Studies*, and adapted by *JBL*.

Tiede: D. Tiede, *The Charismatic Figure as Miracle Worker* (SBL Diss. Ser., 1) (Missoula, MT: Scholars Press, 1972).

Vermes: G. Vermes, "Ḥanina ben Dosa," *JJS* 23 (1972) 28-50; 24 (1973) 51-64.

Vorsokr: H. Diels (ed.), *Die Fragmente der Vorsokratiker*, 7th ed. Kranz (Berlin: Weidmannsche, 1954). Cited according to volume and page number, and fragment of author.

Weinreich: O. Weinreich, *Antike Heilungswunder* (Giessen: Töpelmann, 1909).

y.: *Talmud Yerushalmi*, ed. Krotoshin. Cited according to folio and column.

PART I

OLD TESTAMENT STORIES

ABRAHAM AND PHARAOH

This incident is a good example of a literary event that achieves multiple and profoundly modified narration. The ruler who wishes to take the Patriarch's wife for his own is thwarted by God. In this account, the ruler is Pharaoh. In the other two accounts in Genesis, Gen 20:1-18 (Abraham) and Gen 26:6-11 (Isaac), the ruler is Abimelech of Gerar. The *Genesis Apocryphon* borrows and embellishes motifs from Gen 20:1-18 in its narration, while Josephus omits the motif of prayer from his retelling of the second account in Genesis.

OT 1
Pharaoh, Chastened, Restores Sarah to Abraham.
Gen 12:10-20.

Now there was a famine in the land. So Abram went down to Egypt to sojourn there, for the famine was severe in the land. When he was about to enter Egypt, he said to Sarai his wife, "I know that you are a beautiful woman to behold; and when the Egyptians see you, they will say, 'This is his wife;' then they will kill me, but they will let you live. Say you are my sister, that it may go well with me because of you, and that my life may be spared on your account." When Abram entered Egypt, the Egyptians saw that the woman was very beautiful. And when the princes of Pharaoh saw her, they praised her to Pharaoh. And the woman was taken into Pharaoh's house. And for her sake, he dealt well with Abram; and he had sheep, oxen, he-asses, menservants, maidservants, she-asses, and camels.

But the Lord afflicted Pharaoh and his house with great plagues because of Sarai, Abram's wife. So Pharaoh called Abram, and said, "What is this you have done to me? Why did you not tell me that she was your wife? Why did you say, 'She is my sister,' so that I took her for my wife? Now then, here is your wife, take her and be gone." And Pharaoh gave men orders concerning him; and they set him on the way, with his wife and all that he had.

OT 2
How Pharaoh Took and Returned Sarah.
Jubilees 13,10-15 (Hebrew/Ethiopic). Charlesworth 2,83.

And he arose from there and he went toward the South and he reached Hebron—and Hebron was built then. And he dwelt there two years. And he went to the land of the South as far as Bealoth. And there was a famine in the land. And Abram went into Egypt in the third year of the week and he stayed in Egypt five years before his wife was taken from him. And Tanis of Egypt was built then, seven years after Hebron.

And it came to pass when Pharaoh took Sarai, the wife of Abram, that the Lord plagued Pharaoh and his house with great plagues on account of Sarai, the wife of Abram. And Abram was honored with many possessions: sheep and oxen and asses and horses and camels and male and female servants and silver and much gold. And Lot, his brother's son, also had possessions. And Pharaoh returned Sarai, the wife of Abram. And he sent him out from the land of Egypt.

OT 3
Abraham Prays and Drives Away the Evil Spirit That Had Been Afflicting Pharaoh.
Genesis Apocryphon 20,21-34 (Aramaic). Fitzmyer, 65-67.[1]

> [Abraham has a dream which warns him of the danger Sarah's beauty poses to his life. After three of the Pharaoh's ministers describe this beauty, Pharaoh takes Sarah, but at the prayer of Abraham a "pestilential," "evil" spirit afflicts Pharaoh and his household: Pharaoh cannot approach Sarah. This lasts two years.]

Then Hirqanos came to me and begged me to come and pray over the king and lay my hands upon[2] him that he might be cured, for [he had seen me] in a dream.

But Lot said to him: Abram, my uncle, cannot pray for the king while his wife Sarai is with him. Now go, tell the king that he should send his wife away from him, (back) to her own husband. Then he (Abram) will pray for him that he might be cured (*wyḥh*).

When Hirqanos heard Lot's words, he went (and) said to the king: All these plagues and afflictions with which my lord, the king, is beset and afflicted (are) due to Sarai, the wife of Abram. Let Sarai be returned to her husband, Abram, and this plague will depart from you, as well as the spirit of purulence.

So he (the Pharaoh) summoned me to him and said to me: What have you done to me for [Sar]ai's sake, in telling me, 'She is my sister,' when she was (really) your wife? And I took her to be my wife. Here is your wife; take her away; go, depart from all the provinces of Egypt. But now pray for me and for my household that this evil spirit may be commanded (to depart)[3] from us.

So I prayed for that [. . . .] and I laid my hands upon his [he]ad. The plague was removed from him and the evil [spirit] was commanded (to depart) [from him] and he was cured (*why*).

And the king rose [and] [made] known to me [. . .]; and the king swore an oath to me that [he had] not [touched her?].

And then [they brought] Sarai to [me].

The king gave her [m]uch [silver and go]ld; many garments of fine linen and purple [. . . and he laid them] before her, and Hagar too. H[e hand]ed her over to me and appointed men to escort me [out of Egypt . . . .]

[1] In Fitzmyer's system, brackets = a lacuna in the Aramaic text, parentheses enclose explanatory additions.
[2] Motif: Matt 9:1/Mark 5:23; Mark 6:5; 7:32; 8:23.25; 16:18; Luke 4:40; 13:13; Acts 9:12. 17-18; 28:8.
[3] Fitzmyer points out that the root *g'r* is rendered in the LXX by *epitiman*. This same notion of "rebuking" used in connection with a demon, mentioned or implied, is found in Matt 8:26; 12:16/Mark 4:39/Luke 8:24; Matt 17:18/Mark 9:25/Luke 9:42; Mark 1:25; 3:12; Luke 4:35.39.41.55(?); Jude 9.

OT 4
How God Upheld Abraham.
Philo, *On Abraham* 19. Loeb 6,49-53.

This is the opening of the story of the friend of God, and it is followed by actions which call for anything but contempt. But their greatness is not clear to everyone, but only to those who have tasted virtue and who recognize the greatness of the good things which belong to the soul and therefore are wont to deride those which win the admiration of the multitude. God, then, approving of the action just related, at once rewards the man of worth with a great gift; for when his marriage was threatened through the designs of a licentious potentate, God kept it safe and unharmed. The occasion which led up to the attempted outrage originated in the following way. There had been a failure of the crops for a considerable period, at one time through a great and excessive rainfall, at another through drought and stormy weather; and the cities of Syria, hard pressed through continual famine, were stripped of their inhabitants who scattered in different directions to seek for food and to procure necessities. Abraham, then, learning that there was a rich and abundant supply of corn in Egypt, where the river by its seasonal flooding had turned the plains into pools, and well-tempered winds had produced and fostered a fine growth of corn, set off thither with his whole household. He had a wife distinguished greatly for her goodness of soul and beauty of body, in which she surpassed all the women of her time. When the chief people of Egypt saw her and admired her beauty, since the highly placed leave nothing unobserved, they told the king. He sent for the woman and, marking her surpassing comeliness, paid little regard to decency or the laws enacted to shew respect to strangers, but gave rein to his licence and determined nominally to take her in marriage, but in reality to bring her to shame. She who in a foreign country was at the mercy of a licentious and cruel-hearted despot and had no one to protect her, for her husband was helpless, menaced as he was by the terror of stronger powers, joined him in fleeing for refuge to the last remaining championship, that of God. And God, who is kindly and merciful and shields the wronged, had pity for the strangers and plied the king with almost intolerable pains and grievous penalties. He filled him body and soul with all manner of scarce curable plagues. All appetite for pleasure was eradicated and replaced by visitations of the opposite kind, by cravings for release from the endless tortures which night and day haunted and racked him almost to death. The whole household, too, shared the punishment with him, since none had shewn indignation at the outrage, but all by consenting were almost accomplices in the misdeed. Thus the chastity of the woman was preserved, while the nobility and piety of the man was evidenced by God, who deigned to grant him this signal boon, that his marriage, which would have been in almost immediate danger of violation, should remain free from harm and outrage, that marriage from which was to issue not a family of a few sons and daughters, but a whole nation, and that the nation dearest of all to God, which, as I hold, has received the gift of priesthood and prophecy on behalf of all mankind.

[As usual, Philo goes on to give an allegorical interpreta-

tion of the incident. Abraham = a good mind; Sarai
("Sovereign Lady") = virtue.]

OT 5
Pharaoh and Sarah: Josephus' Account of the Incident.
Jewish Wars 5,379-82. Loeb 3,319.

Nechaos, also called Pharaoh, the reigning king of Egypt,
came down with a prodigious host and carried off Sarah, a prin-
cess and the mother of our race. What action, then, did her husband Abraham, our forefather, take? Did he avenge himself on
the ravisher with the sword? He had, to be sure, three hundred
and eighteen officers under him, each in command of a bound-
less army. Or did he not rather count these as nothing, if un-
aided by God, and uplifting pure hands towards this spot which
you have now polluted enlist the invincible Ally on his side?
And was not the queen, after one night's absence, sent back im-
maculate to her lord, while the Egyptian, in awe of the spot
which you have stained with the blood of your countrymen and
trembling at his visions of the night, fled, bestowing silver and
gold upon those Hebrews beloved of God?

OT 6
Pharoah and Sarah: Another Version by Josephus.
Jewish Antiquities 1,8,1. Loeb 4,81-83.

Some time later, Canaan being in the grip of a famine, Abraham, hearing of the prosperity of the Egyptians, was of a mind
to visit them, alike to profit by their abundance and to hear
what their priests said about the gods; intending, if he found
their doctrine more excellent than his own, to conform to it, or
else to convert them to a better mind should his own beliefs
prove superior. He took Sarra with him, and fearing the Egyptians' frenzy for women, lest the king should slay him because of
his wife's beauty, he devised the following scheme: he pre-
tended to be her brother and, telling her that their interest required it, instructed her to play her part accordingly.

On their arrival in Egypt all fell out as Abraham had sus-
pected: his wife's beauty was noised abroad, insomuch that
Pharaothes, the king of the Egyptians, not content with the reports of her, was fired with a desire to see her and on the point
of laying hands on her. But God thwarted his criminal passion
by an outbreak of disease and political disturbance; and when he
had sacrifices offered to discover a remedy, the priests declared
that his calamity was due to the wrath of God, because he had

wished to outrage the stranger's wife. Terrified, he asked Sarra who she was and who was this man she had brought with her. On learning the truth, he made his excuses to Abraham: it was, he said, in the belief that she was his sister, not his wife, that he had set his affections on her; he had wished to contract a marriage alliance and not to outrage her in a transport of passion. He further gave him abundant riches, and Abraham consorted with the most learned of the Egyptians, whence his virtue and reputation became still more conspicuous.

Moses' First Encounters in Midian

OT 7
Moses Aids the Daughters of Reuel.
Exod 2:15-22.

And Pharaoh heard of this thing [the killing of the Egyptian], and he sought to kill Moses; and Moses fled from before Pharaoh, and he dwelt in Midian, and he sat down by a well.[1]

Now the priest of Midian had seven daughters; and they came and drew water, and filled the troughs to water their father's flock. The shepherds came and drove them away; but Moses rose up and saved them and watered their flock.

When they came to their father Reuel, he said: How is it that you have come so soon today? They said: An Egyptian rescued us from the hand of the shepherds, and he even drew water for us and watered the flock.

He said to his daughters: And where is he? Why have you left the man? Call him that he may eat bread.

And Moses was content to dwell with the man, and he gave Moses his daughter Zipporah. She bore a son and he called his name Gershom; for he said: I have been a sojourner in a foreign land.

[1] Motif: Gen 24:11; 29:1-8; 1 Sam 9:11; John 4:6.

OT 8
Moses' First Encounters and Adventures in Midian.
Tg. Yer. I Exod 2:15-22.

And Pharaoh heard of this thing and wanted to kill Moses; and Moses fled from before Pharaoh, and he dwelt in the land of Midian, and he sat down by a well.

Now the lord of Midian had seven daughters, and they came and drew water, and they filled the troughs to water the flock of their father. And shepherds came and drove them away; and Moses rose up in the strength of his power, and redeemed them and watered their flock.

And they came to Reuel their grandfather; and he said: How is it that you have come early today? They said: The Egyptian man saved us from the hand of the shepherds, and he himself drew water and watered the flock. And he said to his son's daughters: And where is he? Why did you leave the man? Call him and let him eat bread.

And when Reuel learned that Moses had fled from Pharaoh, he cast him into a pit. But Zipporah, the daughter of his son, sustained him with food secretly for ten years. And at the end of ten years, he brought him up out of the pit. And Moses went into the garden of Reuel and gave thanks and prayed before Yhwh who would work miracles and mighty acts through him. And there was shown to him the rod which had been created between the twilights, and on which there was engraved the great and glorious Name with which he was to perform the wonders in Egypt, divide the Sea of Reeds, and bring forth water from the rock. And it was fixed in the middle of the garden; and he stretched forth his hand immediately and took it.

Then, behold, Moses was content to dwell with the man; and he gave him Zipporah, the daughter of his son, to Moses, and she bore a male child; and he called his name Gershom because, he said, I have been a sojourner in a strange land that is not mine.

OT 9
Moses Saves the Shepherd Girls at the Well in Midian.
Philo, *Life of Moses* 1,10-11. Loeb 6,303-07.

I will describe an action of his at this time which, though it may seem a petty matter, argues a spirit of no petty kind. The Arabs are breeders of cattle, and they employ for tending them not only men but women, youths and maidens alike, and not only those of insignificant and humble families but those of the highest position. Seven maidens, daughters of the priest, had come to a well, and, after attaching the buckets to the ropes, drew water, taking turns with each to share the labour equally. They had with great industry filled the troughs which lay near, when some other shepherds appeared on the spot who, disdaining the weakness of the girls, tried to drive them and their flock away, and proceeded to bring their own animals to the place where the water lay ready, and thus appropriate the labours of others.

But Moses, who was not far off, seeing what had happened, quickly ran up and, standing nearby, said: "Stop this injustice. You think you can take advantage of the loneliness of the place. Are you not ashamed to let your arms and elbows live an idle life? You are masses of long hair and lumps of flesh, not men. The girls are working like youths, and shirk none of their duties, while you young men go daintily like girls. Away with you: give place to those who were here before you, to whom the water belongs. Properly, you should have drawn for them, to make the supply more abundant; instead, you are all agog to take from them what they have provided. Nay, by the heavenly eye of justice, you shall not take it; for that eye sees even what is done in the greatest solitude. In me at least, it has appointed a champion whom you did not expect, for I fight to succour these injured maidens, allied to a mighty arm which the rapacious may not see, but you shall feel its invisible power to wound if you do not change your ways."

As he proceeded thus, they were seized with fear that they were listening to some oracular utterance, for as he spoke he grew inspired and was transfigured into a prophet. They became submissive, and led the maidens' flock to the troughs, after removing their own.

The girls went home in high glee, and told the story of the unexpected event to their father, who thence conceived a strong desire to see the stranger, which he showed by censuring them for their ingratitude. "What possessed you," he said, "to let him depart? You should have brought him straight along, and pressed him if he showed reluctance. Did you ever have to charge me with unsociable ways? Do you not expect that you may again fall in with those who would wrong you? Those who forget kindness are sure to lack defenders. Still, your error is not yet past cure. Run back with all speed, and invite him to receive from me first the entertainment due to him as a stranger, secondly some requital of the favour which we owe to him."

They hurried back and found him not far from the well, and, after explaining their father's message, persuaded him to come home with them.

Their father was at once struck with admiration of his face, and soon afterwards of his disposition, for great natures are transparent and need no length of time to be recognized. Accordingly, he gave him the fairest of his daughters in marriage and, by that one action, attested all his noble qualities, and showed that excellence standing alone deserves our love, and

needs no commendation from aught else, but carries within itself the tokens by which it is known.

OT 10
Moses at the Well in Madian.
Josephus, *Jewish Antiquities* 2,11,1-2. Loeb 4,277-79.

On reaching the town of Madian(e), situated by the Red Sea
and named after one of Abraham's sons by Katura, he sat down
on the brink of a well and there rested after his toil and hard-
ships, at midday, not far from the town.[1]

Here he was destined to play a part, arising out of the customs of the inhabitants, which exhibited his merits and proved
the opening of better fortune.

For, those regions being scant of water, the shepherds used
to make a first claim on the wells, for fear that, the water being
exhausted by others beforehand, there should be nothing for
their flocks to drink.

Now there came to this well seven sisters, virgin daughters of
Raguel, a priest held in high veneration by the people of the
country; they were in charge of their father's flocks, for this
function is customarily undertaken by women also among the
Troglodytes, and, arriving first, they drew from the well sufficient water for their flocks into troughs constructed to receive
it.

But when shepherds appearing set upon the young women,
in order to appropriate the water for themselves, Moses, deem-
ing it monstrous to overlook this injury to the girls and to suffer
these men's violence to triumph over the maidens' rights, beat
off the arrogant intruders, and afforded the others opportune
aid.

And they, after this beneficent act, went to their father and,
recounting the shepherds' insolence and the succour which the
stranger had lent them, besought him not to let such charity go
for nought or unrewarded.

The father commended his children for their zeal for their
benefactor and bade them bring Moses to his presence to receive the gratitude that was his due.

On his arrival, he told him of his daughters' testimony to the
help which he had rendered, and, expressing admiration for his
gallantry, added that he had not bestowed this service upon
those who had no sense of gratitude but on persons well able to
requite a favour, indeed to outdo by the amplitude of the reward the measure of the benefit.

He therewith adopted him as his son, gave him one of his

daughters in marriage, and appointed him keeper and master of his flocks, for in those consisted of yore all the wealth of the barbarian races.

¹ Motif: Jn 4:6.

Moses and Israel at the Red Sea

OT 11
The Miracle at the Red Sea.
Exod 14:21-31.

Then Moses stretched out his hand over the sea; and Yhwh forced the sea back by a strong east wind all night; and he made the sea into dry land, and the waters were divided. And the sons of Israel went into the midst of the sea on dry land, and the waters were a wall to them on their right hand and left. And Egypt pursued and went in after them, all the horses of Pharaoh and his chariots and his chariot drivers, into the midst of the sea. And in the morning watch, Yhwh looked down on the army of Egypt, from the pillar of fire and cloud; and he threw the army of Egypt into a panic. And he clogged the wheels of their chariots and they lumbered along heavily. And Egypt said: "Let us flee from Israel because Yhwh is fighting for them against Egypt."

Then Yhwh said to Moses: stretch out your hand over the sea, and let the waters come back over Egypt, over his chariots and chariot drivers. And Moses stretched out his hand over the sea, and the sea returned to its place at morning; and Egypt was fleeing before it, and Yhwh threw Egypt into the midst of the sea. And the waters came back and covered the chariots and the chariot drivers and the whole force of Pharaoh which went in after them in the sea; there was not left even one of them. And the sons of Israel walked on dry land in the midst of the sea, and the waters were a wall to them on their right hand and their left.

Thus Yhwh saved Israel that day from the hand of Egypt; and Israel saw Egypt dead on the shore of the sea; and Israel saw the mighty work which Yhwh performed against Egypt; and the people feared Yhwh and put their faith in him and in Moses his servant.

OT 12
The Departure from Egypt and the Crossing over the Sea.
Biblical Antiquities 10,2-6 (Hebrew/Latin). Charlesworth
2,317.

And while they were going forth from there and setting out,
the heart of the Egyptians was hardened once more, and they
continued to pursue them and found them by the Red Sea. And
the sons of Israel cried out to their Lord and said to Moses, saying, "Behold now the time of our destruction has come. For the
sea is ahead of us, and the throng of enemies is behind us, and
we are in the middle. Is it for this that God has brought us forth,
or are these the covenants that he established with our fathers,
saying, 'To your seed will I give the land in which you dwell'
that now he might do with us whatever is pleasing in his sight?"
Then in considering the fearful situation of the moment, the
sons of Israel were split in their opinions according to three
strategies. For the tribe of Reuben and the tribe of Issachar and
the tribe of Zebulun and the tribe of Simeon said, "Come, let us
cast ourselves into the sea. For it is better for us to die in the
water than to be killed by our enemies." But the tribe of Gad
and the tribe of Asher and the tribe of Dan and that of Naphtali
said, "No, but let us go back with them; and if they are willing to
spare our lives, we will serve them." But the tribe of Levi and
the tribe of Judah and that of Joseph and the tribe of Benjamin
said, "Not so, but let us take up our weapons and fight with
them, and God will be with us."

And Moses cried out to the Lord and said, "Lord God of our
fathers, did you not say to me, 'Go and tell the sons of Israel,
"God has sent me to you" '? And now behold you have brought
your people to the edge of the sea, and the enemy has pursued
them; but you, Lord, remember your name." And God said,
"Why have you cried out to me? Lift up your rod and strike the
sea, and it will be dried up." And when Moses did all this, God
rebuked the sea and the sea was dried up. And the seas of water
piled up and the depths of the earth were visible, and the foundations of the world were laid bare by the fearful din of God and
by the breath of the anger of the Lord. And Israel passed
through the middle of the sea on dry ground.

And the Egyptians saw this and continued following them.
And God hardened their perception, and they did not know
that they were entering the sea. And while the Egyptians were
in the sea, God again commanded the sea and said to Moses,
"Strike the sea yet once more." And he did so. And the Lord

commanded the sea, and it started flowing again and covered
the Egyptians and their chariots and horsemen.

OT 13
The Escape from Egypt.
Jubilees 48,12-14 (Hebrew/Ethiopic). Charlesworth 2,139-40.

And despite all the signs and wonders, Prince Mastema was
not shamed until he had become strong and called to the Egyptians so that they might pursue after you with all the army of
Egyptians, with their chariots, and with their horses, and with
all the multitude of the peoples of Egypt.

And I stood between the Egyptians and Israel, and we delivered Israel from his hand and from the hand of his people. And
the Lord brought them out through the midst of the sea as
through dry land. And all of the people whom he brought out to
pursue after Israel the Lord our God threw into the middle of
the sea into the depths of the abyss beneath the children of
Israel. Just as the men of Egypt cast their sons into the river he
avenged one million. And one thousand strong and ardent men
perished on account of one infant whom they threw into the
midst of the river from the sons of your people.

OT 14
The Escape through the Red Sea.
Philo, *Life of Moses* 1,32. Loeb 6,367-69.

At sunset a south wind of tremendous violence arose, and, as
it rushed down, the sea under it was driven back and, though
regularly tidal, was on this occasion more so than usually, and
swept as into a chasm or whirlpool, when driven against the
shore. No star appeared, but a thick black cloud covered the
whole heaven, and the murkiness of the night struck terror into
the pursuers. Moses now, at God's command, smote the sea
with his staff, and as he did so it broke and parted into two. Of
the waters thus divided, one part rose up to a vast height, where
the break was made, and stood quite firmly, motionless and still
like a wall; those behind were held back and bridled in their
forward course, and reared as though pulled back by invisible
reins; while the intervening part, which was the scene of the
breaking, dried up and became a broad highway. Moses, seeing
this, marvelled and was glad, and in the fullness of his joy encouraged his men and bade them move on with all speed.

And, when they were about to begin the passage, a most extraordinary sign occurred. The guiding cloud, which at other

times stood in front, turned round to the back of the multitude
to form its rearguard, and thus posted between the pursuers and
pursued regulated the course of the latter and drove them
before it under safe protection, but checked and repelled the
former as they strove to advance. When the Egyptians saw this,
tumult and confusion prevailed everywhere among them. In
their terror, their ranks fell into disorder. They tumbled over
each other, and sought to escape, but it was of no avail; for,
while the Hebrews with their women and children, still mere
infants, crossed on a dry road in the early dawn, it was otherwise
with the Egyptians.

Under the north wind, the returning tide was swept back,
and hurled its lofty billows upon them. The two sections of the
sea rolled upon them from either side, united and submerged
them, horses, chariots and all, with not even a torchbearer left
to announce to the people of Egypt the sudden disaster. This
great and marvelous work struck the Hebrews with amazement
and, finding themselves unexpectedly victorious in a bloodless
conflict, and seeing their enemies, one and all, destroyed in a
moment, they set up two choirs, one of men and one of women,
on the beach, and sang hymns of thanksgiving to God. Over
these choirs, Moses and his sister presided, and led the hymns,
the former for the men and the latter for the women.

OT 15
Moses at the Red Sea.
Philo, *Life of Moses* 2,45-46. Loeb 6,573-77.

Having completed this necessary account of the oracles of
mixed character, I will proceed next to describe those delivered
by the prophet himself under divine inspiration, for this was included in my promise. The examples of his possession by God's
spirit begin with one which was also the beginning of the prosperity of the nation, when its many myriads set out as colonists
from Egypt to the cities of Syria. Men and women alike, they
had traversed a long and pathless wilderness, and arrived at the
Red Sea, as it is called. They were then naturally in great difficulties, as they could not cross the sea for want of boats, and did
not think it safe to retrace their steps. When they were in this
state of mind, a greater misfortune burst upon them. The king
of Egypt, accompanied by a very formidable body of infantry
and cavalry, came in hot pursuit, eager to overtake them and so
chastise them for leaving the country. . . . But, while in these
helpless straits, they were at death's door with consternation the
prophet, seeing the whole nation entangled in the meshes of

panic, like a draught of fishes, was taken out of himself by divine possession and uttered these inspired words: "Alarm you needs must feel. Terror is near at hand: the danger is great. In front is a vast expanse of sea; no haven for a refuge, no boats at hand: behind, the menace of the enemy's troops, which march along in unresting pursuit. Whither can one turn or swim for safety? Everything has attacked us suddenly from every side—earth, sea, man, the elements of nature. Yet be of good courage, faint not. Stand with unshaken minds, look for the invincible help which God will send. Self-sent it will be with you anon, invisible it will fight before you. Ere now you have often experienced its unseen defence. I see it preparing for the contest and casting a noose round the necks of the enemy. It drags them down through the sea. They sink like lead into the depths. You see them still alive: I have a vision of them dead, and to-day you too shall see their corpses."

So he spake with words of promise exceeding anything they could hope for. But they began to find by the experience of facts the truth of the heavenly message. For what he prophesied came to pass through the might of God, though harder to credit than any fable. Let us picture the scene. The sea breaks in two, and each section retires. The parts around the break, through the whole depth of their waters, congeal to serve as walls of vast strength: a path is drawn straight, a road of miracle between the frozen walls on either side: the nation makes its passage, marching safely through the sea, as on a dry path or a stone-paved causeway; for the sand is crisped, and its scattered particles grow together into a unity: the enemy advance in unresting pursuit, hastening to their own destruction: the cloud goes behind the travellers' rear to guide them on their way, and within is the vision of the Godhead, flashing rays of fire. Then the waters which had been stayed from their course and parted for a while return to their place: the dried-up cleft between the walls suddenly becomes a sea again: the enemy meet their doom, sent to their last sleep by the fall of the frozen walls, and overwhelmed by the tides, as they rush down upon their path as into a ravine! that doom is evidenced by the corpses which are floated to the top and strew the surface of the sea: last comes a mighty rushing wave, which flings the corpses in heaps upon the opposite shore, a sight inevitably to be seen by the saved, thus permitted not only to escape their dangers, but also to behold their enemies fallen under a chastisement which no words can express, through the power of God and not of man.

Compare: *The Confusion of Tongues* 10 and 16; *On Dreams* 2; *The Contemplative Life* 11. This incident provides Philo with many occasions for his allegorical applications.

OT 16
The Miraculous Passage of the Red Sea.
Josephus, *Jewish Antiquities* 2,16,1-3. Loeb 4,311-15.

Having spoken thus far, he [Moses] led them towards the sea under the eyes of the Egyptians; for these were in view but, exhausted with the fatigue of the pursuit, judged it well to defer battle until the morrow. Then, when he reached the shore, Moses took his staff and made supplication to God, invoking His alliance and aid in these words: "Thus thyself knowest full well that escape from our present plight passes alike the might and the wit of man; nay, if there be any means of salvation at all for this host which at thy will has left Egypt, thine it is to provide it. For our part, despairing of other hope or resource, we fling ourselves upon thy protection alone, and expectantly, if aught be forthcoming from thy providence or might to snatch us from the wrath of the Egyptians, we look to thee. May it come quickly, this aid that shall manifest to us thy power; raise the hearts of this people, whom hopelessness has sunk into the depths of woe, to serenity and confidence of salvation. Nor are these straits in which we find ourselves without thy domain; nay, thine is the sea, thine the mountain that encompasseth us: this then can open at thy command, or the deep become dry land, or we might e'en find escape through the air, should it please thine almighty power that after this manner we should be saved."

After this solemn appeal to God, he smote the sea with his staff. And at that stroke it recoiled and, retreating into itself, left bare the soil, affording passage and flight for the Hebrews. Moses, beholding this clear manifestation of God and the sea withdrawn from its own bed to give them place, set the first foot upon it and bade the Hebrews follow him and pursue their way by this God-sent road, rejoicing at the peril awaiting their advancing foes and rendering thanks to God for the salvation thus miraculously brought by him to light.

They, without more ado, sped forth with zest, assured of God's attendant presence; whereupon the Egyptians at first deemed them mad, thus rushing to a certain death, but when they saw them far advanced unscathed, unchecked by obstacle or discomfiture, they made speed to pursue them, imagining that the sea would remain motionless for them also, and with the cavalry leading they proceeded to descend. But the Hebrews, while their enemies were arming and wasting time over that, had outstripped them and emerged unharmed on the opposite shore; this, however, but stimulated the ardour of the Egyptians for the pursuit, in the belief that they too would suffer nothing. Little dreamed they that it was a road reserved for the Hebrews, no public highway, whereon they were setting foot, a road created solely for the salvation of those in jeopardy, not for the use of them that were bent upon their destruction. When, therefore, the entire army of the Egyptians was once within it, back poured the sea, enveloping and with swelling wind-swept billows descending upon the Egyptians: rain fell in torrents from heaven, crashing thunder accompanied the flash of lightning, aye and thunderbolts were hurled. In short, there was not one of those destructive forces which in token of God's wrath combine to smite mankind that failed to assemble then; for withal a night of gloom and darkness overwhelmed them. Thus perished they to a man, without a single one remaining to return with tidings of the disaster to those whom they had left at home.

The Waters of Marah

OT 17
Moses at the Waters of Marah.
Exod 15:22-25.

And Moses had Israel set out from the Sea of Reeds; and they went up into the desert of Shur, and they walked three days in the desert, and they found no water; and they came to Marah, and they could not drink the water from Marah, because it was bitter—that is why they called its name Marah.

And the people murmured against Moses saying: What shall we drink? And he cried to Yhwh; and Yhwh showed him a tree, and he threw it into the water, and it became sweet.

Compare: OT 22; OT 25; OT 51.

OT 18
Moses at the Waters of Marah.
Tg. Yer. I Exod 15:22-26.

And Moses had Israel journey from the Sea of Reeds, and they went to the desert of Ḥaluṣa; and they journeyed three days in the desert, lax in instruction[1] and they did not find water. And they came to Marah, and they could not drink the water from Marah, because it was bitter—that is why its name is called Marah. And the people murmured against Moses, saying: What shall we drink? And he prayed before Yhwh; and Yhwh showed him the bitter tree Ardiphne; and he wrote the great and glorious Name on it, and threw it into the midst of the waters, and the waters were sweetened.[2]

[1] See the similar expression in a fuller form in OT 23 and the discussion there.

[2] *Tg. Neof.* says that at Moses' prayer, the Lord showed him a tree, "and the Word of the Lord took from it a word of the Law and he cast it into the midst of the water and the waters were made sweet." Other targums vary the theme slightly.

OT 19

How Moses Receives the Tree of Life.
Biblical Antiquities 11,15 (Hebrew/Latin). Charlesworth 2,319.

And all the people stood far off, but Moses drew near the cloud, knowing that God was there. And then God told him his statutes and his judgments, and he detained him forty days and forty nights. And there he commanded him many things and showed him the tree of life, from which he cut off and took and threw into Marah, and the water of Marah became sweet. And it followed them in the wilderness forty years and went up to the mountain with them and went down into the plains.[1]

[1] Motif: Philo, *Allegorical Interpretation* 2,86; CD 6,4; *t. Sukk.* 4,9; *Tg. Neof.* Deut 2:6; 1 Cor 10:4. See further, note 1 of OT 25.

OT 20

Moses' Prayer at Marah.
Philo, *Life of Moses* 1,33. Loeb 6,369-73.

They set out from the sea coast, and travelled for some time, no longer in any fear of danger from the enemy. But after three days the water failed, and thirst once more reduced them to despondency. Again they began to grumble at their lot, as though nothing good had befallen them hitherto. For, under the onset of the present terror, we always lose sense of the pleasantness of past blessings.

Then they saw some springs and ran to draw from them, full

of joy, but in their ignorance of the truth were deceived. For the water was bitter and, when they had tasted it, the disappointment broke them down. Their bodies were exhausted and their souls dejected, not so much for themselves as for their infant children, the sight of whom, as they cried for something to drink, was more than they could face without tears. Some of the more thoughtless, men of feeble piety, even denounced the past events as not having been intended for their benefit, but rather to bring them into worse misfortunes. It were better, they said, to die thrice, not merely once, at the hands of enemies, than to perish, or worse than perish, by thirst. To depart from life swiftly and easily is, in the eyes of the wise, the same thing as never dying, and death in the true sense is that which comes slowly and painfully, whose terrors appear not in the state of death, but only in the process of dying.

While they were engaged in such lamentations, Moses again addressed his supplications to God, that, knowing the weakness of his creatures, and particularly of mankind, and the necessities of the body, which depends on food, and is tied to those stern mistresses, meat and drink, he should pardon the despondent and also satisfy the needs of all, not at some distant time but with a boon bestowed promptly and swiftly, considering the inborn short-sightedness of mortality, which desires that assistance should be rendered quickly and at the moment.

Hardly had he so prayed, when God sent in advance the power of his grace and, opening the vigilant eye of the suppliant's soul, bade him lift and throw into the spring a tree which he shewed him, possibly formed by nature to exercise a virtue which had hitherto remained unknown, or possibly created on this occasion for the service which it was destined to perform.

Moses did as he was bid, whereupon the springs became sweet, and were converted into drinkable water, so that no one could even guess that they had originally been bitter, since no trace or tang remained to remind one of its former badness.

OT 21
How God Showed Moses the Way to Sweeten the Waters at Marah.
Josephus, *Jewish Antiquities* 3,1,1-2. Loeb 4,321-25.

> [Josephus, following closely the order of events in Exod 15: 22ff, accents the barren and harsh experience of the desert.]

Journeying thus, they arrived towards evening at Mar, a place which they so named from the vileness of its water, *mar* meaning "bitterness;" and there, worn out with ceaseless marching and lack of food, which had now completely failed them, they halted. There was a well—a further reason for stopping there—doubtless by itself insufficient for so large an army, yet a source of slight encouragement to them when found in those regions; for they had heard from their scouts that none was to be had by proceeding further. That water, however, proved bitter, and not only could the men not drink it, but even the beasts of burden found it intolerable.

Moses, seeing their despondency and the indisputable gravity of the case—for this was no sound army, capable of meeting the stress of necessity with manly fortitude, but one whose nobler instincts were vitiated by a rabble of women and children, too feeble to respond to oral admonition—Moses, I say, was in yet more serious straits, in that he made the sufferings of all his own. For it was to no other than to him that they all flocked, imploring him, wives for their infants, husbands for their wives, not to neglect them, but to procure them some means of salvation.

He therefore betook himself to prayer, entreating God to change that present evil property of the water and to render it drinkable.

And, God having consented to grant that favour, he picked up the end of a stick that lay at his feet, cleft it in twain, lengthwise, and then, flinging it into the well, impressed upon the Hebrews that God had lent an ear to his prayers and had promised to render the water such as they desired, provided that they executed his orders with no remissness, but with alacrity.

On their asking what they must do to procure the amelioration of the water, he bade those in the prime of life stand in a ring and draw, declaring that what remained, after they had drained off the larger part, would be drinkable. So, they set to work, and the water, belaboured and purified by these incessant blows, at length became good to drink.

Compare: OT 52.

The Waters of Meribah: at Rephidim

OT 22
Moses at the Waters of Meribah.
Exod 17:1-7.

And the whole congregation of the sons of Israel set out from the desert of Sin; by stages, at the command of Yhwh; and they camped at Rephidim, and there was no water for the people to drink. And the people contended with Moses, and they said: Give us water that we may drink.

And Moses said to them: Why do you contend with me? Why do you tempt Yhwh? And the people were thirsty there for water, and the people murmured against Moses, and they said to him: Why this? You brought us up from Egypt, to kill us and our children and our cattle with thirst!

And Moses cried out to Yhwh saying: What shall I do for this people? A little more and they will stone me. And Yhwh said to Moses: Pass before the people, and take with you some of the elders of Israel; and your staff with which you struck the Nile, take it in your hand and go. Behold [as for] me, I will stand before you there on the rock at Horeb; and you will strike on the rock, and water will come forth from it, and the people will drink. And Moses did so in the eyes of the elders of Israel.

And he called the name of the place Massah and Meribah, because of the contention of the sons of Israel and because of their tempting Yhwh, saying: Is Yhwh in our midst or not?

OT 23
Moses at the Waters of Meribah.
Tg. Yer. I Exod 17:1-7.

And the whole congregation of the sons of Israel journeyed from the desert of Sin; their journeyings [were regulated] by the Word of Yhwh. And they camped at Rephidim, the place where their hands were lax in the commandments of the Torah.[1]

And the fountains were dry and there was no water for the people to drink. And the wicked of the people contended with Moses; and they said: Give us water that we may drink.

And Moses said to them: Why do you contend with me, and why do you tempt before Yhwh?

And the people thirsted there for water, and the people murmured against Moses and they said: Why did you bring us up out of Egypt to kill us and our children and our cattle with thirst? And Moses prayed before Yhwh, saying: What shall I do for this people? Just a little more and they will stone me. And

Yhwh said to Moses: Pass before the people, and take with you some of the elders of Israel; and your rod with which you struck the Nile, take [it] in your hand and go standing before you there in the place where you will see a footprint on the mountain of Horeb. And you shall strike the stone with your rod, and water will flow from it for drinking and the people will drink.

And Moses did just this before the elders of Israel.

And he called the name of the place "Temptation and Strife" because the sons of Israel strove with Moses, and because they tempted before Yhwh saying: Does the Glory of the Shekinah of Yhwh truly dwell among us or not?

[1] This phrase probably represents the full formulation of the enigmatic expression in *Tg. Yer. I* Exod 15:22 (OT 18). Only *Tg. Yer. I* associates the lack of water with the lack of practice of the commandments, just as it is only *Tg. Yer. I* that associates the presence of water with Miriam's innocence and its subsequent lack to her death in Num 20:1. The mention of "lax" or "slack" hands reflects an interpretation of Rephidim. Jerome is aware of this interpretation when he says the name means *"remissio manuum"* (Letter 77; *PL* 22,706). Philo seems to be aware of the same tradition when he speaks of those unfaithful to the Law as being like weary athletes who "drop their hands in weakness" (*The Preliminary Studies*, 29). A similar phrase can be found in vices enumerated in 1QS 4;9 (*š*pôl yādayim).

OT 24
Moses at the Waters of Meribah.
Josephus, *Jewish Antiquities* 3,1,7. Loeb 4,335-37.

When, departing thence, they reached Raphidin, in extreme agony from thirst—for having on the earlier days lit upon some scanty springs, they then found themselves in an absolutely waterless region—they were in sore distress and again vented their wrath on Moses.

But he, shunning for a while the onset of the crowd, had recourse to prayer, beseeching God, as he had given meat to them in their need, so now to afford them drink, for their gratitude for the meat would perish were drink withheld. Nor did God long defer this boon, but promised Moses that he would provide a spring with abundance of water when they looked not for it; he then bade him strike with his staff the rock which stood there before their eyes, and from it accept a plenteous draught of what they needed; for he would moreover see to it that this water should appear for them without toil or travail.

Moses, having received this response from God, now approached the people, who were expectant and had their eyes fixed upon him, having already observed him hastening from the hill. When he arrived, he told them that God would deliver them from this distress also and had even vouchsafed to save them in unexpected wise; a river was to flow for them out of the rock. And while they at this news were aghast at the thought of being forced, all spent as they were with thirst and travel, to cleave the rock, Moses struck it with his staff, whereupon it opened and there gushed out a copious stream of most pellucid water.

Amazed at this marvellous prodigy, the mere sight of which already slaked their thirst, they drank and found the current sweet and delicious, and all that was to be looked for in a gift from God.

Therefrom too they conceived an admiration for Moses, so high in God's esteem, and they offered sacrifices in return for God's care for their welfare. A writing deposited in the temple attests that God foretold to Moses that water would thus spring forth from the rock.

The Waters of Meribah: at Kadesh

OT 25
The Waters of Meribah at Kadesh.
Num 20:1-13.

And the sons of Israel, the whole congregation, came into the desert of Sin, in the first month; and the people dwelt in Kadesh; and Miriam died there and was buried.

And there was no water for the congregation, and they assembled against Moses and against Aaron; and the people contended with Moses and they said: Would that we had expired when our brethren expired before Yhwh! Why have you brought the assembly of Yhwh to this desert to die here, we and our cattle? And why have you brought us up out of Egypt to bring us to this evil place? It is no place for grain, or figs or vines or pomegranates; and there is no water to drink!

Then Moses and Aaron went from the presence of the assembly to the door of the tent of meeting; and they fell on their faces. And the Glory of Yhwh appeared to them; and Yhwh spoke to Moses saying: Take your staff, and assemble the congregation, you and Aaron your brother; and you shall speak to the rock before their eyes, and it will yield its water; and you will draw out for them water from the rock, and you will give drink to the congregation and to their cattle.

And Moses took his staff from before Yhwh, as he had commanded him. And Moses and Aaron assembled the assembly before the rock; and he said to them: Now listen rebels! From this rock shall we draw out water for you? And Moses lifted up his hand, and he struck the rock with his staff twice; and much water came out,[1] and the congregation drank, and their cattle.

And Yhwh said to Moses and to Aaron: because you did not believe me, to sanctify me in the eyes of the sons of Israel; therefore you will not bring this assembly into the land which I have given to them.

These are the waters of Meribah where the sons of Israel contended with Yhwh, and he was sanctified among them.

[1] Motif: John 7:37-39. For a complete list of the texts gathered around this theme in Rabbinic tradition, see: P. Grelot, "Jean VII, 38: Eau du Rocher ou Source du Temple?" *RB* 70 (1963) 43-51.

OT 26
The Waters of Meribah at Reqem.
Tg. Neof. Num 20:1-13.

And the sons of Israel, all the people of the congregation, entered the desert of Sin, in the first month; and the people camped at Reqem. And Miriam died there and was buried there.

And there was no water for the people of the congregation, and they assembled against Moses and against Aaron; and they contended with him, the people of the congregation, and they said thus: Would that we had died as our brethren died before Yhwh! And why now have you brought the assembly of the congregation of Yhwh to this desert to die here, we and our cattle? And why now have you brought us up from Egypt to bring us to this evil place? It is not a good place as a place for seed, without plants, without fig trees, without vines, without pomegranates; even there is no water for us to drink!

And Moses and Aaron went from before the assembly to the door of the tent of meeting; and they prostrated on their faces, and the Glory of the Shekinah of Yhwh was revealed to them; and Yhwh spoke with Moses saying: Take your staff, and gather the people of the congregation, you and Aaron your brother; and you will speak with the rock before them, before their eyes;

and it will give water, and you will draw out for them water
from the rock, and you will give drink to the people of the congregation and to their cattle.

And Moses took the staff from before Yhwh, as he had commanded him. And Moses and Aaron gathered the assembly
before the rock, and he said to them: Listen now people who
teach its teachers, who need to be taught! From this rock are
we going to draw out water for you? And Moses raised his staff,
and he struck the rock with his staff, the second time, two times[1]
and much water came out of it; and the people of the congregation drank, and their cattle. And Yhwh said to Moses and to
Aaron: Because you have not believed in me, in the name of my
Word, to sanctify my Name in the eyes of the sons of Israel, of an
oath you will not bring this assembly into the place which I have
given them.

These are the waters of the Contention, because the sons of
Israel contended before Yhwh, and he sanctified his Name
among them [or "by them," i.e., the waters].

[1] As the editors of the Díez-Macho text remark, probably
tnyn ("the second time") should be eliminated.

OT 27
The Water That Flowed From the Rock.
Philo, *Life of Moses* 1,38. Loeb 6,385.

[After combining the accounts in Exod 16 and Num 11 of
the sending of the quail, Philo goes on to tell the story of
Meribah, depending more on Num 20:1-13 than on Exod
17:1-7.]

Though this supply of food never failed and continued to be
enjoyed in abundance, a serious scarcity of water again
occurred.

Sore pressed by this, their mood turned to desperation,
whereupon Moses, taking that sacred staff with which he accomplished the signs in Egypt, under inspiration smote the steep
rock with it.

It may be that the rock contained originally a spring and now
had its artery clean severed, or perhaps that then for the first
time a body of water collected in it through hidden channels
was forced out by the impact.

Whichever is the case, it opened under the violence of the
stream and spouted out its contents, so that not only then did it

provide a remedy for their thirst but also abundance of drink for a longer time for all these thousands.

For they filled all their water vessels, as they had done on the former occasion, from the springs that were naturally bitter but were changed and sweetened by God's directing care.

> [Philo continues with a philosophical apologia for "these things," appealing to the greater but more familiar wonders of the stars, the seasons, etc. For the same type of argumentation, see Augustine's discussion of the Multiplication of the Loaves: *Comm. on John*, Tr. 24,1-2 (*PL* 35, 1592-93.)

Moses Overcomes Amalek

OT 28
How Moses Overcame Amalek.
Exod 17:8-16.

And Amalek came in, and fought with Israel at Rephidim.

And Moses said to Joshua: Choose out men for us; and go out, fight with Amalek; tomorrow I will stand on the top of the hill, and the staff of God will be in my hand. And Joshua did as Moses told him; fighting with Amalek; and Moses, Aaron, and Hur went up to the top of the hill.

And it happened that as Moses raised his hands, Israel prevailed; and when he let his hands down, Amalek prevailed. And Moses' hands grew heavy, and they took a stone, and they put it under him, and he sat on it; and Aaron and Hur took hold of his hands, one on this side and one on the other[1]; and so his hands were firm until the going down of the sun. And Joshua mowed down Amalek and his people with the edge of the sword.

And Yhwh said to Moses: Write this memorial in a book, and repeat it in the ears of Joshua; surely I will wipe out the remembrance of Amalek from under heaven. And Moses built an altar, and he called its name Yhwh Nissi; and he said: A hand upon the banner of Yhwh[2]; war between Yhwh and Amalek from generation to generation.

---

[1] Motif: John 19:18.

[2] Reading *yd ' l ns Yh*: for a discussion of this phrase, see B. Childs, *The Book of Exodus* (OT Lib.) (Philadelphia: Westminster Press, 1974) 311-12.

OT 29

Moses' Prayers and the Merits of the Fathers Overcome Amalek.

Tg. Neof. Exod 17:8-16. McNamara, 458-59.

And the lords of Amalek came and set battle-array with Israel in Rephidim.

And Moses said to Joshua: Choose out for us warrior men, and go out and set battle-array with those of the house of Amalek tomorrow. Behold, I will stand ready on the top of the height and in my hand the staff by which signs were done before Yhwh.

And Joshua did as Moses, his master, said to him, setting battle-array with those of the house of Amalek; and Moses and Aaron and Hur went up to the top of the height.

And it happened that when Moses raised his hands in prayer, those of the house of Israel prevailed and were victorious; and when he withheld his hands from praying, those of the house of Amalek prevailed, and they fell by the sword.

And the hands of Moses were raised in prayer, and they took a stone and placed it under him, and he sat on it and Aaron and Hur took hold of his hands, one at one side and one at the other side; and the hands of Moses were raised in prayer, recalling the faith of the just fathers, Abraham, Isaac, and Jacob, and recalling the faith of the just mothers, Sarah, Rebekah, Rachel and Leah, until the sun sank.

And Joshua blotted out Amalek and his people at the edge of the sword.

And Yhwh said to Moses: Write this as a good memorial in the book and place [repeat?] it in the hearing of Joshua; that I will surely blot the memory of Amalek from beneath the heavens.

And Moses built an altar, and prayed there in the name of the Word of Yhwh who had worked signs[1] for him. And he said: An oath has gone out from beneath the throne of the Glory of the Lord of all the world: the first king who is to arise from the tribe of Benjamin shall be Saul, the son of Kish. He shall wage war on the house of Amalek, and shall kill kings with rulers; and Mardocai and Esther shall blot out what remains of them.[2]

And the Lord decreed in his Word to blot out the memory of Amalek for all generations.

[1] The Aramaic translators, perhaps baffled by the *nissî* of the Masoretic text, change it to *nîsîn* ("signs").

2 For a reflection of these traditions, see: 1 Sam 15:8-32;
Esth 3:1; *b. Meg.* 13a; *Bib. Ant.* 58,1-4.

OT 30
Moses in the Battle Against Amalek.
Philo, *Life of Moses* 1,39. Loeb 6,387-91.

After traversing a long and pathless expanse, they came
within sight of the confines of habitable land, and the outlying
districts of the country in which they proposed to settle. This
country was occupied by Phoenicians.

Here they had thought to find a life of peace and quiet, but
their hopes were disappointed. For the king who ruled there,
fearing pillage and rapine, called up the youth of his cities and
came to meet them, hoping to bar their way or, if that were not
feasible and they attempted violence, to discomfit them by force
of arms, seeing that his men were unwearied and fresh for the
contest, while the others were exhausted with much journeying
and by the famine and drought which had alternately attacked
them.

Moses, learning from his scouts that the enemy was not far
distant, mustered his men of military age and, choosing as their
general one of his lieutenants named Joshua, hastened himself
to take a more important part in the fight. Having purified himself according to the customary ritual, he ran without delay to
the neighbouring hill and besought God to shield the Hebrews
and give a triumphant victory to the people whom he had saved
from wars and other troubles still more grievous than this, dis-
persing not only the misfortunes with which men had menaced
them, but also those so miraculously brought about in Egypt by
the upheaval of the elements and by the continual dearth which
beset them in their journeying.

But, when they were about to engage in the fight, his hands
were affected in the most marvellous way. They became very
light and very heavy in turns and, whenever they were in the
former condition and rose aloft, his side of the combatants was
strong and distinguished itself the more by its valour, but whenever his hands were weighed down, the enemy prevailed. Thus,
by symbols, God shewed that earth and the lowest regions of the
universe were the portion assigned as their own to the one
party, and the ethereal, the holiest region, to the other; and
that, just as heaven holds kingship in the universe and is superior to earth, so this nation should be victorious over its oppo-
nents in war.

While, then, his hands became successively lighter and

weightier, like scales in the balance, the fight, too, continued to be doubtful; but, when they suddenly lost all weight, the fingers serving them as pinions, they were lifted on high like the tribe that wings its way through the air, and remained thus soaring until the Hebrews won an undisputed victory and their enemies were slaughtered wholesale, thus justly suffering the punishment which they wrongly strove to deal to others.

Then, too, Moses set up an altar, and called it from the event "Refuge of God" [*Theou kataphygēn*; LXX *Kyrios mou kataphyg*], and on this, with prayers of thanksgiving, he offered sacrifices in celebration of the victory.

OT 31
The Battle with Amalek.
Josephus, *Jewish Antiquities* 3,2,1-5. Loeb 4,341-45, 347.

[Josephus' long account begins with a description of how the Kings of Gobolitis and Petra, the Amalekites, stirred up their neighbors to put down the upstart Hebrews. Moses, when apprised of the imminent danger, assembled his destitute troops and urged them to courage and faith in God.]

With such words did Moses embolden the multitude, and calling up the heads of the tribes and the other officers singly and all together, he exhorted the juniors to obey their elders and these to hearken to their general. And they, with hearts elated at the peril, were ready to face the horror of it, hoping ere long to be quit of their miseries, and they urged Moses to lead them instantly and without procrastination against the enemy, since delay might damp their ardour.

Moses then, having selected from the crowd all of military efficiency, put at their head Joshua, son of Naukos, of the tribe of Ephraim, a man of extreme courage, valiant in endurance of toil, highly gifted in intellect and speech, and withal one who worshipped God with a singular piety which he had learnt from Moses, and who was held in esteem by the Hebrews. He also posted a small force of armed men around the water as a protection for the children and women and for the camp in general.

All that night they passed in preparations, repairing any damaged arms and attentive to their generals, ready to plunge into the fray so soon as Moses gave them the order. Moses too passed a wakeful night, instructing Joshua how to marshal his forces. At the first streak of dawn he once more exhorted Joshua to prove himself in action no whit inferior to the hopes that were built upon him and to win through this command a reputation with his troops for his achievements; he next exhorted the most notable of the Hebrews one by one, and finally addressed stirring words to the whole host assembled in arms. For himself, having thus animated the forces by his words and by all these active preparations, he withdrew to the mountain, consigning the campaign to God and to Joshua.

The adversaries met and a hand-to-hand contest ensued, fought with great spirit and with mutual shouts of encouragement. So long as Moses held his hands erect, the Amalekites were discomfited by the Hebrews. Moses, therefore, unequal to the strain of this extension of his arms, and seeing that as often as he dropped them so often were his men worsted, bade his brother Aaron and his sister Mariamme's husband, by name Ur, stand on either side of him to support his hands and by their aid not suffer them to flag. That done, the Hebrews inflicted a crushing defeat on the Amalekites, who would all have perished, had not night supervened to stay the carnage.

A most noble victory and most timely was this that our forefathers won; for they defeated their assailants, terrified the neighbouring nations, and withal acquired by their efforts great and magnificent riches, having captured their enemy's camp and thereby obtained stores of wealth both for public and private use, they who but now had lacked even the necessaries of life.

[Then follows a detailed description of how the Hebrews despoiled the vanquished.]

On the morrow, Moses had the corpses of the enemy stripped and all the armour shed by the fugitives collected; he presented rewards to the valiant and eulogized their general Joshua, whose exploits were attested by the whole army. Indeed of the Hebrews not a man had perished, while the enemy's dead were past numbering.

Offering sacrifices of thanksgiving, he erected an altar, calling God by the name of "Giver of victory" [*nikaion onomasas ton Theon*]; and he predicted that the Amalekites were to be utterly exterminated and not one of them should survive to after ages, because they had set upon the Hebrews at a time when they were in desert country and in sore distress.

Moses' Intercession at Sinai

OT 32
Moses' Prayer Assuages the Lord.
Exod 32:1-14.

And the people saw that Moses took a long time to come down from the mountain; and the people assembled against Aaron, and they said to him: Up, make gods for us who will go before us; for this Moses, the man who brought us up from the land of Egypt, we don't know what happened to him. And Aaron said to them: Take off the golden rings which are in the ears of your wives, sons, and daughters, and bring them to me. And all the people took off the golden rings which were in their ears and they brought them to Aaron. And he took them from their hands, and he formed them with a graving tool, and he made a molten calf. And they said: These are your gods, O Israel, who brought you up from the land of Egypt. And Aaron saw, and he built an altar before it; and Aaron called out and said: A feast for Yhwh tomorrow! And they got up early on the next day, and they sent up burnt offerings, and brought peace offerings; and the people sat down to eat and drink, and they rose up to play.

And Yhwh spoke to Moses: Go, descend; for corrupt are your people whom you brought up from the land of Egypt; they have swerved swiftly from the way that I commanded them, they have made for themselves a molten calf, and they worshipped it and sacrificed to it and said: These are your gods, O Israel, who brought you up from the land of Egypt. And Yhwh said to Moses: I have seen this people, and behold it is a stiff-necked people. And now leave me be, and my anger will burn them and I will finish them. And Moses assuaged Yhwh his God, and he said: Why, Yhwh, does your anger burn against your people whom you brought out from the land of Egypt with great strength and a mighty hand? Why should Egypt say: Evilly he brought them out, to kill them in the mountains, to finish them from off the face of the earth? Come back from the heat of your anger, and repent of this evil against your people. Remember Abraham, Isaac, and Israel, your servants; that you swore to them by yourself, and you spoke to them: I will make your seed great, like the stars of the heavens; and all this land which I promised, I will give to your seed, and they will possess it forever.

And Yhwh repented of the evil he had proposed to do against his people.

Compare: Deut 9-10; Num 14:1-38; Josephus, *Ant.* 3,5,7-8; Exod 32:30-34; 33:12-17; 34:8-10.

OT 33
How the Lord Relented at Moses' Prayer.
Tg. Yer. I Exod 32:1-14.

And the people saw that Moses took time to come down from the mountain; and the people gathered against Aaron, as they saw that the time he [Moses] had appointed for them had passed, and the Satan came and misled them and he turned their hearts in panic *and they said to him: Up, make deities for us who will go before us;*[1] for Moses, the man who brought us up from the land of Egypt—he was consumed on the mountain by the consuming fire before Yhwh; we don't know what happened to him in the end.

And he took [it] from their hands, and tied it in a cloak, and cast it in a mold; and made a molten calf; and they said: These are your deities, O Israel, who brought you out of the land of Egypt.

And Aaron saw Hur slain in front of him and he was frightened; and he built an altar in front of him; and Aaron called out with a loud voice and he said: A feast before Yhwh tomorrow; from the killing of these dead who ignored their Lord and repelled the Glory of his Shekinah with this calf. And they rose early on the next day, and they sent up burnt offerings and they brought sacrifices; and the people sat down to eat and drink and they rose up to amuse themselves in alien worship.

And Yhwh spoke with Moses: Go, descend from the greatness of your honor, because I have not bestowed greatness upon you except for the sake of Israel. But now they have corrupted their ways, your people whom you brought up from the land of Egypt. They have swerved quickly from the way that I commanded them at Sinai: You shall not make for yourselves an image or a form or a likeness. *And now they have made for themselves the molten calf and worshipped it and sacrificed to it and proclaimed before it: These are your deities, O Israel, who brought you up from the land of Egypt.*

And Yhwh said to Moses: It is revealed before me, the pride of this people; that it is a stiff-necked people. And now cease from your prayer and do not cry out on their behalf before me; and I will let my fierce anger burn as a fire against them, and I will do away with them; I will make you into a great people.

And Moses was shaken with fear, and he began to pray

before Yhwh his God, and he said: Why, Yhwh, is your anger so strong against your people whom you brought out of the land of Egypt with great power and a strong hand? Why should the Egyptians who are left say: Evilly he brought them out to kill them among the mountains, Tabor, Hermon, Sirion, and Sinai, so that he could do away with them from the face of the earth? Come back from the strength of your anger, and let there be relenting before you over the evil you are thinking of doing to your people. Remember Abraham, Isaac, and Israel, your servants to whom you swore by your Word, and you spoke to them: I will make your children numerous as the stars of the heavens; and all this land which I have promised to you, I will give to your children and they will possess it forever.

And there was relenting from before Yhwh over the evil which he thought of doing to his people.

> 1 The words between asterisks are left in Hebrew in *Tg. Neof.*, conforming to the injunction of *m. Meg.* 4,10 that they should be read but not translated.

OT 34
The Episode of Moses' Prayer.
Philo, *Life of Moses* 2,31. Loeb 6,527-31.

> [Philo recounts this episode as the background for an understanding of how the Levites came to be the priestly tribe.]

The story of that deed is as follows: When Moses had gone up into the mountain, and was there several days communing privately with God, the men of unstable nature, thinking his absence a suitable opportunity, rushed into impious practices unrestrainedly, as though authority had ceased to be and, forgetting the reverence they owed to the Self-Existent, became zealous devotees of Egyptian fables. Then, having fashioned a golden bull, in imitation of the animal held most sacred in that country, they offered sacrifices which were no sacrifices, set up choirs which were no choirs, sang hymns which were very funeral chants, and, filled with strong drink, were overcome by the twofold intoxication of wine and folly. And so, revelling and carousing the livelong night, and unwary of the future, they lived wedded to their pleasant vices, while justice, the unseen watcher of them and the punishments they deserved, stood ready to strike.

But, since the continuous shouting in the camp which arose

from the great masses of men gathered together carried for a long distance, so that the echoes reached even to the mountain-top, Moses, as they smote upon his ear, was in a dilemma between God's love for him and his love for man. He could not bear to leave his converse with God, in which he talked with him as in private with none other present, nor yet to disregard the multitude, brimful of the miseries which anarchy creates.

For, skilled as he was to divine in an inarticulate and meaningless noise the distinguishing marks of inward passions which to others were obscure and invisible, he recognized the tumult for what it was, saw that drunkenness caused the prevailing confusion, since intemperance begets satiety, and satiety riot. So, drawn backwards and forwards, hither and thither, by the two sides of his being, he was at a loss what he should do. And, as he considered, this divine message came. "Go quickly hence. Descend. The people have run after lawlessness. They have fashioned a god, the work of their hands, in the form of a bull, and to this god, who is no god, they offer worship and sacrifice, and have forgotten all the influences to piety which they have seen and heard."

Struck with dismay, and compelled to believe the incredible tale, he yet took the part of mediator and reconciler and did not hurry away at once, but first made prayers and supplications, begging that their sins might be forgiven.

Then, when this protector and intercessor had softened the wrath of the Ruler, he wended his way back in mingled joy and dejection. He rejoiced that God accepted his prayers, yet was ready to burst with the dejection and heaviness that filled him at the transgression of the multitude.

OT 35

Moses at Sinai.
Josephus, *Jewish Antiquities* 3,5,7-8. Loeb 4,361-65.

Such was the position of affairs when Moses again went up into Mount Sinai, after forewarning the Hebrews, before whose eyes he made the ascent. Then, as time dragged on—for he was full forty days parted from them—a fear seized the Hebrews that something had befallen Moses, and of all the horrors that they had encountered none so deeply distressed them as the thought that Moses had perished. There was conflict of opinions: some said that he had fallen a victim to wild beasts—it was principally those who were ill disposed towards him who voted for that view—others that he had been taken back to the divinity. But the sober-minded, who found no private satisfaction in either statement—who held that to die under the fangs of beasts was a human accident, and that he should be translated by God to himself by reason of his inherent virtue was likely enough— were moved by these reflections to retain their composure. Imagining themselves, however, to have been bereft of a patron and protector, the like of whom they could never meet again, they continued in the deepest distress; and while their earnest expectation of some good news of their hero would not permit them to mourn, so neither could they restrain their grief and dejection. Nor durst they break up the camp, Moses having charged them to abide there.

At length, when forty days had passed and as many nights, he came having tasted of no food of such sort as is customary with men.[1] His appearance filled the army with joy; and he proceeded to disclose the care which God had for them, telling them that he had during these days shown him that manner of government which would promote their happiness, and that he desired that a tabernacle should be made for him, whither he would descend whensoever he came among them, "to the intent," said he, "that when we move elsewhere we may take this with us and have no more need to ascend to Sinai, but that he himself, frequenting the tabernacle, may be present at our prayers. This tabernacle shall be fashioned of the dimensions and with the equipment which he himself has indicated, and ye are diligently to apply yourselves to the task." Having so said, he showed them two tables on which were graven the ten words, five on either of them; and the writing thereon was from the hand of God.

[1] Motif: Matt 4:2/Luke 4:2.

Moses Provides a Remedy for a Rebellious People

OT 36
Moses is Shown How to Provide a Remedy for the
Punishment of the People.
Num 21:4-9.

And they set out from Mount Hor, by the way of the Sea of Reeds, to go around the land of Edom; and the soul of the people gave out on the journey, and the people spoke against God and against Moses: Why have you brought us up out of Egypt to die in the desert? For there is no food and no water, and our souls are fed up with this worthless food!

And Yhwh sent the burning serpents among the people; and they bit the people, and a great crowd of the people died.

And the people came to Moses, and they said: We have sinned, because we spoke against Yhwh and against you. Pray to Yhwh, and the serpent will go away from us.

And Moses prayed on behalf of the people.

And Yhwh said to Moses: Make for yourself a burning serpent, and put it on a standard; and it shall come about that all who are bitten, and see it, will be restored to life.

And Moses made a bronze serpent, and he put it on a standard. And it happened that if a serpent bit a man, and he looked at the bronze serpent, he was restored to life.

OT 37
How God Directed Moses to Save the People From Their Just Punishment.
Tg. Neof. Num 21:4-9. McNamara, 578-79.

And they journeyed from Hor the Mountain, by way of the Red Sea, to go around the land of the Edomites; and the soul of the people was afflicted on the way; and the people spoke against the Word of Yhwh, and murmured against Moses: Why, now, have you brought us out of Egypt to kill us in the desert? For there is no bread for us to eat, and no water to drink, and our souls are exasperated with this bread whose nourishment is little!

And the Bat Qol [the divine voice] came forth from the earth and its voice was heard on high: Come, see, all you creatures; and come give ear, all you sons of the flesh; the serpent was cursed from the beginning and I said to it: Dust shall be your food. I brought my people out from the land of Egypt and I had manna come down for them from heaven, and I made a well come up for them from the abyss, and I carried quail from the sea for them; and my people has turned to murmur before me concerning the manna, that its nourishment is little. Let the serpent which does not murmur concerning its food come and rule over the people which has murmured concerning their food.

Whereupon Yhwh let loose [read *gry*] burning serpents among the people; and they bit the people, and many people of Israel died. And the people came to Moses and said: We have sinned, for we have spoken against the Word of Yhwh and murmured against you. Pray before Yhwh that he make the serpents pass from us.

And Moses prayed for the people.

And Yhwh said to Moses: Make a bronze serpent and set it on an elevated place; and it shall come to pass that everyone who is bitten by the serpent, and sees it, he will be restored to life. And Moses made a bronze serpent and put it on an elevated place; and if the serpent bit a man, he would look upon the bronze serpent, and he would live.[1]

Compare: John 3:14.

[1] For the textual confusion in the last two lines of this text, see the apparatus in Díez-Macho. In *Tg. Yer. I*, these last lines run: "And Yhwh said to Moses: Make for yourself a burning serpent of bronze, and put it on an elevated place; and it shall come to pass that all whom the serpent bites, and they look on it, shall be restored to life, if his heart be directed to the Name of the Word of Yhwh. And Moses made a bronze serpent and put it on an elevated place; and it came to pass that if the serpent bit a man, and he would look on the bronze serpent, and fix his heart on the Name of the Word of Yhwh, he would live."

OT 38
A Reinterpretation of the Incident of the Bronze Serpent. Wis 16:5-14.

For when the fearful anger of beasts came upon them [God's people], and they were being destroyed by the bites of writhing serpents, your wrath did not last to the finish.

As a warning, they were shaken for a little while, having a sign of salvation as a memorial of the commandment of your law. For he who turned toward it was saved, not by what was seen, but by you, the Savior of all.

And in this, too, you convinced our enemies that it is you who deliver from every evil. For the bites of locusts and flies killed them, and there was found no healing for their soul, because they were worthy of being afflicted by such things. But not even the fangs of poisonous serpents overcame your sons, for your mercy came to their help, and healed them.

As a reminder of your words were they stung, and quickly saved; lest falling into deep forgetfulness, they should become unresponsive to your beneficence. For neither herb nor poultice cured them, but rather your Word, O Lord, which heals all.

For you have the power of life and death, you lead down to the gates of Hades, and you lead back up. But man kills in his wickedness; the spirit leaves and he does not bring it back, nor does he free the soul once confined.

OT 39
The Bronze Serpent.
Philo, *Allegorical Interpretation* 2,79-81. Loeb 1,274-77.

How, then, is a healing of their suffering brought about? By the making of another serpent, opposite in kind to that of Eve, namely the principle of self-mastery. For self-mastery runs counter to pleasure, a variable virtue to a variable affection, and a virtue that defends itself against pleasure its foe. So then God bids Moses make the serpent that expresses self-mastery, and says: "Make for thyself a serpent and set it upon a standard." You notice that Moses makes this serpent for no one else, but for himself, for God's bidding is, "Make it for thyself." This is that you may know that self-mastery is not a possession of every man, but only of the man beloved of God.

We must consider why Moses makes a brazen serpent, no direction having been given him as to material. Possibly these are the reasons. In the first place, matter is not an element in God's gifts making them to be of this or that sort; but the gifts of us mortals are always looked upon embodied in matter. A second reason: Moses loves excellence without bodily form, whereas our souls, being unable to get out of our bodies, crave for excellence in bodily shape. But the principle of self-mastery, being forcible and unyielding, is likened to the strong and firm substance of brass, perhaps also because, whereas the self-mastery found in the man beloved of God is most precious and like gold, that which is found in him who has absorbed wisdom by gradual progress holds the second place. Everyone, then, "whom a serpent shall have bitten, when he looks on it shall live." This is quite true. For if the mind, when bitten by pleasure, the serpent of Eve, shall have succeeded in beholding in soul the beauty of self-mastery, the serpent of Moses, and through beholding this, beholds God himself, he shall live; only let him look and mark well.

Aaron's Intercession at the Plague

OT 40
Aaron Saves the People From the Plague.
Num 17:6-15.

On the morrow, all the congregations of the people of Israel murmured against Moses and Aaron saying: You have killed the people of Yhwh.

And when the congregation had assembled against Moses and against Aaron, they turned toward the tent of meeting; and behold the cloud covered it, and the glory of Yhwh appeared. And Moses and Aaron came to the front of the tent of meeting and Yhwh said to Moses: Get away from the midst of this congregation, that I may consume them in a moment. And they fell on their faces.

And Moses said to Aaron: Take your censer and put fire therein from off the altar and lay incense on it and carry it quickly to the congregation, and make atonement for them; for wrath has gone forth from Yhwh and the plague has begun. So Aaron took it as Moses said, and ran into the midst of the assembly; and behold the plague had already begun among the people; and he put on the incense and made atonement for the people.

And he stood between the dead and the living; and the plague was stopped. Now those who died by the plague were fourteen thousand seven hundred, besides those who died in the affair of Korah. And Aaron returned to Moses at the entrance of the tent of meeting, and the plague had stopped.

OT 41
Aaron Saves the People From Anger.
Tg. Yer. I Num 17:6-15.

On the next day, all the congregation of the sons of Israel murmured against Moses and against Aaron saying: You are the reasons for the death sentence against the people of Yhwh.

And as the congregation was gathered against Moses and against Aaron to kill them, they turned toward the tent of meeting and behold the cloud of the glory of the Shekinah covered it, and there was revealed there the glory of Yhwh. And Moses and Aaron went up from the assembly to the door of the tent of meeting. And Yhwh spoke with Moses saying: Separate yourselves from the midst of this congregation, and I will make an end of them in a brief time. And they prostrated on their faces in prayer.

And Moses said to Aaron: Take the censer and put fire in it from off the altar and place perfumed incense on the fire and carry it quickly to the congregation, and make atonement on their account. For the destruction which consumed them at Horeb whose name is *Qeṣep* [Anger], from before Yhwh, has, by commandment, begun to kill.

And Aaron took [the censer] just as Moses said and ran into the midst of the assembly and behold *Qeṣep* had begun the destruction by destroying the people. And he put on the perfumed incense and he made atonement for the people. And

Aaron stood in prayer in the midst and make a sacred partition with the censer between the dead and the living; and the plague came to an end. And the number of those who died in the plague was fourteen thousand seven hundred, besides those who died in the schism of Korah. And Aaron returned to Moses at the door of the tent of meeting: and the plague had stopped.

OT 42
A Meditation on Aaron's Saving of the People.
Wis 18:20-25.

The experience of death touched even the just, and a plague in the desert occurred to the multitude; but the wrath did not last for long.

For a blameless man hastened to fight as champion bearing the weapon of his service: prayer and the propitiation of incense. He withstood the anger and put an end to the calamity, showing that he was your servant.

He overcame the bitterness, not by strength of body, not by power of arms, but by word he subdued the Smiter, recalling the promises of the Fathers, and the covenants.

For when the dead had already fallen on one another in heaps, standing in the midst, he stopped the wrath; he partitioned off the way to the living. For on his full-length robe was the whole world and the glories of the Fathers carved on the four rows of stones, and your greatness was the diadem of his head.

To these the destroyer yielded, these he feared; for the experience of the wrath was enough.

Samuel Saves the People at Mizpah

OT 43
How Samuel's Prayer and Sacrifice save Israel.
1 Sam 7:5-11.

And Samuel said: Gather all Israel at Mizpah, and I will pray on your behalf to Yhwh.

And they gathered at Mizpah; and they drew water and poured it out before Yhwh, and they fasted on that day, and they said there: We have sinned against Yhwh; and Samuel judged the sons of Israel at Mizpah; and the lords of the Philistines went up against Israel.

And the sons of Israel heard, and they were afraid in face of the Philistines; and the sons of Israel said to Samuel: Do not lose interest in us, in crying out to Yhwh our God that he deliver us from the hand of the Philistines! And Samuel took one suckling lamb and sent it up as a whole offering to Yhwh; and Samuel cried out to Yhwh on behalf of Israel; and Yhwh answered him.

And it came to pass, as Samuel was sending up the offering, the Philistines came near to wage war on Israel; and Yhwh thundered in a mighty voice that day against the Philistines; and they were set in confusion, and they were beaten before Israel.

And the men of Israel went out from Mizpah, and smote the Philistines, and harried them, as far as below Beth-car.

> [The story goes on to tell of Samuel's setting up of the "stone of help;" and how the Philistines never again had power within the boundaries of Israel.]

OT 44
How God defeated the Philistines at Samuel's Prayer.
Josephus, *Jewish Antiquities* 6,2,1-2. Loeb 5,177-81.

> [Josephus expands the speech of Samuel in 1 Sam 7:3-4; and then makes the episode in the following verses part of the same complex of incidents.]

Samuel then gathered them to a city called Masphate, which in the Hebrew tongue signifies "espied." There, having drawn water, they made libations to God and, fasting throughout the day, gave themselves unto prayer.

However, their gathering at this spot did not pass unperceived by the Philistines who, having learnt of their mustering, advanced upon the Hebrews with an army mighty in strength, hoping to surprise them while off their guard and unprepared. Dismayed by this attack and plunged into confusion and alarm, the Hebrews, hastening to Samuel, declared that their courage had flagged through fear and the memory of their former defeat. "That," said they, "was why we sat still, in order not to stir up the enemy's forces. But when thou hadst brought us hither for prayers, sacrifices and oaths, now the enemy are upon us while we are naked and unarmed. Other hope of salvation therefore have we none, save from thee alone and from God, should he be entreated by thee to afford us escape from the Philistines."

But Samuel bade them be of good cheer and promised that God would succour them. Then, taking a suckling lamb, he sacrificed it on behalf of the throng and besought God to extend his right hand over them in the battle with the Philistines and not suffer them to undergo a second reverse.

And God hearkened to his prayers and, accepting the sacrifice in gracious and befriending spirit, gave them assurance of victory and triumph. God's victim was still upon the altar and he had not yet wholly consumed it through the sacred flame, when the enemy's forces issued from their camp and drew up for battle, expectant of victory, thinking to have caught the Jews in a hopeless plight, seeing that they were without arms and had assembled there with no intention of battle.

But the Philistines encountered what, had one foretold it, they would scarcely have believed. For, first, God vexed them with earthquake, rocking and making tremulous and treacherous the ground beneath them, so that from its reeling their footsteps staggered, and at its parting, they were engulfed in sundry of its chasms. Next, he deafened them with thunderclaps, made fiery lightning to flash around them as it were to burn out their eyes, struck the arms from their hands, and so turned them weaponless to flight.

But Samuel now rushed upon them with his people and, having massacred many, pursued them to a certain place called Korraea; and there he set up a stone as landmark of the victory and of the flight of the foe, and called it "Strong(stone)" [ischyros], in token of the strength which God had lent them against their enemies.

Elijah and the Widow of Zarephath

OT 45
The Lord Provides for Elijah.
1 Kgs 17:8-16.

And it happened, the word of Yhwh came to him, saying: Rise up, go to Zarephath which belongs to Sidon, and dwell there. Behold, I have commanded a widow woman there to feed you. And he rose up and he went to Zarephath; and he entered the gate of the city, and behold a widow woman there gathering sticks, and he called to her and he said: Bring me, please, a little water in a vessel that I may drink.

And she went to get it; and he called to her and he said: Bring me, please, a morsel of bread in your hand. And she said: As Yhwh your God lives, if I have anything but a handful of meal in a jar, and a little oil in a jug; and behold me, gathering a couple of sticks, and I am going in and prepare it for me and my son, and we will eat it, and die.

And Elijah said to her: Do not fear; go and do as you have spoken, but make for me from it a little cake first, and bring it out to me; and prepare it for yourself and your son afterwards. For thus speaks Yhwh, the God of Israel: The jar of meal shall not be spent, and the jug of oil shall not fail up to the day of Yhwh's giving rain upon the face of the earth.

And she went and did as Elijah had said: and she ate, and he, and her household, for days. And the jar of meal was not spent, and the jug of oil did not fail; according to the word of Yhwh which he spoke by Elijah.

OT 46
Elijah's Prophecy of the Drought and How God Provided for Him.
Josephus, *Jewish Antiquities* 8,13,2. Loeb 5,745-47.

> [Josephus follows the biblical text closely; he briefly establishes the context, introducing Elijah and reports his prophecy of the drought and his residence "in the south country."]

But, when the river dried up for want of rain, he came to the city of Sarephtha, not far from Sidon and Tyre—it lies between them—at the command of God, for he said that he would there find a widow who would provide him with food.

Now when he was a little way from the city gate, he saw a labouring woman who was gathering wood. Thereupon, as God revealed to him that this was she who was to give him food, he went up to her and, after greeting her, asked her to fetch him some water to drink, but, when she started out, he called her back and bade her bring some bread as well.

But she swore that she had nothing in the house except a handful of meal and a little oil, and she said that she was setting out for home, after gathering the wood, to knead the meal and make bread for herself and her child; after this was eaten they must perish, consumed by hunger, for there was no longer anything left.

Whereupon he said, "Even so, be of good courage and go your way in hope of better things; but first prepare a little food and bring it to me, for I prophesy to you that neither the bowl of meal nor the jar of oil shall be empty until God sends rain."

When the prophet had said these things, she went to her home and did as he had told her; and she had enough food for herself and her child as well as for the prophet, nor did they lack anything to eat until the drought finally ended.

This rainless time is also mentioned by Menander in his account of the acts of Ithōbalos, the king of Tyre, in these words: "There was a drought in his reign, which lasted from the month of Hyperberetaios until the month of Hyperberetaios in the following year. But he made supplication to the gods, whereupon a heavy thunderstorm broke out. He it was who founded the city of Botrys in Phoenicia, and Auza in Libya." This, then, is what Menander wrote, referring to the drought which came in Achab's reign, for it was in his time that Ithōbalos was king of Tyre.

Elijah Raises the Widow's Son

OT 47
Elijah Raises the Widow's Son.
1 Kgs 17:17-24.

And it happened after these things; the son of the woman, the mistress of the house, fell sick; and the sickness was very strong, so that there was no breath left in him.

And she said to Elijah: What is it between you and me, man of God; have you come to me to cause the remembrance of my sin and the death of my son?

And he said to her: Give me your son. And he took him from her bosom, and he brought him up to the upper rooms where he dwelt, and he laid him on his bed.

And he cried out to Yhwh, and he said: Yhwh, my God, even upon the widow with whom I sojourn, have you brought evil, causing her son to die? And he stretched out upon the child three times; and he called out to Yhwh, and he said: Yhwh, my God, please let the soul of this child return to his body!

And Yhwh listened to the voice of Elijah; and the soul of the child returned to his body; and he lived.

And Elijah took the child, and brought him down from the upper room into the house; and gave him to his mother.[1] And Elijah said: Look, your son is alive.

And the woman said to Elijah: This time I know that you are a man of God; and the word of Yhwh is in your mouth truly.

[1] Motif: Luke 7:15.

OT 48
How God, at the Prayers of Elijah, Raised a Boy Who Seemed
to be Dead.
Josephus, *Jewish Antiquities* 8,13,3. Loeb 5,747-49.

Now the woman of whom we spoke above, who gave food to
the prophet—her son fell ill so seriously that he ceased to
breathe and seemed to be dead,[1] whereupon she wept bitterly,
injuring herself with her hands and uttering such cries as her
grief prompted; and she reproached the prophet for having
come to her to convict her of sin and on that account causing
the death of her son.

But he urged her to take heart and give her son over to him,
for he would, he said, restore him to her alive.

So she gave him over, and he carried him into the chamber
in which he himself lived, and placed him on the bed; then he
cried aloud to God, saying that he would ill requite the woman
who had received him and nourished him, if he took her son
from her, and he prayed God to send the breath into the child
again and give him life.

Thereupon God, because he took pity on the mother and also
because he wished graciously to spare the prophet from seeming to have come to her for the purpose of harming her, beyond
all expectation brought the child back to life.

Then the mother thanked the prophet and said that now she
clearly realized that the Deity spoke with him.

> [1] The notice that the boy seemed to be dead is very much
> in keeping with the Hellenistic accounts of raising from
> the dead: see H 205; H 208-11; H 215.

The Call of Elisha

OT 49
Elijah Calls Elisha.
1 Kgs 19:21-22.

And he went from there; and he found Elisha, son of Shapat;
and he was plowing with twelve yoked teams in front of him,
and he was with the twelfth team.

And Elijah passed over towards him, and he threw his cloak
over him. And he left the oxen, and ran after Elijah, and he
said: Let me embrace my father and my mother,[1] and I will
walk after you.

And he said to him: Go, return; for what have I done to you?
And he turned back, and he took the team of oxen and he

sacrificed them; and with the plowing equipment of the oxen, he cooked them; and he gave them to the people,[2] and they ate.

And he rose up, and he walked after Elijah; and he served him.[3]

> Comparable Narratives (structure): Matt 4:18-22/Mark 1:16-20.
>
> [1] Motif: Luke 9:61-62.
> [2] Motif: Luke 5:29/Mark 2:15/Matt 9:10.
> [3] Motif: Matt 8:15 (Mark 1:31/Luke 4:39); Luke 8:3.

OT 50
How Elisha Began to Prophesy and Became Elijah's Attendant.
Josephus, *Jewish Antiquities* 8,13,7. Loeb 5,763.

When Elijah heard these words [spoken at Horeb], he returned to the country of the Hebrews and came upon Elisha, the son of Saphates, as he was ploughing and some others with him, who were driving twelve yoke of oxen, and, going up to him, he threw his own mantle over him.

Thereupon, Elisha immediately began to prophesy and, leaving his oxen, followed Elijah. But he asked to be allowed to take leave of his parents and, when Elijah bade him do so, he parted from them and then went with the prophet; and so long as Elijah was alive, he was his disciple and attendant [*diakonos*].

Such, then, is the history of this prophet.

Elisha Heals the Noxious Water

OT 51
Elisha Heals the Water.
2 Kgs 2:19-22.

And the men of the city [Jericho] said to Elisha: Behold, if you please, the site of the city is good, as my lord sees: but the water is bad, and the land does not bear.

Bring me a new bowl, and put salt in it. And they brought it to him.

And he went out to the spring of water, and he threw salt in it, and he said: Thus speaks Yhwh: I have healed this water, there will not come from here any more either death or incapacity to bear.

And the waters were healed up to this day; according to the word of Elisha which he spoke.

OT 52
Elisha and the Spring at Jericho.
Josephus, *Jewish Wars* 4,8,3. Loeb 3,135-39.

Hard by Jericho, however, is a copious spring of excellent value for irrigation; it gushes up near the old town, which was the first in the land of the Canaanites to fall before the arms of Jesus the son of Naue, general of the Hebrews. Tradition avers that this spring originally not only blighted the fruits of the earth and of trees but also caused women to miscarry, and that to everything alike it brought disease and destruction, until it was reclaimed and converted into a most salubrious and fertilizing source by a certain prophet Elisha, the disciple and successor of Elijah.

Having been the guest of the people of Jericho and been treated by them with extreme hospitality, he requited their kindness by conferring a boon for all time upon them and their country. For he went out to this spring and cast into the stream an earthenware vessel full of salt, and then raising his righteous right hand to heaven and pouring propitiatory libations upon the ground, he besought the earth to mollify the stream and to open sweeter channels, and heaven to temper its waters with more genial airs and to grant to the inhabitants alike an abundance of fruits, a succession of children, and an unfailing supply of water conducive to their production, so long as they remained a righteous people. By these prayers, supplemented by various ritual ceremonies, he changed the nature of the spring, and the water which had before been to them a cause of childlessness and famine thenceforth became a source of fecundity and plenty.

Such, in fact, are its powers of irrigation, that if it but skim the soil, it is more salubrious than waters which stand and saturate it. Hence, too, while the benefit derived from other streams is slight, though they use them more lavishly, this little rill yields an ample return.

The Widow Whose Oil was Multiplied

OT 53
How Elisha Saves a Widow From Debt.
2 Kgs 4:1-7.

And a woman, one of the wives of the sons of the prophets,

cried out to Elisha saying: Your servant my husband is dead, and you know that your servant feared Yhwh; and the creditor has come to take my two children for himself as slaves.

And Elisha said to her: What shall I do for you? Tell me, what have you in the house?

And she said: Your maidservant has nothing in the whole house except a jar of oil.

And he said: Go, borrow vessels from outside, from all your neighbors; empty vessels, and don't spare the number. Then go in, shut the door on yourself and your sons; and pour into all these vessels, and the full one set aside.

And she went from him, and she closed the door on herself and her sons; they passed [the vessels] to her, and she poured. And it came to pass, as the vessels were filled, she said to her son: Pass me another vessel.

And he said to her: There are no more vessels. And the oil stopped.

And she went and told the man of God; and he said: Go, sell the oil and satisfy your creditors; you and your sons can live from the rest.

OT 54
How Elisha Helped the Widow of Obadiah.
Tg. Yer. I 2 Kgs 4:1-7.

And a certain woman from the wives of the disciples of the prophets cried out before Elisha saying: Your servant Obadiah my husband is dead; and you know that your servant feared Yhwh; when Jezebel killed the prophets of Yhwh, he took one hundred of them and hid them, fifty here, fifty there, in caves; and he used to borrow and feed them, so as not to feed them from the possessions of Ahab because they were unjustly acquired; and now the creditor has come to take my two sons for himself as slaves.[1] And Elisha said to her: What can I do for you? Indicate to me what you have in the house.

And she said to him: Your handmaid has absolutely nothing in the house except a jar of oil.

And he said: Go, borrow vessels from the outside, from all your neighbors; empty vessels, do not have a few. And go in and close the door on yourself and your sons; and pour the oil into all these jars; and the jar that is full, set aside.

And she went from him, and she closed the door on herself and on her sons; they were bringing [the jars] to her and she was pouring the oil. And it came about as she filled the jars. that she said to her son: Bring me another jar. And he said to her: There are no more jars. And the oil stopped.

And she went and made it known to the prophet of Yhwh; and he said: Go, sell the oil, and satisfy your creditors; and you and your sons can be provided for from the rest.

> [1] The notion, based on 1 Kgs 18:3-4, that it was the widow of Obadiah who came to Elisha is well attested in the Rabbinic tradition: see Josephus in OT 55 and Ginzberg, *Legends* 4,240-42.

OT 55
How Elisha Freed Obadiah's Widow From Debt.
Josephus, *Jewish Antiquities* 9,4,2. Loeb 6,27-29.

It is said that there came to him the wife of Obedias, the steward of Achab, saying that he was not ignorant of how her husband had saved the lives of the prophets who were to have been slain by Achab's wife Jezabela, for, she said, a hundred of them had been fed by him with money he had borrowed and had been kept in hiding; now, after her husband's death, both she and her children were being taken away into slavery by her creditors, and she besought him, because of this good deed of her husband, to pity her and give her some assistance.

When he inquired what she had in the house, she replied that there was nothing but a very little oil in a jar. But the prophet bade her go and borrow from her neighbours many empty vessels and then shut the doors of her chamber and pour some of the oil into all of them, for God, he said, would fill them.

And the woman did as he had bidden, and instructed her children to bring every one of the vessels; and, when all were filled and not a single one was left empty, she came to the prophet and told him of these things. Then he advised her to go and sell the oil and pay her creditors what was owing, saying that something would be left over from the price of the oil which she could use for the maintenance of her children.

In this way, then, did Elisha free the woman of her debts and deliver her from the harsh treatment of her creditors.

PART II

RABBINIC STORIES

THE EARLIEST SAGES

R 56
Simeon the Just's Knowledge of His Death.
b. Yoma 39b. Soncino, 185-86.

Our Rabbis taught: The same year that Simeon the Just died, he said to them that he would die in that year.[1]

They said to him: How do you know?

He said to them: On every Day of Atonement, an old man dressed in white and wrapped in white would join me and go in with me [to the Holy of Holies] and go out with me. And this day, I was joined by an old man dressed in black, wrapped in black, who entered and did not leave with me.

After the festival of Sukkot, he was sick for seven days and died.

[1] About 330 BCE.

R 57
R Joshua b Peraḥiah's Reluctance to Assume Office as Nasi, and His Refusal to Renounce it.
b. Menaḥ. 109b. Soncino, 678.

It was taught: Joshua b Peraḥiah[1] said: At first whoever were to say to me, "Go up" [take the honor], I would bind him and put him in front of a lion. But now, whoever were to say to me: "Give up the honor," I would pour over him a kettle of boiling water. For we see that Saul shunned [his throne], but after he had taken it, he sought to kill David.

> Comparable Narrative: *'Abot R. Nat.* A,10; B,20 (Schechter, 43), where this saying is attributed to R Judah b Ṭabbai; *y. Pesah.* 6,1; 33a, where it is found in the name of Joshua b Kabasi.

[1] About 125 BCE.

R 58

Judah b Ṭabbai's Overhasty Zeal in Condemning a False Witness.
b. Ḥag. 16b. Soncino, 106-07.

R Judah b Ṭabbai said: May I [not] see the consolation if I did not have a false witness put to death as a demonstration against the Sadducees who say that the false witnesses should not be put to death unless the accused has already been put to death.

Simeon b Sheṭaḥ said to him: May I [not] see the consolation if you have not shed innocent blood. For the Sages say: False witnesses are not to be put to death until both of them have been proven false witnesses, and they are not to be flogged until both have proven to be false witnesses, and they are not to be required to pay money until both are proven false witnesses.

Thereupon Judah b Ṭabbai undertook never to make a decision except in the presence of Simeon b Sheṭaḥ. All the days of his life, he prostrated himself on the grave of the executed man. And his voice was heard. The people believed that it was the voice of the executed man. He said to them: It is my voice. You shall know this, that on the morrow [when] I die, the voice shall not be heard.

> [There then follows a series of remarks on the predominance of the two Rabbis over the Court.]
> Same Narrative: *y. Sanh.* 6,3; 23b.
> Comparable Narrative: *'Abot.* 1,8.9.

R 59

Simeon b Sheṭaḥ's Honesty.
Deut. Rab. 3,3. Soncino, 71.

It is related of R Simeon b Sheṭaḥ: Once he bought an ass from an Ishmaelite. His disciples came and found a precious stone hanging from its neck.

They said to him: Rabbi, Master, "The blessing of the Lord makes rich [Prov 10:22]."

R Simeon b Sheṭaḥ said to them: I have purchased an ass, but I have not purchased a precious stone. He went and returned it to the same Ishmaelite.

The Ishmaelite exclaimed regarding him: Blessed be the Lord God of Simeon b Sheṭaḥ!

Thus, from the faithfulness of man, we learn the faithfulness of God, who is faithful to pay the reward of the precepts which [Israel] performs.

R 60
A Snake Brings Justice to a Murderer.
t. Sanh. 8,3. Danby Tr. 79.

Said R Simeon b Sheṭaḥ: May I not live to see the consolation
if I have not seen a man running after his companion with a
sword in his hand. He entered into a [deserted] building; the
other entered after him. I entered after him and found the one
slain, and a sword in the hand of the murderer dripping with
blood. I said to him: Wicked man, who slew this man? May I
not live to see the consolation if I did not see him. I or you must
have slain him. But what can I do to you since your condemnation cannot rest on my hands? For the Law says: By the mouth
of two witnesses, or by the mouth of three, shall he who dies be
put to death. But he who knows the thoughts, he exacts ven-
geance from the guilty. For the murderer did not move from
that place before a serpent bit him, so he died.

R 61
Simeon b Sheṭaḥ Before King Alexander Jannaeus.
b. Sanh. 19a-b. Soncino, 98-99.

"The king may neither judge. . ." [*m. Sanh.* 2,2]. R Joseph
said: This refers only to the Kings of Israel, but the Kings of the
House of David may judge and be judged, as it is written [Jer
21:12]: "O House of David, thus says the Lord, execute justice
in the morning". . . But why this prohibition of the Kings of
Israel? Because of an incident which happened in connection
with a slave of King Jannaeus, who killed a man.
    Simeon b Sheṭaḥ said to the Sages: Set your eyes upon him
and let us judge him.
    So they sent [to the King]: Your slave has killed a man. He
sent the man to them.
    They sent to him: You must come, for the Torah says [Exod
21:29]: "If a warning has been given to its owners. . ." The
owner of the ox must come and stand by his ox. The King came
and sat down.
    Simeon b Sheṭaḥ said: Stand on your feet, King Jannaeus,
and let the witnesses testify against you; it is not before us that
you stand, but before him who spoke and the world came into
being, as it is written [Deut 19:17]: "Both the men between
whom the controversy exists, shall stand. . ."
    He said to him: I shall not act in accordance with what you
say, but in accordance with what your colleagues say.
    Simeon turned to the right and to the left, but they all kept

their faces fixed on the ground. Simeon said: Are you trying to
master your thoughts? Let the Master of thoughts come and call
you to account. Instantly Gabriel came and smote them to the
ground and they died.

It was there and then enacted: A King [not of the House of
David] may neither judge nor be judged; testify nor be testified
against.

Comparable Narrative: Josephus, *Ant.* 14,9,4; R 94.

R 62
Simeon b Sheṭaḥ's Son is Faithful to the Process of the Law
Even When the False Witnesses Confess.
y. Sanh. 6,3; 23b.

Simeon b Sheṭaḥ had hands hot [for destroying evil]. A band
of godless people came along and said: Come, let us testify
against his son and have him executed. They testified against
him and his sentence was handed down for death.

As he was going out to be executed, they said to him: My
lord, we are false witnesses. His father wanted to reverse the
decision. He said to him: Father, if you wish salvation to come
through you, make me a threshold [for the law to enter and
have its way].

R 63
Hillel the Elder Resolves the Debate About the Occurrence of
Passover on Sabbath.
b. Pesah. 66a. Soncino, 333-35.

On one occasion, the 14th [of Nissan] fell on the Sabbath.
They forgot and did not know whether the Passover overrides
the Sabbath or not.

They said: Is there any man who knows whether the Passover overrides the Sabbath or not?

They said to him: There is a certain man who has come up
from Babylon, Hillel the Babylonian by name, who studied
under the two greatest men of the generation. He knows
whether the Passover overrides the Sabbath or not.

They called to him and said: Do you know whether the Passover overrides the Sabbath or not?

He said to them: Have we [but] one Passover in the year
that overrides the Sabbath? Surely we have many more than
200 Passovers during the year which override the Sabbath.

They said to him: How do you know it?

He said to them: "In its appointed time" [Num 28:2] is said in connection with the Passover—and it is said "in its appointed time" in connection with the *tamid* [continual daily sacrifice]. And just as "its appointed time," which is said in connection with the *tamid,* overrides the Sabbath, so "in its appointed time," which is said in connection with the Passover, overrides the Sabbath. Therefore, if the *tamid* [whose omission] is *not* punished by *karet* [being cut off] overrides the Sabbath, then is it not logical that the Passover [whose omission] *is* punished by *karet,* overrides the Sabbath?

They immediately set him at their head and appointed him *Nasi* over them, and he was sitting and lecturing the whole day on the laws of Passover.

Same Narrative: *y. Pesah.* 6,1; 33a.

R 64
Hillel the Elder Goes to Perform a Religious Duty.
Lev. Rab. 34,3. Soncino, 428.

Another explanation of the text [Lev 25:25]: "If your brother becomes very poor." It bears on what is written [Prov 11:17]: "The merciful man does good to his own soul."

This applies to Hillel the Elder: When he had finished his studies with his disciples, he walked along with them.

His disciples said to him: Where are you going?

He said to them: To perform a religious duty.

They said to him: And what is this religious duty?

He said to them: To wash in a bath house.

They said to him: Is this a religious duty?

He said to them: Yes, if the statues of kings, which are erected in the theatres and circuses are scoured and washed by the man who is appointed to look after them, and this is how he obtains his keep, and he is exalted in the company of the great of the kingdom: how much more I, who have been created in the image and likeness, as it is written [Gen 9:6]: "For, in the image of God, he made man."

R 65
Hillel the Elder Does Good to a Guest.
Lev. Rab. 34,3. Soncino, 428-29.

Another illustration of: "The merciful man does good to his own soul [Prov 11:17]."

In regard to Hillel the Elder: When he had finished his studies with his disciples, and was walking along, they walked with him.

His disciples said to him: Rabbi, where are you going?

He said to them: To do good to a guest in the house.

They said to him: Do you have a guest every day?

He said to them: And this poor soul, is it not a guest in the body? Today it is here, and tomorrow it is here no longer.

A Series of Stories about R Hillel and R Shammai

(1) R 66
Two Men Test Hillel's Patience.
b. Sabb. 30b-31a. Soncino, 138-39.

Our Rabbis taught: A man should always be gentle like Hillel, and not impatient like Shammai. It once happened that two men made a wager with each other. They said: He who goes and makes Hillel angry shall receive four hundred *zuz*.

Said one: I will go and incense him. That day was the Sabbath eve, and Hillel was washing his head. He went, passed by the door of his house, and called out: Is Hillel here, is Hillel here? Hillel wrapped himself and called to him.

He said: My son, what do you wish?

He said to him: I have a question to ask.

He said to him: Ask, my son.

He asked: Why are the heads of the Babylonians round?

He said to him: My son, you have asked a great question: because they have no skilful midwives.

He went, counted one hour, returned and said: Is Hillel here, is Hillel here? He wrapped himself and went out to call him.

He said: My son, what do you wish?

He said: I have a question to ask.

He said: Ask my son.

He said: Why are the eyes of the Palmyreans bleared?

He said to him: My son, you have asked a great question: because they live in sandy places.

He went, waited an hour, returned and said: Is Hillel here, is Hillel here? He wrapped himself, went out to call him.

He said: My son, what do you wish?

He said to him: I have a question to ask.

He said to him: Ask, my son.

He asked: Why are the feet of the Africans wide?

He said to him: My son, you have asked a great question: because they live in watery marshes.

He said to him: I have many questions to ask, but fear that you may become angry.

Thereupon he wrapped himself, sat before him and said: Ask all the questions you have to ask.

He said to him: Are you the Hillel who is called the Nasi of Israel?

He said to him: Yes.

He said to him: If that is you, may there not be many like you in Israel.

He said to him: Why, my son?

He said to him: Because I have lost four hundred *zuz* through you.

He said to him: Be careful of your moods. Hillel is worth it that you should lose four hundred *zuz* and yet another four hundred *zuz* through him; yet Hillel shall not lose his temper.

Same Narrative: *'Abot R. Nat.* A,15 (Schechter, 60).

(2) R 67
A Proselyte Learns About the Oral Law From Hillel.
b. Šabb. 31a. Soncino, 139-40.

Our Rabbis taught: Once a gentile came before Shammai and said to him: How many *Torot* have you?

He said to him: Two, the Written Torah and the Oral Torah.

He said to him: I believe you with respect to the Written, but not with respect to the Oral Torah; make me a proselyte on condition that you teach me the Written Torah [only]. He rebuked him and pushed him away in anger.

He went before Hillel; he accepted him as a proselyte. On the first day he taught him alef, beth, gimmel, daleth; the following day he reversed [them] to him.

He said to him: Yesterday you did not say them to me thus.

He said to him: Must you then not rely upon me? Then rely upon me with respect to the Oral [Torah] too.

Same Narrative: *'Abot R. Nat.* A,15 (Schechter, 61).

(3) R 68
Hillel Teaches a Proselyte the Golden Rule.
b. Šabb. 31a. Soncino, 140.

Another story: A gentile went to Shammai and said to him: Make me a proselyte on condition that you teach me the whole

Torah while I stand on one foot. He pushed him away with the measuring stick that was in his hand. He went to Hillel.

He said to him: What is hateful to you, do not do to your neighbor. This is the whole Torah, and the rest is its commentary. Go and learn.[1]

Compare the use of Lev 19:18 in Rom 13:8-10; Gal 5:14; Jas 2:8. See also Matt 22:39 and par.

[1] Motif: Luke 8:37: "Go and you do likewise."

(4) R 69
The Proselyte Who Desired to Become the High Priest.
b. Šabb. 31a. Soncino 140-41.

Again it happened that a certain gentile was passing behind a Beth Hamidrash and he heard the voice of a scribe who was saying [Exod 28:4]: "And these are the garments which they shall make, a breastplate and an ephod."

He said: For whom are these?

He said: For the High Priest.

The gentile said to himself: I will go and become a proselyte that I may be appointed a High Priest. So he went before Shammai and said to him: Make me a proselyte on condition that you appoint me a High Priest. But he repulsed him with the measuring stick which was in his hand.

He then went before Hillel, who made him a proselyte.

He said to him: Can any man be made a king but he who knows the arts of government? Do you go and study the arts of government! He went and read. When he came to [Num 1:51]: "And the stranger that comes near will be put to death," he said to him: About whom is this written? He said to him: [It applies] even to David, King of Israel.

The proselyte reasoned within himself: If Israel, who are called sons of the Omnipresent, and who in his love for them he called them, "Israel is my son, my firstborn [Ezek 4:22]," yet it is written of them, "and the stranger who comes near shall be put to death;" how much more so a mere proselyte who comes with his staff and wallet! Then he went before Shammai and said to him: Am I then eligible to be a High Priest; is it not written in the Torah, "And the stranger who comes near shall be put to death"?

He went before Hillel and said to him: O gentle Hillel, blessings rest on your head for bringing me under the wings of the *Shekinah*.

Some time later the three met in one place.

They said: Shammai's impatience sought to drive us from the world, but Hillel's gentleness brought us under the wings of the *Shekinah*.

Same Narrative: *'Abot R. Nat.* A,15 (Schechter, 61).

R 70
Hillel the Elder's Wife Gives Dinner Away to a Poor Man.
Der. Er. Rab. 57a. Soncino MT, 551.

A man should never mind at all what he shall have for his meal. Once it happened that Hillel the Elder had a certain man to a meal, and a poor man came and stood by his door, and said: I am to marry today, but I have no provisions at all. Hillel's wife then took the entire meal and gave it to him. Afterwards she kneaded fresh dough, cooked another dinner, and placed it before them.

He said to her: My dear, why did you not bring it to us sooner? She told him all that had happened.

He said to her: My dear, I did not judge you in the scale of guilt, but in the scale of merit, because everything which you did was only in the name of heaven.

R 71
A Hasid Prays for Rain.
t. Ta'an. 3,8.

It happened in regard to a certain hasid that they said to him: Pray in order that rain might fall. He prayed and the rain fell. They said to him: As you prayed, and the rain fell, so pray and it will stop.

He said to them: Go out and see. If there is a man standing on the keren ophel and dangling his feet in the Kedron brook, we will pray that the rain will not fall. However, we are confident that God is not bringing destruction on the world.

R 72 and R 73
Ḥoni's Prayer for Rain.
m. Taʿan. 3,8; *b. Taʿan.* 23a, Soncino, 115-17.

R 72 *m. Taʿan.* 3,8	R 73 *b. Taʿan.* 23a
It happened:	Our rabbis taught: one time, most of the month of Adar had passed and rain had not fallen.
they said to Ḥoni the Circle-Drawer: Pray that rain might fall.	they sent [a message] to Ḥoni the Circle-Drawer: Pray in order that rain might fall.
He said to them: Go and take in the passover ovens so that they do not dissolve. He prayed, but the rain did not fall; he drew a circle, stood in the middle,	He prayed, but the rain did not fall; he drew a circle and stood in the middle, just as Habakkuk the prophet did as it is said, "I will stand upon my watch" [2:1].
and said before God: Master of the world, your children look to me because I am like a child of your household before you. I swear by your great name that I will not move from here until you have mercy on your children. The rain began in drops.	He said before God: Master of the world your children look to me because I am like a child of your household before you. I swear by your great name that I will not move from here until you have mercy on your children. The rain began in drops. His disciples said to him: Rabbi, we see you, and we will not die; but it seems to us that this rain is falling only to free you from your oath.
He said: It is not for such that I asked;	He said: It is not for such that I asked;

but a rain for cisterns,
ditches, and caves. It came
down with vehemence.

He said:
It is not for such that I
asked;
but for a rain of
benevolence, blessing and
graciousness. It came down
as it should until the
Israelites went from
Jerusalem up to the Temple
Mount on account of the
rain.
They said to him:
As you prayed for the rain to
fall so pray for it to stop.

He said to them:
Go out and see whether the
Losers' Stone has been
washed away.

but a rain for cisterns,
ditches, and caves. It came
down with vehemence, each
drip as big as a barrel
mouth, and the sages
estimated that none was less
than a *log*. His disciples said
to him: Rabbi, we see you,
and we will not die; but it
seems to us that this rain is
falling only to destroy the
world.
He said before God:
It is not for such that I
asked;
but for a rain of
benevolence, blessing and
graciousness. It came down
as it should until the people
went up to the Temple
Mount on account of the
rain.

They said to him:
Rabbi, as you prayed that
the rain fall, so pray that it
stop.
He said to them:

This is what was handed on
to me, that one should not
pray, about an excess of
good. However, bring me a
bullock of thanksgiving
[offering]. They brought to
him the bullock of
thanksgiving [offering]; he
laid both his hands on it and
said: Master of the world,
your people Israel whom you

	brought out from Egypt are not able to stand an excess of good or an excess of punishment. When you were angry with them, they could not stand it; when you showered upon them an excess of good, they could not stand it; let it be your good pleasure that there be respite in the world. Immediately, the wind blew, the clouds dispersed, and the sun shone. The people went out to the fields and brought in mushrooms and truffles.
Simeon b Sheṭaḥ sent word to him:	Simeon b Sheṭaḥ sent word to him: Were you not Ḥoni
You deserve to be excommunicated.	I would decree your excommunication; if these years were like the years of Elijah, would not the name of God be profaned because of you?
But what can I do since you are petulant before God as a petulant son before his father, and still the father does what he wants.	But what can I do since you are petulant before God as a petulant son before his father, And still the father does what he wants. If he says to him Abba,[1] bathe me in warm water, he bathes him; wash me in cold water, he washes him; give me nuts, peaches, almonds and pomegranates, and he gives them.
The text is about you which says: "Let your father and mother be glad, and let her who bore you rejoice." [Prov 23:25.]	The text is about you which says: "Let your father and mother be glad, and let her who bore you rejoice."

Same Narrative: R 71.
Comparable Narratives: Josephus, *Ant.* 14,2; *Meg. Ta῾an.*
(H. Lichtenstein, "Die Fastenrolle, eine Untersuchung
zur Jüdisch-Hellenistischen Geschichte," *HUCA* 8-9,
1931-32, 257-352, esp. p. 348); Tanḥuma, Ki Tabo 4;
Midr. Ps 77,1; *'Abot R. Nat.* 9 (Schechter, 41).

1 This is one of two instances in Rabbinic literature where
it is possible that God is being addressed as Abba. See: J.
A. Fitzmyer: "*Abba* and Jesus' Relation to God," in *A
Cause de L'Evangile.* (Mélanges offertes à Dom Jacques
Dupont) (Paris: Cerf, 1985) 15-38, esp. pp. 26-27. The
other instance is found in R 93.

R 74
Ḥoni's Long Sleep.
b. Ta῾an. 23a. Soncino, 117-18.

Said R Yoḥanan: All his life long this righteous man [Ḥoni]
was troubled about this verse [Ps 126:1], "When the Lord
brought back those that returned to Zion, we were like them
that dream."

He said: Did anyone ever sleep 70 years? One day while
walking on the road he noticed a man planting a carob-tree. He
[Ḥoni] said to him: You know it takes 70 years before a carob-
tree bears fruit; are you so sure that you will live 70 years to eat
therefrom?

He said to him: I have found this world provided with carob-
trees, as my ancestors planted them for me, so I plant them for
my progeny.

Thereupon Ḥoni sat down to eat and was overcome by sleep:
As he slept, a grotto was formed around him, so that he was
screened off from human eyes, and then he slept for 70 years.
When he awoke, he saw a man gathering carobs from the carob-
tree and eating them.

He said to him: Do you know who planted this carob-tree?
He said to him: My grandfather.
Said Ḥoni: I must have slept 70 years. [He saw many herds
that had descended from his she-ass.] Then he went to his house
and inquired whether the son of Ḥoni the Circle-Drawer was
still alive. He was told that the son was no longer among the
living; but that his grandson was still alive. He said to them: I
am Ḥoni. But the people did not believe him. He took himself
to the Bet ha-Midrash and he heard the scholars say: Our studies are as clear to us today as they used to be in the times of Ḥoni
the Circle-Drawer, for when he came to the Bet ha-Midrash he

used to explain to the scholars all their difficulties. He said to
them: I am Ḥoni, but they would not believe him nor show him
the respect due him. [This grieved him very much], and therefore he prayed to God that he should die, and he died.

Comparable Narratives: *y. Taʿan.* 3,10; 66d; H 206.

THE FIRST GENERATION OF TANNAIM
APPROXIMATELY 1-90 C.E.

R 75 and R 76
R Ḥanina b Dosa Heals the Son of Gamaliel.
b. Ber. 34b, Soncino, 215-16, and *y. Ber.* 9d.[1]

R 75 *b. Ber.* 34b	R 76 *y. Ber.* 9d
Our masters taught: It happened that the son of Rabban Gamaliel fell sick. He sent out two disciples to R Ḥanina b Dosa	It happened to Rabban Gamaliel that his son fell sick. He sent two disciples to R Ḥanina b Dosa in his town.
to ask mercy for him. As soon as Ḥanina saw them	He said to them: Wait while I mount to the upper room;
he mounted to an upper room and asked mercy for him. When he came down, he said to them: Go, for the fever has left him.	he mounted to the upper room and he came down and said to them:
	I am assured that the son of R Gamaliel has recovered from his illness.
They said to him: Are you a prophet?[2] He said to them: I am not a prophet nor a son of a prophet; but I have learned this: if my prayer is fluent in my mouth I know that it is accepted, and if not, I know that it is rejected.	

They sat down and noted, determining the exact hour. And as they were coming in to Rabban Gamaliel, he said to them: By the Worship! You are not too soon or too late, but as it happened, it was exactly at that hour that the fever left him and he asked us for some water to drink.	They noted.
	At that exact hour
	he requested food.[3]

1 Story: John 4:46-54.
2 See R 78, note 1.
3 Motif: Mark 5:43.

R 77
Hanina Heals the Son of Yohanan b Zakkai.
b. Ber. 34b, Soncino, 216.

Another story about R Hanina b Dosa: He went to learn To-rah from R Yohanan b Zakkai, and the son of R Yohanan b Zak-kai was sick.

He said to him: Hanina, my son, ask mercy for him that he may live. He put his head between his knees;[1] and he asked mercy for him, and he lived.

R Yohanan b Zakkai said: If ben Zakkai had squeezed his head between his knees all day, no notice would have been taken of him.

His wife said to him: Is Hanina greater than you?

He said to her: No, but he is like a servant before the king, and I am like a nobleman before the king.

1 Motif: 1 Kgs 18:42.

R 78 and R 79
R Hanina Rescues the Daughter of Nehuniah.
b. B. Qam. 50a, Soncino, 287-88, and *b. Yebam.* 121b.

R 78 *b. B. Qam.* 50a	R 79 *b. Yebam.* 121b
Our rabbis taught: It happened in regard to the daughter of Nehuniah the trench-digger, that she fell into a deep well.	[The same.]

They came   [The same.]
and informed R Ḥanina b
Dosa.
The first hour he came and
said to them: Shalom.
The second hour he came
and said to them:
She has come up.   ●
They said to her: He said to her:
who drew you up?   My daughter who drew you
                                             up?
She said: She said to him:
A ram came to me in time   A ram came to me in time
and an old man led it.   and an old man led it.
They said to him: [The same but for the one
Are you a prophet?   word indicated.]
He said to them:
I am not a prophet,
nor am I the son of a
prophet;[1]
but this is what I said to
myself:
Shall the very thing in which
this just man troubles   [engages himself]
himself be a stumbling block
to his posterity?
R Aḥa said: [The same.]
All the same his son died of
thirst; as it is written: "He is
awesome to all round about
him" [Ps 89:8]. Which
teaches that the Holy One,
blessed be he, deals strictly
with those round about him,
to a hair's breadth. . . .

Comparable Narrative: R 166.

[1] Motif: the same question and answer occur in R 75.
This is an instance of a "floating formula."

R 80
The Snake Which Bites R Ḥanina Dies.
t. Ber. 3,20.

They say concerning R Ḥanina b Dosa, that he was praying and a snake bit him, and he did not interrupt his prayer. His disciples went and found the snake dead at the mouth of its hole.

They said: Woe to the man whom a snake bites, but woe to the snake who bites ben Dosa!

Comparable Narratives: *y. Ber.* 9a; *b. Ber.* 33a, H 199b.

A Catena of Stories Concerning R Ḥanina

(1) R 81
Ḥanina Prays for the Starting and Stopping of Rain.
b. Ta'an. 24b. Soncino, 127.

R Ḥanina b Dosa was journeying on the road when it began to rain.

He said: Master of the Universe, the whole world is at ease but Ḥanina is in distress; the rain then ceased.

When he returned home he said: Master of the Universe, the whole world is in distress and Ḥanina is at ease. Whereupon the rain fell.

Same Narrative: *b. Yoma* 53b.

(2) R 82
Ḥanina's Wife and the Full Oven.
b. Ta'an. 24b-25a. Soncino, 128.

Rab Judah said in the name of Rab: Every day a heavenly voice is heard declaring:[1] The whole world draws its sustenance because [of the merit] of Ḥanina my son, and Ḥanina my son has enough with a qab of carobs from one Sabbath eve to another.

Every Friday his wife would light the oven and throw twigs into it, so as not to be put to shame. She had a certain bad neighbor who said: I know that these people have nothing, what then is the meaning of [this] smoke? She went and knocked at the door. [The wife of R Ḥanina] feeling humiliated retired into a room. A miracle[2] happened for her and she [her neighbor] saw the oven filled with loaves of bread and the kneading trough full of dough.

She said to her: You, you, bring your shovel, for your bread is getting charred.

She said: I just went to fetch it.

A Tanna taught: She actually had gone to fetch the shovel because she was accustomed to miracles.

1 See R 100, note 2.

2 Literally "sign" (*nissa'*). This is a common designation for miracle in this literature. The Fourth Gospel uses "sign" (*semeia*) in the same way.

(3) R 83
The Golden Table Leg.
b. Ta'an. 25a. Soncino, 128-29.

Once his wife said to him [Ḥanina]: How long shall we go on suffering so much?

He said to her: What shall we do?

She said to him: Pray that something may be given to you. He prayed and there emerged the figure of a hand reaching out to him a leg of a golden table. Thereupon he saw in a dream that the pious would one day eat at a three-legged golden table, but he would eat at a two-legged table.

He said to her: Are you content that everybody shall eat at a perfect table and we at an imperfect table?

She said: Pray that the leg should be taken away from you. He prayed and it was taken away.

A Tanna taught: The latter miracle was greater than the former, for there is a tradition that a thing may be given but once; it is never to be taken away again.

(4) R 84
Ḥanina's Daughter and the Confusion of the Oil and Vinegar.
b. Ta'an. 25a. Soncino, 129.

One Friday eve he noticed that his daughter was sad and he said to her: My daughter, why are you so sad?

She said: My oil jar got mixed up with my vinegar jar and I kindled the Sabbath light with it.

He said to her: My daughter, why should this trouble you? He who commanded the oil to burn will also command the vinegar to burn.

A Tanna taught: The light continued to burn the whole day until they took of it light for the "Habdalah."

(5) R 85
R Ḥanina's Goats.
b. Taʿan. 25a. Soncino, 129.

R Ḥanina had goats. On being told that they were doing damage he said: If they indeed do damage may bears devour them, but if not may they each of them at the evening time bring home a bear on their horns. In the evening each of them brought home a bear on its horns.

(6) R 86
Ḥanina and the Projection of the Beams.
b. Taʿan. 25a. Soncino, 129.

R Ḥanina had a neighbor who once said to him: I have built a house but the beams will not reach the walls. He said to her: What is your name?

She said to him: Aiku [Ikku].

He said to her: Aiku, that your beams stretch!

A Tanna taught: They projected one cubit on either side. Some say new pieces joined themselves [miraculously] to the beams.

It has been taught: Polemo says: I saw that house and its beams projected one cubit on either side, and people told me: This is the house which R Ḥanina b Dosa covered with beams, through his prayer.

(7) R 87
Ḥanina and the Hens.
b. Taʿan. 25a. Soncino, 130.

[This story explains how Ḥanina, a poor man, possessed goats. See: R 85.]

R Pinḥas said: Once it happened that a man passed by his house and left hens there. The wife of R Ḥanina b Dosa found them.

R Ḥanina said to her: Do not eat of their eggs. As the eggs and the chickens increased in number he was very troubled by them and therefore he sold them and with the proceeds he purchased goats. One day the man who lost the hens passed by and said to his companions: Here I left my hens.

R Ḥanina heard and said: Have you any sign?

He said to him: Yes. He gave him the sign and took away the goats. These were the goats that had brought bears on their horns.

Comparable Narratives: R 160; R 59.

R 88
The Donkey Who Wouldn't Eat When Stolen.
'*Abot R. Nat.* 8 (Schechter, 38). Goldin, 53.

Once the ass of R Ḥanina b Dosa was stolen by brigands. They tied up the ass in a yard, and put before it straw and barley and water.

But it would not eat or drink. They said: Why should we let it die and befoul our yard? So they opened the gate before it, and drove it out. It walked along braying until it reached the house of R Ḥanina b Dosa. When it reached his house, his son heard its voice.

He said: Father, this sounds like our beast.

R Ḥanina said to him: My son, open the door for it, for it has almost died of hunger. He arose and opened the door, and put before it straw, barley and water. And it ate and drank.

Therefore it was said: Even as the righteous of old were saintly, so were their beasts saintly, like their masters.

Comparable Narrative: R 159.

R 89
R Ḥanina Warned Before Eating Untithed Spices.
y. Dem. 1,3; 22a. Vermes, p. 45.

On a Sabbath night, when R Ḥanina b Dosa was sitting down to eat, his table collapsed.

They said to him: What is this?

She [his wife] said to him: I have borrowed spices from my neighbor, but have not tithed them. He caused it to be remembered a second time, and the table rose again.

Comparable Narrative: *y. Ber.* 9d.

R 90
R Ḥanina's Control Over Demons.
b. Pesaḥ. 112b. Soncino, 579-80.

One must not go out alone at night, neither on the night of the fourth day, nor on the night of the Sabbath, because Agrat bat Maḥlat sets out with eighteen myriads of angels of destruction, each of which singly has full power to destroy. At first they

were to be met with daily. But once she encountered R Ḥanina
b Dosa.

She said to him: Had someone not cried out in heaven concerning you, "Beware of Ḥanina b Dosa and his teaching," I
should have tried to harm you.

He said to her: If I enjoy such esteem in heaven, then I declare that you shall never wander upon inhabited land!

She said to him: I beg you, grant me some space! Thereupon
he conceded to her the nights of the Sabbath and the fourth
day.[1]

> [1] For a similar dialogue, see: Matt 8:31-32 par. (A similar
> power is attributed to R Abaye in the story which follows
> immediately in *b. Pesah.* 112b.)

R 91
Angels Carry Ḥanina's Gift to the Temple.
Qoh. Rab. 1,1. Soncino, 1.

The words of Qoheleth, the son of David, King in Jerusalem
[1,1]. That is what Scripture declares by the Holy Spirit through
Solomon, King of Israel [Prov 22:29], "Do you see a man diligent
in his business? He shall stand before kings."

Once R Ḥanina b Dosa saw the inhabitants of his city taking
vowed offerings and free-will offerings up to Jerusalem. He said:
All are taking vowed offerings and free-will offerings up to Jerusalem, but I take nothing! What did he do? He went out to the
waste land of his city and saw there a stone which he chipped,
chiselled, and polished. He then said: Behold I take it upon myself to convey it to Jerusalem. He sought to hire workmen, and
five men chanced to come his way. He said to them: Will you
carry up this stone for me to Jerusalem? They answered, "Give
us five *selas* and we will carry it up to Jerusalem." He wanted to
give them the money, but he had none with him at the time, so
they left him and departed. The Holy One, blessed be he, arranged for five angels to appear to him in the likeness of men.

He said to them: Will you carry up this stone for me?

They said to him: Give us five *selas* and we will carry your
stone up for you to Jerusalem, but on condition that you place
your hand and finger with ours. He placed his hand and finger
with theirs and they found themselves standing in Jerusalem.
He wanted to pay them their hire but could not find them. He
entered the Hall of Hewn Stone and inquired about them.

[The men in the Hall] said to him: Probably ministering angels carried your stone up to Jerusalem.

And they applied to him this text: "Do you see a man diligent in his business? He shall stand before kings;" [m^elakim]— read the phrase as "He shall stand before angels" [mal'akim].

Same Narrative: *Cant. Rab.* 1,1.

R 92
Ḥanina Eats a Poisonous Onion.
b. 'Erub. 29b. Soncino, 202.

Our Rabbis taught: No one should eat an onion on account of the poisonous fluid it contains. It happened once that R Ḥanina ate half an onion and half of its poisonous fluid, and became so ill that he was on the point of dying. His colleagues, however, begged for heavenly mercy, and he recovered because his contemporaries needed him.

R 93
Ḥoni's Grandson Ḥanan ha-Neḥba.
b. Ta'an. 23b. Soncino, 120.

Ḥanan ha-Neḥba was the son of the daughter of Ḥoni the Circle-Drawer. When the world was in need of rain, the Rabbis would send him school children and they would take hold of the hem of his garment and say to him: Abba, Abba, give us rain.

He said: Master of the Universe, do it for the sake of these who are unable to distinguish between the Abba[1] who gives rain and the abba who does not. And the rain came.

[1] See the note on R 74.

R 94
The Glance of R Yoḥanan b Zakkai Strikes a Man Dead.
b. Sanh. 100a. Soncino, 678.

But if you have heard something it is this:
R Yoḥanan was sitting and teaching: The Holy One, blessed be he, will bring jewels and precious stones, each thirty cubits long, and thirty cubits high, and make an engraving in them, ten by twenty cubits, and set them up as the gates of Jerusalem, for it is written [Isa 54:12]: "And I will make your windows of agates, and your gates of carbuncles."

A certain disciple derided him saying: We do not find a jewel even as large as a dove's egg, yet such huge ones are to exist!

Some time later, he took a sea journey and saw the ministering angels cutting precious stones and pearls.

He said to them: For what are these:

They said: The Holy One, blessed be he, will set them up as the gates of Jerusalem.

On his return, he found R Yoḥanan sitting and teaching.

He said to him: Expound, O Master, and it is indeed fitting for you to expound; for even as you did say, so did I myself see.

He said to him: Wretch, had you not seen, you would not have believed! You deride the words of the Sages.[1]

He set his eyes upon him, and he turned into a heap of bones.[2]

[1] Motif: John 20:29.
[2] Comparable Narratives: R 61; b. Šabb. 34a.

R 95

R Yoḥanan Answers a Gentile About the Red Heifer.
Pesiq. R. 14,13 (Friedman 65a). Braude, 291-92.

A gentile asked Rabban Yoḥanan b Zakkai, saying: These things that you Jews do appear to me to be some kind of sorcery. A heifer is brought, it is burned, is pounded into ashes, and its ashes are gathered up. Then, when one of you gets defiled by contact with a corpse, two or three drops of the ashes mixture are sprinkled upon him, and he is told: You are cleansed.[1]

He said to him: Has the spirit of madness ever possessed you?

He said to him: No.

[He said to him]: But have you ever seen a man whom the spirit of madness has possessed?

He said to him: Yes.

[He said to him]: And you have not seen what is done to this man?

[The gentile said]: Roots[2] are brought, they are made to smoke under him, water is splashed upon him until the spirit flees.

He said to him: Do not your ears hear what your mouth is saying? A man defiled is like a man possessed of a spirit. This spirit is a spirit of uncleanness, and Scripture says [Zech 13:2]: "And I will cause the prophets of the spirit of uncleanness to pass out of the land." And then he went out.

His disciples said to him: Rabbi, you have thrust this man away with a reed, and what will be the reply to us?

He said to them: It is not the corpse that defiles, nor the mixture of ash and water that purifies, but the rite of the Red Heifer is a decree of the Lord. The Holy One, blessed be he, said: I have set down a law and issued a decree. You are not permitted to transgress my decree. [See Num 19:2.]

1 See: Heb 9:13.
2 Motif: R 170 and note 1.

R 96
R Yoḥanan b Zakkai Meets Vespasian and Predicts his Future Reign.
b. Git. 56a-b. Fraenkel, 81-82.

Abba Siqra (the father of the Sicarii), the head of the bandits of Jerusalem, was the son of R Yoḥanan b Zakkai's sister. He [Yoḥanan] sent to him: Come to me secretly. He came.

He said to him: How long are you going to carry on in this way and kill all the people with starvation?

He said to him: What can I do? If I say a word to them, they will kill me.

He said to him: Devise some plan for me to get out, perhaps it will save a little.

He said to him: Pretend to be ill, and let everyone come to inquire about you, and let them say you are dead, and bring something evil-smelling and put it by you. Let then your disciples attend on you, since they know that a living being is lighter than a corpse.

He did so; and R Eliezer went on one side and R Joshua on the other. When they reached the gate, they [the Sicarii] wanted to stab him.

He [Siqra] said to them: Shall they say, they have stabbed their master?

They wanted to push him.

He said to them: Shall they say that they pushed their master? Then they opened the gate.

When he [Yoḥanan] came to him [Vespasian], he said: Peace to you O king, peace to you O king.

He said to him: You have to be condemned to death on two accounts: firstly, because I am not a king and you call me king; and again, if I am a king, why did you not come to me before now?

He said to him: As for you saying that you are not a king, in truth you are a king, since if you were not a king, Jerusalem would not be delivered into your hand, as it is written [Isa

10:34]: "And Lebanon shall fall by a mighty one," and "mighty one" means nothing but a king, as it is written [Jer 30:21]: "And their mighty one shall be of themselves, and their governor shall proceed from the midst of them." As for your saying, 'If I am a king, why did you not come to me before now?', the bandits among us did not let me.

He said to him: If there is a jar of honey round which a serpent is wound, would they not break the jar because of the serpent?

He did not answer.

R Joseph applied to him the verse [Isa 44:25]: "[God] turns wise men backward and makes their knowledge foolish."

He ought to have said to him: We take a pair of tongs, and grip the serpent and kill it, leaving the jar intact.

Just then, a messenger came to him [Vespasian] and said to him: Arise, for the emperor [Nero] is dead and the notables of Rome decided to make you head.

> Comparable Narrative: H 217.
> Josephus (*J. W.* 3,8,9) applies the same type of prophecy to himself, and this is confirmed by Suetonius, *Vesp.*, 5. Tacitus also makes mention of the aura of prophecy that surrounded Vespasian at this time (*Hist.* 2,78; 5,13; etc.), and this is repeated, in regard to Josephus, by Dio Cassius, *Epitome* 66,1. For a full discussion, see: R. Lattimore, "Portents and Prophecies in Connection with the Emperor Vespasian," *Classical Journal* 29 (1934) 441-49. For some other portents, see H 187-H 189.

THE SECOND GENERATION OF TANNAIM
APPROXIMATELY 90-130 C.E.

R 97
Two Rabbis Prove That Sea Water Absorbs Fresh Water.
Qoh. Rab. 1,7. Soncino, 20-21.

Another interpretation of Qoh 1:7: "All the rivers run into the sea; yet the sea is not full." This refers to the ocean which is never full.

Once R Eliezer and R Joshua were traveling on the great sea. The ship entered a place where water did not flow.

R Eliezer said to R Joshua: We have only come here so that we would be able to make a test. They filled a cask with water from that place. When they arrived at Rome, Hadrian said to them: What are the waters of the ocean?

They said to him: It consists of water which absorbs water.

He said to them: Is it possible that rivers should run into it without becoming full?

They said to him: It absorbs all the water in the world. He said to them: I will not believe you until you prove it to me. They took the water which they had drawn from the ocean, filled a flask with it and then poured further water into it which was absorbed by the ocean-water.

Same Narrative: *Gen. Rab.* 13,9.

R 98
Rabbis Eliezer and Joshua and the Fire From Sinai.
y. Ḥag. 2,1; 77b.

[Elisha b Abuyah is telling the story.]

Abuyah my father was one of the leading men of Jerusalem. It happened on a Sabbath day, when I was to be circumcised, that he invited all the leading men of Jerusalem and he seated them in one room; but R Eliezer and R Joshua he put in another room. When they [all the guests] had finished eating and drinking, they began to clap and dance.

R Eliezer said to R Joshua: As they are busy about their affairs, so let us be busy about ours. And they sat down and busied themselves with the words of the Torah, from the Torah to the

Prophets and from the Prophets to the Writings. And a fire came down and enveloped them.[1]

Abuyah said to them: Masters, have you come to burn my house down on me?

They said to him: Far be it from us! But we were sitting and stringing together the words of the Torah, from the Torah to the Prophets and from the Prophets to the Writings. And the words were full of joy as when they were delivered from Sinai. The fire was lapping at them as it lapped at them [coming] from Sinai. Originally, when they were given from Sinai, they were only given in fire: "And the mountain was burning with fire right up to the heart of heaven." [Deut 4:11.]

Abuyah my father said to them: Masters, if that is the power of the Torah, then if this son is left to me, I dedicate him to the Torah.

Because his proposal was not [really] directed to God, the man [Elisha] was not left to him completely. [There follows a remark conveying the Pharisees' conviction that Elisha was a heretic.]

Comparable Narrative: *Cant. Rab.* 1,10.

[1] For a comparable use of the themes of stringing together Torah, Prophets and Writings, and the burning of Sinai, see Luke 24:27-32.44.

R 99
Cucumbers Produced by a Command.
b. Sanh. 68a. Soncino, 462.

I [R Eliezer] have studied three hundred [some say three thousand] laws about the planting of cucumbers by magic and no one except R Aqiba b Joseph ever questioned me thereon. Once he and I were walking together on a road.

He said to me: My master, teach me about the planting of cucumbers. I said one command and the whole field was filled with cucumbers. He said to me: Master, you have taught me how to plant them, now teach me how to pick them.

I said one command, and all the cucumbers were gathered in one place.

Same Narrative: *m. Sanh.* 7,11; *y. Sanh.* 7; 25d; *t. Sanh.* 11,5; *'Abot R. Nat.* A,25 (Schechter, 81).

R 100
R Eliezer Works Wonders to Support His Opinion.
b. B. Mes. 59b. Soncino, 352-53.

A Tanna taught: On that day, R Eliezer brought forth all the arguments in the world, but they did not accept them.

Said he to them: If the halakah agrees with me, let this carob-tree prove it! Thereupon, the carob-tree was torn a hundred cubits out of its place[1]—others affirm, four hundred cubits.

They said to him: No proof can be brought from a carob-tree.

And he said to them: If the halakah agrees with me, let the stream of water prove it! Whereupon the stream of water flowed backwards.

They said to him: No proof can be brought from a stream of water!

And he said to them: If the halakah agrees with me, let the walls of the schoolhouse prove it! Whereupon the walls inclined to fall.

But R Joshua said: When scholars are engaged in a halakic dispute, why do you interfere? Hence they did not fall, in honour of R Joshua; nor did they become upright, in honour of R Eliezer; and they are still standing.

Again he said to them: If the halakah agrees with me, let it be proved from Heaven! Whereupon a Heavenly Voice[2] came and said: Why do you dispute with R Eliezer, seeing that in all matters the halakah agrees with him?

But R Joshua arose and said: It is not in heaven. [Deut 30:12.] What did he mean by this? Said R Jeremiah: That the Torah had already been given at Mount Sinai; we pay no attention to a Heavenly Voice, because you have long since written in the Torah at Mount Sinai, "After the majority must one incline" [Exod 23:2].

> Same Narrative: *y. Kil.* 3,1; 81c-d. See: A. Guttmann, "The Significance of Miracles for Talmudic Judaism," *HUCA* 20 (1947) 363-406.

[1] Motif: Luke 17:6.
[2] Motif: Matt 3:17/Mark 1:11/Luke 3:22; Matt 17:5/Mark 9:7/Luke 9:35; see also R 82.

R 101
R Gamaliel's Prayer to Calm a Storm at Sea.
b. B. Mes. 59b. Soncino, 354.[1]

[This is one of the sequels to R 100.]

A Tanna taught: How great was the calamity that befell that day, for everything at which R Eliezer cast his eyes was burned. R Gamaliel too was traveling in a ship when a wave arose to drown him. He said: It seems to me that this is on account of none other than R Eliezer b Hyrcanus. He arose and said: Sovereign of the Universe, it is known to you that I have not acted for my honor, nor for the honor of my father's house, but for your honor, that strife may not be multiplied in Israel. At that, the sea subsided.

[1] Story: R 173; Matt 8:23-27/Mark 4:35-41/Luke 8:22-25.

R 102
How R Eliezer Parried Questions With Counter-Questions.
b. Yoma 66b. Soncino, 310.

R Eliezer was asked: What about carrying it [the scapegoat] on his shoulder?
He said to them: It is possible for him to carry me and you.
[They said]: If he who was to send it away became sick, may he send it away through someone else?
He said to them: Surely I wish to be in peace, I and you.
[They said]: If he pushed it down, and it did not die, should he go down after it and kill it?
He said to them [Judg 5:31]: "So perish all your enemies, O Lord! But the Sages say: If it became sick, he may load it on his shoulder; if he pushed it down and it did not die, he shall go down and kill it.

R 103
R Eliezer is Asked Various Questions.
b. Yoma 66b. Soncino, 310-11.

They asked R Eliezer: What about "Peloni"[1] in the world to come?
He said to them: Have you not asked me anything but about "Peloni?"
[They said]: May one save the lamb from the lion?
He said to them: Have you not asked me anything but about the lamb?

They said: May one save the shepherd from the lion?

He said to them: Have you not asked me anything but about the shepherd?

[They said]: May a bastard inherit [from his father]?

[He said]: May he likewise marry the wife of his brother who died without issue?

[They said]: May one whitewash his house?

[He said]: May one whitewash his grave? [His evasion was due] not to his desire to divert them with words, but because he never said anything that he had not heard from his teacher.

> 1 The use of Peloni ("somebody") may be veiling an original question concerning Solomon, Absalom or some other ancestor.

R 104
R Joshua b Hananiah Prays and the Lion of Be-Ila 'i Comes.
b. Hul. 59b. Soncino, 328.

The Emperor once said to R Joshua b Hananiah: Your God is like a lion, for it is written [Amos 3:8]: "The lion has roared, who will not fear? The Lord has spoken, who can but prophesy?" But what is the greatness of this? A horseman can kill a lion!

He said to him: He has not been likened to the ordinary lion, but to the lion of Be-Ila 'i!

He said to him: I desire that you show it to me.

He said to him: You cannot behold it.

He said to him: Indeed, I will see it.

He [R Joshua b Hananiah] prayed and the lion set out from its place. When it was four hundred parasangs distant, it roared once and all pregnant women miscarried and the walls of Rome fell. When it was three hundred parasangs distant, it roared again, and all the molars and incisors of man fell out; even the Emperor himself fell from his throne to the ground.

He said to him: Please, pray that it return to its place. He prayed and it returned to its place.

R 105
R Joshua Convinces the Emperor That He Cannot See God.
b. Hul. 59b-60a. Soncino, 328.

The Emperor said to R Joshua b Hananiah: I wish to see your God.

He said to him: You cannot see him.

He said to him: Indeed, I shall see him.

He went and placed the Emperor facing the sun during the summer solstice.

He said to him: Look up at it.

He said to him: I cannot.

He said to him: If you cannot look at the sun, which is but one of the ministers that attend the Holy One, blessed be he, how can you look upon the divine presence?

R 106
The Emperor Learns About the Greatness of God.
b. Ḥul. 60a. Soncino, 328-29.

The Emperor said to R Joshua b Ḥananiah: I wish to prepare a banquet for your God.

He said to him: You cannot do this.

He said to him: Why?

Because his attendants are too numerous.

He said to him: Indeed, I will do it!

He said to him: Then go and prepare it on the spacious banks of Rebitha'. He spent the six months of summer in making preparations, when a tempest arose and swept everything into the sea. He then spent the six months of winter in making preparations, when rain fell and washed everything into the sea.

He said to him: What is this?

He said to him: They are but the sweepers and sprinklers that march before him!

He said to him: If so, then I cannot do it.

R 107
R Joshua b Ḥananiah Illustrates the Teaching That the Words of the Torah Abide With the Meek.
b. Ta ʿan. 7a-b. Soncino, 27.

> [The story illustrates a saying of R Oshaia that the words
> of the Torah are like water, wine and milk: all precious
> liquids stored in ordinary vessels.]

This explains the story of the daughter of the Roman Emperor who said to R Joshua b Ḥananiah: What glorious wisdom in such an ugly vessel.

He said to her: Does not your father keep wine in an earthenware vessel?

She said to him: In what [else] shall he keep it?

He said to her: You who are nobles should keep it in vessels of gold and silver. Thereupon, she went and told this to her father and he had the wine put into vessels of gold and silver and it became sour. When they told [this] to him, he said to his daughter: Who told you this?

She said to him: R Joshua b Hananiah. He was called before him, and [the Emperor] said to him: Why did you tell her [to do] this?

He said to him: I spoke to her according to the way she spoke to me.

Are there not good-looking people who are learned? If these very people were ugly, they would be still more learned.

Another explanation: Just as these three liquids can become unfit for consumption only through inattention, so too the words of the Torah are forgotten only through inattention.

R 108
R Joshua Answers Hadrian's Objections About the Ten Commandments.
Pesiq. R. 21,2-3 (Friedman 99a-b). Braude, 415-16.

Another exposition on [Ps 92:4]: "With an instrument of ten strings, with the psaltery," are read as, "For me the ten, for me the psaltery." Hadrian—may his bones crumble to dust—asked R Joshua b Hananiah, saying to him: The Holy One, blessed be he, bestowed a great honor upon the nations of the world when he gave five commandments to Israel and offered five to the nations of the world. In the first five commandments, which the Holy One, blessed be he, gave to Israel, his name is involved with the commandments, so that if Israel sin, God raises a cry against them. But in the second five commandments, which he offered to the nations of the earth, his name is not involved with the commandments, so that when the nations of the earth sin, he raises no cry against them.

He said to him: Come walk in the city square with me. And in each and every place where [R Joshua] led him, Hadrian saw a statue of himself standing.

[R Joshua] said: This: What is it?

He said to him: It is a statue of me. And this one here—what is it? The Emperor replied: It is a statue of me. Finally, he drew him along and led him into a privy.

He said to him: My lord king, I see that everywhere in this city you are a ruler, because in each and every place a statue of yourself is standing, but in this place, none stands.

He said to him: Would this be the honor due to a king, to have a statue of himself standing in such a place, a place that is loathsome, a place that is polluted?

He said to him: Do not your ears hear what your mouth is saying? Would it be an improvement to the praise of the Holy One, blessed be he, to have his name mentioned with murderers, with adulterers, with thieves?

[Hadrian] dismissed him, and he went.

After [Hadrian] went away, his disciples said to him: Master, you have thrust off that one [with a broken reed of an answer]. What answer will you give to us?

> [There then follows a long story relating how God searched for a people who would accept all ten commandments, and found only Israel willing.]

R 109
R Joshua Proves to Hadrian the Superiority of Moses as a Law-Giver.
Qoh. Rab. 9,4. Soncino, 228-29.

[Qoh 9:4]: "For a living dog is better than a dead lion." Hadrian—may his bones crumble to dust—asked R Joshua b Ḥananiah saying: Am I [not] better than your teacher Moses?

He said to him: Why?

Because I am living and he is dead, as it is written: "For a living dog is better than a dead lion."

He said to him: Are you able to declare that no man light a fire for three days?

He said to him: Yes [and he issued the command]. When the evening of that day came, they both went up to the roof of the palace and saw smoke going up in the distance.

He said to him: What is that there?

He said to him: One of my officers is ill and a physician went to visit him and said to him: Until you have hot drinks, you will not be cured.

He said to him: May this breath be your last! While you are alive your order is annulled. But Moses, our teacher, in the hour that he decreed upon us [Exod 35:3], "You shall kindle no fire throughout your dwellings on the Sabbath day," no Jew has kindled a fire on the Sabbath from his days, and still his decree has not been annulled throughout all these years until now. And yet you say: I am better than he.

Same Narrative: *Ruth Rab.* 3,2; *Qoh. Zuta* 9,4.

R 110
The Four Rabbis on Their Trip to Rome; Their Debate With a Sectarian About the Sabbath.
Exod. Rab. 30,9. Soncino, 355-56.

Another explanation of Exod 21:1: "And these are the judgments." This is what is written [Ps 147:19]: "He declares his word to Jacob"—these are the [ten] commandments; "his statutes and judgments to Israel"—these are the judgments. Because the ways of God are not like the ways of man. The ways of a man: he teaches others to do something, and he does nothing. God is not like that: what he does, he tells Israel to do and observe.

A story about Rabban Gamaliel, R Joshua, R Eleazar b Azariah, and R Aqiba: They went to Rome and taught there: The ways of God are not like man who makes a decree and tells others to do it and he does nothing—God is not like that.

There was a sectarian there. As they were going out, he said to them: Your words are nothing but lies. Did you not say that God commands and does? Why doesn't he keep the Sabbath?

They said to him: Wretch! Is not a man permitted to carry something in his own courtyard on the Sabbath?

He said to them: Yes.

They said to him: The upper and lower regions [of the universe] are God's courtyard, as it is said [Isa 6:3], "The whole earth is full of his glory." And is it not true that a man does not transgress even if he carries something the distance of his own height?

He said to them: Yes.

They said to him: It is written [Jer 23:24], "Do I not fill the heavens and the earth?"

R 111
The Elders and Philosophers Debate About Idolatry.
m. 'Abod. Zar. 4,7.

They asked the elders in Rome: If God has no pleasure in idolatry, why does he not make an end of it?

They said to them: If it were a thing not necessary for the world that they worshipped, he would make an end of it. But look, they worship the sun and the moon and the stars and the planets: shall he destroy his world because of fools?

They said to them: If that is the case, let him destroy what is not necessary for the world, and let him leave what is necessary for the world.

They said to them: He would but strengthen the hands of those who worship them. They would say: "Know that these are deities, for look, they have not been made an end of."

R 112
A Different Version of the Debate About Idolatry.
b. 'Abod. Zar. 54b. Soncino, 279.

Gemara: Our Rabbis taught: Philosophers asked the elders in Rome: If your God has no pleasure in idolatry, why does he not make an end of it?

They said to them: If it were a thing not necessary for the world that they worshipped, surely he would make an end of it. But look, they worship the sun and the moon and the stars and the planets: shall he destroy the world because of fools? The world continues to go on its natural course, and the fools who act perversely will have to give an account.

Another exposition: Suppose a man stole a measure of wheat and went and sowed it in the ground: is it right that it should not grow? The world continues to go on its natural course, and the fools who act perversely will have to give an account.

Another exposition: Suppose a man goes to his neighbor's wife: is it right that she should not conceive? The world continues to go on its natural course, and the fools who act perversely will have to give an account.

R 113
Gamaliel and a Philosopher on the Same Topic.
b. 'Abod. Zar. 54b-55a. Soncino, 279-80.

A philosopher asked R Gamaliel: It is written in your Torah [Deut 4:24], "Yhwh your God is a consuming fire, he is a jealous God." Why is he jealous of its worshippers and not of the idol itself?

He said to him: I will give you a parable. To what is this like? It is like a human king who had a son, and this son reared a dog to which he gave the name of his father. Whenever he took an oath, he said, "By the life of this dog, my father." When the father hears of it, with whom is he angry: is he angry with the son or with the dog? Surely he is angry with the son!

He said to him: You call the idol a dog, but there is some reality in it.

He said to him: What do you see?

He said to him: One time a fire broke out in our city and the whole city was burnt except the shrine of the idol.

He said to him: I will give you a parable. To what is this like? It is like a human king against whom a province rebelled. When he makes war, is it against the living that he makes it, or against the dead? Surely it is against the living!

He said to him: You call the idol a dog and you call it dead. If that is the case, let him destroy it from the world!

He said to him: If it were a thing not necessary for the world that they worshipped, surely he would make an end of it. But look, they worship the sun and the moon and the stars and the planets, and the brooks and the glens. Should he destroy his world because of fools? And thus he says [Zeph 1:2]: "Am I to make an end of all things from off the face of the earth, a saying of Yhwh, am I to make an end of man and beast, am I to make an end of the birds of the heavens and the fish of the sea, and that which makes the wicked stumble?" Just because the wicked stumble over them, should he destroy them from the world? Don't they worship man? "Am I to cut man off from the face of the earth?" [Zeph 1:3.]

Same Narrative: *Mek. Baḥod* 6 (Horowitz, 226).

R 114
Gamaliel and General Agrippa.
b. 'Abod. Zar. 55a. Soncino, 280.

General Agrippa asked R Gamaliel: It is written in your Torah [Deut 4:24], "Yhwh your God is a consuming fire, he is a jealous God." But is anyone ever jealous except that it be one wise man of another, one strong man of another, one rich man of another?

He said to him: I will give you a parable. To what is this like? It is like a man who takes a wife in addition to his first wife: if the second is superior, the first is not jealous; if she is inferior, then the first is jealous.

R 115
Rabbi Gamaliel's Rejoinder While in the Bath of Aphrodite.
m. 'Abod. Zar. 3,4. Danby, 440.

Proklos, the philosopher, asked R Gamaliel in Akko, while he was bathing in the Bath of Aphrodite, and said to him: It is written in your law [Deut 13:17]: "None of the devoted things shall cleave to your hand." Why are you bathing in the Bath of Aphrodite?

He said to him: One may not answer in the bath.

And when he came out, he said: I did not come into her borders, she came within mine. They do not say, "Let us make a bath for Aphrodite," but "Let us make an Aphrodite as an adornment for the bath." Moreover, if they gave you a lot of money, you would not enter into service of your goddess naked, or after being polluted, or urinate before her. Yet this goddess stands at the mouth of the gutter and all the people urinate before her. It is written [Deut 12:3]: "Their gods" [only]; thus what is treated as a god is forbidden, but what is not treated as a god is permitted.

R 116
The Emperor's Daughter Explains Gen 2:21 to Her Father.
b. Sanh. 39a. Soncino, 247-48.

The Emperor said to Rabban Gamaliel: Your God is a thief, for it is written [Gen 2:21]: "And the Lord caused a deep sleep to fall upon man, and while he slept took out one of his ribs."

Thereupon, his daughter said to him: Leave him to me and I will answer him. She said to him [the Emperor]: Give me a commander.

He said to her: Why do you need him?

[She said]: Thieves came to us at night and took from us a pitcher of silver, but left us a pitcher of gold.

He said to her: If only they would come to us every day!

[She said]: Then was it not better for the first man that a rib was taken from him, and instead a hand-maiden was presented to him for his use?

He said to her: That is what I mean: he should have taken it from him openly.

She said to him: Give me a piece of raw meat. It was given to her. She placed it under her armpit, then took it out.

She said to him: Eat from it.

He said to her: I find it loathsome.

She said to him: Even so would she [Eve] have been to Adam, if she had been taken from him openly.

> Comparable Narratives: *Gen. Rab.* 17,7; *'Abot R. Nat.* B,8 (Schechter, 23-24).

R 117
R Gamaliel Refutes the Emperor's Pretensions.
b. Sanh. 39a. Soncino, 248.

The Emperor said to Rabban Gamaliel: I know what your

God is doing, and where he is seated. [Rabban Gamaliel] became faint and sighed.

He said to him: What is the matter?

He said to him: I have a son in one of the cities of the sea, and I have a longing for him. Pray, tell me about him.

He said: Do I then know where he is?

He said to him: Then you do not know what is on earth, and yet [claim to] know what is happening in heaven!

R 118
Two Other Examples of R Gamaliel's Dialogue With the Emperor.
b. Sanh. 39a. Soncino, 248.

Again the Emperor said to Rabban Gamaliel: It is written [Ps 147:4]: "He counts the number of the stars." In what way is that remarkable? I too can count them!

Rabban Gamaliel brought some quinces, put them into a sieve, whirled them around, and said: Count them.

He said to him: Keep them still.

He said to him: But the heavens also revolve!

It has been said that the Emperor said to him: The number of the stars is known to me.

Thereupon Rabban Gamaliel said to him: How many molars and [other] teeth have you? Putting his hand to his mouth, he began to count them.

He said to him: You do not know what is in your mouth and yet you know what is in heaven!

> [The text in *b. Sanh.* continues with a debate between R Gamaliel and the Emperor concerning whether the one who "forms" is the same as the one who "creates." This is followed by an additional remark loosely connected to the debate and an account of another debate between R Tanhum and the Emperor. The text resumes with the following story.]

R 119
R Gamaliel Illustrates God's Omnipresence to the Emperor.
b. Sanh. 39a. Soncino, 249-50.

The Emperor said to Rabban Gamaliel: You have said that in every gathering of ten, the Shekinah rests. How many Shekinahs are there then?

Rabban Gamaliel called [Caesar's] servant, and tapped him

on the neck. He said to him: Why does the sun enter into Caesar's house?

He said to him: But the sun rests upon the whole world!

Then if the sun, which is but one of the countless myriads of the servants of the Holy One, blessed be he, rests on the whole world, how much more the Shekinah of the Holy One, blessed be he, himself!

A Cycle of Debates About the Resurrection

(1) R 120
Gamaliel Debates With the Sectarians.
b. Sanh. 90b. Soncino, 604-05.

It has been taught: R Simai said: From where do we learn resurrection? From the Torah? It is written [Exod 6:4]: "And I also have established my covenant with them, to give them the land of Canaan;" "[to give] you" is not said, but "to give them." Thus resurrection is proved from the Torah. Ṣdk Gm Gšm Qm.[1]

Sectarians [minim][2] asked Rabban Gamaliel: From where do we know that the Holy One, blessed be he, will resurrect the dead?

He said to them: From the Torah, the prophets, and from the Writings.

But they would not accept it from him.

From the Torah, for it is written [Deut 31:16]: "And the Lord said to Moses, 'Behold you will sleep with your fathers and rise up [again].'" They said to him: But perhaps, "and the people shall rise up." From the Prophets, as it is written [Isa 26:19]: "Your dead men shall live, together with my dead body they shall arise. Awake and sing, you that dwell in the dust, for your dew is as the dew of herbs, and the earth shall cast out its dust." But perhaps this refers to the dead whom Ezekiel resurrected? From the Writings, as it is written [Cant 7:9]: "And the roof of your mouth, like the best wine of my beloved, that goes down sweetly, causing the lips of those that are asleep to speak." But perhaps it means only that their lips will move, even as R Joḥanan said: If a halakah is said in any person's name in this world, his lips speak in the grave, as it is written, "causing the lips of those who are asleep to speak." But he did not satisfy them until he said this verse [Deut 11:21]: "[in the land] which the Lord swore unto your fathers to give them." Not "to you" it is said, but "to them" [is it said]. Hence, resurrection is derived from the Torah.

¹ Ṣdk Gm Gšm Qm. It is impossible at this point to decipher the exact meaning of this mnemonic aid which translates, "The just man, surely his body shall rise." It is meant as a help in memorizing some of the narratives which follow. For an attempt at deciphering, see: M. Heilprin, *Abbreviations, Signs and Surnames* (Heb) (Jerusalem, 1930) 215.

² In the first story of the cycle according to a variant, Gamaliel's interlocutors are Sadducees, which is much more likely, unless the *minim* are gnostics or Samaritans since, contrary to the note in Soncino at this point, the Christians not only maintained that resurrection of the dead was taught in the Torah, but preserved this opinion as a teaching of Jesus himself (Matt 22:31-32 par.) in an argument much like that attributed to R Simai.

(2) R 121
R Joshua b Hananiah Debates With the Romans.
b. Sanh. 90b. Soncino, 605-06.

The Romans asked R Joshua b Hananiah: From where do we know that the Holy One, blessed be he, will resurrect the dead and knows the future?

He said: Both are deduced from this verse [Deut 31:16]: "And the Lord said to Moses, 'Behold you will sleep with your fathers, and rise up again; and this people shall go awhoring.'"

But perhaps "will rise up, and go awhoring"?

He said: Then at least you have the answer to half, namely that he knows what the future will be.

It has been stated also: R Johanan in the name of R Simeon b Yohai said: From where do we know that the Holy One, blessed be he, will resurrect the dead and knows what the future will be? As it is written: "Behold you shall sleep with your fathers and rise again."

(3) R 122
R Meir answers Cleopatra.
b. Sanh. 90b. Soncino, 607.

Queen Cleopatra [not the famous one] asked R Meir: I know that the dead will revive, for it is written [Ps 72:16]: "and they [the righteous] shall [in the distant future] blossom forth out of the city [Jerusalem] like the grass of the earth." But when they arise, shall they arise nude or in their garments?¹

He said to her: You may deduce by an *a fortiori* argument [the answer] from a wheat grain: if a grain of wheat, which is buried naked, sprouts forth in many robes, how much more will the righteous, who are buried in their raiment![2]

[1] Comparable Narrative: R 145.
[2] Motif: 1 Cor 15:35-44.

(4) R 123
The Emperor's Daughter Answers her Father's Question to Gamaliel.
b. Sanh. 90b-91a. Soncino, 607.

An Emperor said to Rabban Gamaliel: You say that the dead will revive; but they turn to dust, and can dust come to life?

Thereupon his [the Emperor's] daughter said to him [the Rabbi]: Let me answer him: In our town, there are two potters; one fashions [his products] from water, and the other from clay: who is the more praiseworthy?

He said to her: He who fashions them from water.

She said to him: If he can fashion [man] from water, surely he can do so from clay!

Comparable Narratives: R 142; R 145; Gen. Rab. 14,7.

R 124
Rabbi Aqiba's Daughter is Saved from a Spell.
b. Šabb. 156b. Soncino, 801.

From R Aqiba too [we learn that] Israel is free from planetary influence. R Aqiba had a daughter. Now astrologers had told him: On the day she enters the bridal chamber, a snake will bite her and she will die. He was very worried about this. On that day [of her marriage], she took a brooch and stuck it into the wall and by chance it penetrated into the eye of a serpent. The following morning when she took it out, the snake came trailing after it.

Her father said to her: What did you do?

She said to him: A poor man came to our door in the evening and everybody was busy at the banquet, and there was none to attend to him. So I took the portion which was given to me and gave it to him.

He said to her: You have done a good deed.

Thereupon R Aqiba went out and lectured [on the verse]: "But charity delivers from death" [Prov 10:2]. Not merely from an unnatural death but from death itself.

R 125
R Aqiba Answers Tineius Rufus Regarding the Sabbath.
b. Sanh. 65b. Soncino, 445-46.

And this question was asked by Tineius Rufus[1] the Wicked, of
R Aqiba.

He said to him: How does this day [the Sabbath] differ from
other days?

He replied: Wherein does one man differ from another?

He said to him: Because my lord [the Emperor] wishes it.

[He said]: The Sabbath, too, because my Lord wishes it.

He said to him: I ask this: Who tells you that *this* day is the
Sabbath?

He replied: Let the River Sabbation[2] prove it; let the "Ba'al
ob" prove it; [further] let the grave of your father, from which
no smoke ascends on the Sabbath, serve as evidence.

He said to him: You have shamed him, disgraced him, and
reviled him [by this proof].

> Same Narrative: Tanḥuma, ki Tisa, 33; *Gen. Rab.* 11,5;
> *Pesiq. R.* 23,8 (Friedman 119b-120a).

[1] Tineius Rufus, Governor of Judea at the outbreak of the
Bar Kochba Revolt (132 A.D.).
[2] The River Sabbation. A legendary river, said to flow
with a strong current during the weekdays, carrying
along stones and rubble with tremendous force, but it
rests on the Sabbath. See Pliny, *Natural History* 31,18;
Josephus, *J. W.* 7,5,1.

R 126
R Aqiba Answers Tineius Rufus Regarding the Poor in Israel.
b. B. Bat. 10a. Soncino, 45-46.

It has been taught: R Meir used to say: A critic may bring
against you the argument: If your God loves the poor, why does
he not support them? If so, answer him: So that through them
we may be saved from the punishment of Gehinnom.

This question was asked by Turnus Rufus to R Aqiba: If your
God loves the poor, why does he not support them?

He said to him: So that we may be saved through them from
the punishment of Gehinnom.

He said to him: On the contrary, it is this which condemns
you to Gehinnom. Let me tell you a parable. To what is this
like? It is like an earthly king who was angry with his servant
and put him in prison, and ordered that no food or drink be

given to him. But a man went and gave him food and drink. If the king heard, would he not be angry with him? And you are called "servants," as it is written [Lev 25:55]: "For to me the children of Israel are servants."

R Aqiba said to him: Let me tell you a parable: To what is this like? It is like an earthly king who was angry with his son, and put him in prison and ordered that no food or drink should be given to him, and someone went and gave him food and drink. If the king heard of it, would he not send him a present? And we are called "sons," as it is written [Deut 14:1]: "Sons are you to the Lord your God."

He said to him: You are called both sons and servants. When you carry out the desires of the Omnipresent, you are called sons, and when you do not carry out the desires of the Omnipresent, you are called servants.[1] At the present time, you are not carrying out the desires of the Omnipresent.

He said to him: Certainly it says [Isa 58:6-7]: "Is it not to break your bread with the hungry, and the poor that are cast out to bring [them] into your house?" When do you bring the poor that are cast out to your house? At this time, for it tells us "is it not to break your bread with the hungry?"

[1] See the remark in John 15:15.

R 127
R Aqiba Answers Tineius Rufus Regarding Circumcision.
Tanḥuma, Tazria 5.

It happened: Tineius Rufus, the Wicked, asked R Aqiba: Which works are more beautiful, those of God or those of man?

He said to him: Those of man are more beautiful.

Tineius Rufus said to him: Look at the heavens and the earth; can man do anything like him who produced them?

R Aqiba said to him: Will you not say to me in a word that he is superior to mankind because no one rules over him? But speak words that are more accessible to mankind.

He said to him: Why do you practice circumcision?

He said to him: I knew that you were really asking me about that; and so I was ahead of you, and I said that the works of man are more beautiful than those of God.

R Aqiba brought him some grains of corn and some loaves of white bread. He said to him: These are the work of God, and these are the work of man's hands; are not these latter more beautiful than these grains of corn?

Tineius Rufus said to him: But if God takes delight in circumcision, why does he not produce the child already circumcised from his mother's womb?

R Aqiba said to him: And why does his umbilical cord come out with him, and it hangs down from his stomach, and his mother has to cut it off? And you ask why the child does not come out circumcised? For God gave his commandments to Israel only to refine them. As David said [Ps 18:31; Prov 30:5]: "The word of God is refined."

Comparable Narrative: *Pesiq. R.* 23,4 (Friedman, 117a).

R 128
R Aqiba Explains Why He Laughs at R Eliezer's Deathbed.
b. Sanh. 101a. Soncino, 686.

Rabbah b Bar Ḥana said: When R Eliezer fell sick, his disciples entered [his house] to visit him.

He said to them: There is a fierce wrath in the world![1] They broke into tears, but R Aqiba laughed.

They said to him: Why do you laugh?

He said to them: Because of what are you weeping?

They said to him: Is it possible that the Scroll of the Torah lie in pain and we not weep?

He said to them: For that very reason, I laugh. As long as I saw that my master's vine did not turn sour, nor was his flax disordered, nor his oil spoiled, nor his honey fermented, I said, God forbid that he may have received all his reward in this world [leaving nothing for the next]; but now that I see him lying in pain, I rejoice [knowing that his reward has been treasured up for him in the next].

He [R Eliezer] said to him: Aqiba, have I neglected anything of the whole Torah?

He said to him: You have taught us, O master [Qoh 7:20]: "For there is not a just man upon the earth that does good and sins not."

[1] It seems that R Eliezer's death took place shortly before Trajan's pogrom against the Jews in the empire (c. 116-117 C.E.), and perhaps he is alluding to this impending disaster.

R 129
R Aqiba Explains Why Suffering is Precious.
b. Sanh. 101a-b. Soncino, 686-87.

When R Eliezer fell sick, four elders went to visit him: R Tarphon, R Joshua, R Eleazar b Azariah, and R Aqiba.

R Tarphon said: You are more precious to Israel than the rain, for rain is precious in this world, but you are [precious] in this world and the world to come.

R Joshua observed and said: You are better to Israel than the sun's disc, for the sun's disc is for the present world, but my master is for this world and also for the world to come.

R Eleazar b Azariah observed and said: You are better to Israel than a father and mother; for a father and mother are for this world, but my master is for this world and the one to come.

R Aqiba observed and said: Chastenings are more precious.[1]

Thereupon [R Eliezer] said to them: Support me and I will hear the words of my disciple, Aqiba, who said, "Chastenings are precious."

He said to him: Aqiba, how did this come to you?

He said: I interpreted a verse [2 Kgs 21:1-2]: "Manasseh was twelve years old when he began to reign, and he reigned fifty and five years in Jerusalem . . . and he did that which was evil in the sight of the Lord." Now it is also written [Prov 25:1]: "These are also the proverbs of Solomon, which the men of Hezekiah, King of Judah, copied out." Now would Hezekiah, King of Judah, have taught the Torah to the whole world, yet not to his own son Manasseh? But all the pains he spent upon him, and all the work which he labored upon him, did not bring him back to the right path, save chastening alone, as it is written [2 Chr 33:10-13]: "And the Lord spoke to Manasseh and to his people, but they would not listen to him. Therefore the Lord brought upon them the captains of the army of the King of Assyria who took Manasseh with hooks and bound him with fetters of bronze and carried him to Babylon." And it is further written: "And when he was in distress he besought the Lord his God, and humbled himself greatly before the God of his fathers, and prayed unto him; and he was entreated of him; and heard his supplication, and brought him again to Jerusalem unto his kingdom, and Manasseh knew that the Lord was God."

Thus, you learn how precious are chastenings.

[1] Comparable Narratives: R 167-R 169.

R 130

R Aqiba is not Saddened at Seeing the Prosperity of the
Pagans.
b. Mak. 24a-b. Soncino, 174.

Long ago, Rabban Gamaliel, R Eleazar b Azariah, R Joshua
and R Aqiba were walking on the road, and they heard the noise
of the crowds at Rome from Puteoli, a hundred and twenty
miles away. They [all] began to weep, but R Aqiba laughed.

They said: For what reason are you glad?

He said to them: For what reason are you weeping?

They said to him: These heathens who bow down to images
and burn incense to idols live in safety and ease, whereas our
Temple, the "footstool" of our God, is burnt down by fire, and
should we then not weep?

He said to them: For this reason I am glad. If those that
transgress his will fare thus, how much better is it for those who
do his will?

R 131

R Aqiba Derives Consolation From Zechariah's Prophecy
When Seeing the Destroyed Temple.
b. Mak. 24b. Soncino, 174-75.

Again on another occasion, they were coming up to Jerusalem. Just as they came to Mount Scopus, they saw a fox coming
out of the Holy of Holies. Thereupon, they began to weep, but
R Aqiba seemed glad.

They said to him: Why are you happy?

He said to them: Why are you weeping?

They said to him: A place of which it was once written [Num
1:51], "And the common man that draws near shall be put to
death," is now become the haunt of foxes, and should we not
weep?

He said to them: For this reason, I am glad, for it is written
[Isa 8:2]: "And I will take to Me faithful witnesses to record,
Uriah the priest and Zechariah the son of Jeberechiah." Now
what connection has this Uriah the priest with Zechariah?
Uriah lived during the times of the First Temple, while [the
other] Zechariah lived [and prophesied] during the Second
Temple. Now Holy Writ [linked] the prophecy of Zechariah
[which was later] with the [earlier] prophecy of Uriah. In the
prophecy of Uriah, it is written [Mic 3:12; Jer 26:18-20]: "Therefore shall Zion for your sake be ploughed as a field," etc. [But]
in Zechariah it is written [Zech 8:4]: "Thus says the Lord of

Hosts, old men and old women shall again sit in the broad places of Jerusalem." As long as the prophecy of Uriah [which was threatening] did not come into fulfillment, I was fearful that the prophecy of Zechariah would not be fulfilled. [But] now that Uriah's prophecy has been fulfilled, it is quite certain that Zechariah's prophecy will also be fulfilled.

They said to him: Aqiba, you have comforted us! Aqiba, you have comforted us!

R 132
R Aqiba Explains Why He Continues to Teach and Risk His Life.
b. Ber. 61b. Soncino, 385-86.

Our Rabbis taught: Once the wicked government issued a decree forbidding the Jews to study and practice Torah. Pappus b Judah came and found R Aqiba publicly bringing gatherings together and occupying himself with the Torah.

He said to him: Are you not afraid of the government?

He said to him: I will explain to you with a parable. A fox was once walking alongside of a river, and he saw fishes going in swarms from one place to another. He said to them: From what are you fleeing? They said to him: From the nets cast for us by men. He said to them: Would you like to come up onto the dry land so that you and I can live together in the way that my ancestors lived with your ancestors? They said to him: You are the one that they call the cleverest of animals? You are not clever but foolish. If we are afraid in the element in which we live, how much more in the element in which we would die?

So it is with us. If such is our condition when we sit and study the Torah, of which it is written [Deut 30:20]: "For that is your life and the length of your days," if we go and neglect it, how much worse off we shall be.

R 133
R Aqiba's Martyrdom.
b. Ber. 61b. Soncino, 386.

It was said that soon afterward R Aqiba was arrested and thrown into prison, and Pappus b Judah was also arrested and imprisoned next to him.

He said to him: Pappus, who brought you here?

He said to him: Happy are you, R Aqiba, that you have been seized for busying yourself with the Torah! Alas for Pappus, who has been seized for busying himself with idle things!

When R Aqiba was taken out for execution, it was the hour for the recital of the "Shema" and while they combed his flesh with iron combs, he was accepting upon himself the yoke of the kingdom of heaven [that is, reciting the *Shema*]. His disciples said to him: Our teacher, even at this point?

He said to them: All my days I have been troubled by this verse, "with all your soul," [which I interpret] "even if he takes your soul." I said: When shall this come into my hand, that it may be fulfilled? Now that it has come into my hands, shall I not fulfill it? He prolonged the word "'eḥad" [one] until he expired while saying it.

R 134
R Jose the Priest Resolves Contradictory Texts With a Parable. *b. Roš. Haš.* 17b-18a. Soncino, 70.

Come and hear: Bluria [Valeria] the proselyte asked Rabban Gamaliel: It is written in your Law [Deut 10:17]: "[The Lord is a God] . . . who will not lift up his countenance." And it is also written [Num 6:26]: "The Lord shall lift up his countenance upon you."

R Jose the Priest said to her: Let me tell you a parable. To what is this like? It is like a man who lent his neighbour a "maneh" and fixed a time for payment in the presence of the king, while the other swore [to pay him] by the life of the king. When the time arrived, he did not pay him, and he went to excuse himself to the king. [The king, however] said to him: For the wrong done to me, I excuse you, but go and obtain forgiveness from your neighbour.[1] So also here: one text speaks of offences committed by a man against God, the other of offences committed against his fellow man. [This explanation was generally accepted] until R Aqiba came and taught: One text speaks of God's attitude before the final sentence, the other of his attitude after the final sentence. Here too the case is that of an individual.

1 Motif: Matt 5:23-24.

THE THIRD GENERATION OF TANNAIM
APPROXIMATELY 130-160 C.E.

R 135
R Simeon b Yoḥai Exorcizes a Demon From the Emperor's
Daughter.
b. Me'il. 17a-b. Soncino, 63-64.

The Jews then conferred as to who should go [to Rome] to
work for the annulment of the decrees. Let R Simeon b Yoḥai
go for he is experienced in miracles. And who should go with
him? R Eliezer the son of R Jose.

R Jose said to them: Were my father Ḥalafta still alive, would
you have said to him to give his son for slaughter?

R Simeon said: Were Yoḥai my father still alive, would you
have said to him to give his son for slaughter?

R Jose said to them: I will go with him for I fear that R Simeon may punish him. R Simeon decided not to inflict any punishment on him then, but he did punish him. For when they
were proceeding on the way, the following question was raised
in their presence: Wherefrom do we know that the blood of a
reptile is unclean? R Eliezer curved his mouth and said: It is
written [Lev 11:29]: "And these are they that are unclean. . . ."

R Simeon said to him: From the undertone of your utterance, one can see that you are a scholar, yet the son shall not
return to his father.

Then Ben Temalion [a demon] came to meet them. He said:
Is it your wish that I accompany you?

R Simeon wept and said: The handmaid of my ancestor's
house was found worthy of meeting an angel three times, and I
have not met him even once. However, let the miracle be performed no matter how. Then he [Ben Temalion] went ahead of
them and entered the Emperor's daughter. When he [R Si-
meon] arrived, he said: Ben Temalion leave her, Ben Temalion
leave her. And as he said this, he left her.

He [the Emperor] said to them: Request whatever you desire. They were led into the treasure house to take whatever
they wished. They found the bill [containing the decrees
against Jewish religious practices] and they took it and tore it to
pieces.

R 136
R Jose b Ḥalafta Answers a Roman Matron Regarding the
Jewish God and the Snake God.
Exod. Rab. 3,12. Soncino, 70-71.

"And Moses fled from before it." [Exod 4:3.]
A Roman matron said to R Jose: My god is greater than
yours.
He said to her: In which way?
She said to him: For when your God revealed himself to
Moses at the thorn-bush, he merely hid his face, but when he
saw the serpent, who is my god, immediately he "fled from
before it."
He said to her: When our God revealed himself at the thorn-
bush, there was no room for him to flee anywhere. Where could
he flee? To the heavens? Or to the sea, or dry land? What does
it say about our God? [Jer 23:24]: "Do I not fill the heavens and
earth? says the Lord." But the serpent who is your god, a man
can flee two or three paces and escape from him. For this reason it is written: "And Moses fled from before it."
Another explanation: Why did he flee? Because he sinned
by his words. If he had not sinned, he would not have fled, for
the serpent does not bring death, but sin, as it is written in the
story about Ḥanina b Dosa [R 80].

R 137
R Jose Explains God's Providence to a Roman Matron.
Lev. Rab. 8,1. Soncino, 100-01.

[Lev 6:3]: "This is the offering of Aaron and his sons." R
Levi opened his discourse [with the following verse] [Ps 75:8]:
"For God is a judge; this one he humbles, and this one he lifts
up." A Roman matron asked R Jose b Ḥalafta: In how many
days did the Holy One, blessed be he, create his world?
He said to her: In six days, for it is written [Exod 31:17]:
"For in six days the Lord made heaven and earth."
She said to him: And from that time until now, what has he
been doing?
He said to her: He is joining couples [proclaiming]: A's wife
is to be allotted to A; A's daughter is to be allotted to B; So-and-
so's wealth is for So-and-so."
She said to him: This is a thing which I too can do. See how
many male slaves I have, and how many female slaves I have? I
can make them consort together all at the same time.
He said to her: If in your eyes it is an easy task, it is in the

eyes of the Lord as hard a task as the dividing of the Red Sea. He went away and left her. What did she do? She sent for a thousand male slaves and a thousand female slaves, placed them in rows and said to them: Male A shall take wife B; C shall take D, and so on. She let them consort together for one night. In the morning they came to her. One had a head wounded, another had an eye taken out, another an elbow crushed, another a leg broken. One said: I do not want this one [as my husband]. Another said: I do not want this one [as my wife]. Immediately she sent for R Jose b Halafta and said to him: Rabbi, your Torah is true, fine and excellent. All you have said was well said.

He said to her: Have I not told you that if in your eyes it is an easy task, it is in his eyes a task as hard as the dividing of the Red Sea? As it is said [Ps 68:7]: "He makes the solitary to dwell in a house, he brings out the prisoners into prosperity [ba-kôšarôt]."

What does "ba-kôšarôt" mean? "Weeping" ["baki"] and "singing" ["shiroth"]. He who is pleased [with his match] utters songs, while he who is not pleased weeps. And what does God do [when bringing about matches]? He pairs them together despite themselves, without their goodwill.

Said R Berekiah: In the following manner did R Jose b Halafta answer her: "[Ever since he completed creation], the Holy One, blessed be he, makes ladders by which he makes one go up, and another go down," as it is written [Ps 75:8]: "God is a judge: This one he humbles and this one he lifts up."[1]

> [1] This story is very popular in Rabbinic literature. It can be found in *Gen. Rab.* 68,4; *Num. Rab.* 3,6; 22,8; *Pesiq. Rab. Kah.* 2,4; Tanhuma *passim*. For a complete list, see Herr, p. 146, n. 21.

R 138

R Jose Discusses Divine Justice [Dan 2:21] With a Roman Matron.[1]
Qoh. Rab. 1,7. Soncino, 22.

[This story is found within the discussion of "All the rivers run to the sea" (Qoh 1:7).]

A certain matron asked R Jose b Halafta, saying: What is the meaning of this which is said [Dan 2:21]: "He gives wisdom unto the wise." The text should have stated: He gives wisdom unto them that are not wise and knowledge to them that know not understanding.

He said to her: I will explain with a parable. If two persons

came to borrow money from you, one rich and the other poor,
to whom would you lend, the rich man or the poor?

She said to him: To the rich man.

He said to her: Why?

She said to him: Because, if the rich man loses my money, he
has with which he will repay me; but if the poor man loses my
money, how can he repay me?

He said to her: Do your ears hear what you have uttered
with your mouth? If the Holy One, blessed be he, gave wisdom
to fools, they would sit and meditate upon it in privies, theatres,
and bath-houses; but the Holy One, blessed be he, gave wisdom
to the wise who sit and meditate upon it in synagogues and
houses of study. Hence, "He gives wisdom unto the wise, and
knowledge to them that know understanding."

   1 For other examples of dialogues between R Jose and the
   Roman matron concerning divine justice, see Herr, p.
   146.

R 139
R Jose Explains the Significance of Ezek 4:9 to a Roman
Matron.
Pesiq. R. 18,5 (Friedman 92b-93a). Braude, 389.

And the Rabbis taught: It was this ʿomer of barley that stood
by them in the days of Ezekiel [Ezek 4:9]: "Take also to yourself
wheat, and barley, and beans, and lentils, and millet, and spelt,
and put them in one vessel, and make bread of them. During
the number of days that you lie upon your side, 390 days, you
shall eat it." In order to make this bread, which of the three
grains, wheat, barley, or spelt, did he use most of? Ezekiel put
mostly barley into the dough, an excess of which, according to R
Samuel bar Naḥman, brings on the runs. Samuel said: Over in
Babylonia, it is told that out of dough with an excess of barley
they made a cake for a dog, but he would not eat it.

A Roman matron inquired of R Jose b Ḥalafta. She said to
him: What pain that righteous Ezekiel must have endured!
And to think that every one of the great number of manservants
and maidservants he had looked down upon him because of the
food and drink he chose to live on!

He said to her: His pain was meant to make you understand
that whenever Israel is in pain, the righteous are in pain with
them.

Same Narrative: *Lev. Rab.* 28,6; *Pesiq. Rab. Kah.* 8,3
(Mandelbaum, 143).

R 140
R Jose Illustrates an Aspect of the Mystery of Election.
Num. Rab. 3,2. Soncino, 68.

Come and see. The Holy One, blessed be he, brought Jethro
near to himself, but did not choose him. He brought Rahab
near, but did not choose her. Happy are these whom he
brought near to himself, even though he did not choose them!

A Roman matron asked a question of R Jose. She said to him:
Your God brings near to himself [indiscriminately] whomsoever
he pleases. He brought her a basket of figs and she scrutinized
them well, picking the best and eating them. He said to her:
You apparently know how to select; but does not the Holy One,
blessed be he, know how to select? The one whose actions he
perceives to be good, him he chooses and brings near to himself.

Same Narrative: *Midr. Sam.* 8,2.

R 141
R Jose Explains to the Roman Matron That Enoch Died.
Gen. Rab. 25,1. Soncino, 205.

A Roman matron asked R Jose saying: We do not find death
[stated] of Enoch?

Said he to her: If it said [Gen 5:24]: "And Enoch walked
with God," and no more, I would agree with you. Since, however, it says, "And he was not, for God took him," it means that
he was no more in this world, "for God took him."

R 142
R Jose Discusses Resurrection With a Bereaved Heretic.
Midr. Ps. 2,11. Braude, 42-43.

Ps 2:9: "You shall break them with a rod of iron. You shall
dash them in pieces like a potter's vessel." When one of the
prominent men of Sepphoris, a heretic it is said, lost his son by
death, R Jose went up to comfort him. When he saw the man, R
Jose smiled.

[The man] said to him: Why are you smiling?

[R Jose] said to him: We trust in the Lord of heaven that you
will see your son again in the world to come.

He said to him: The burden of my grief is not enough for

me! Must you come to add to the burden? And he went on: Can the shards of a broken vessel ever be joined together again?

He said to him: No!

He said to him: Not even the likes of you will ever be brought together again. Does not your Scripture say: "You shall dash them in pieces like a potter's vessel"?

R Jose said to him: The verse speaks only of a potter's vessel. For before the clay of a potter's vessel is put through the fire, its form is not fixed; if it is broken it can be shaped by crushing it and making it into another vessel. After it is put through the fire, however, its form is fixed, and if it is broken, it cannot be reshaped. On the other hand, a glass vessel, its form having been fixed before it is put through the fire, cannot be reshaped if it is broken. However, after it is put through the fire, the form of the vessel is no longer fixed, and if it is broken, it can be reshaped.

[The man] said to him: Because a glass vessel is made by having breath blown through it, it can be reshaped.

He said to him: Do you hear what you let come forth out of your mouth? If a vessel of glass, made with breath blown by a mortal, can be reshaped if it is broken, how much more true is this of a human being made with breath blown by the Holy One, blessed be he, as it is said [Gen 2:7]: "The Lord God formed man of the dust of the ground, and breathed into his nostrils the breath of life."

R Isaac said: Scripture does not say, "Like an earthen vessel," but "like a potter's wheel," which can be reshaped before being put through the fire.

> Same Narrative: *Gen. Rab.* 14,7.
> Comparable Narratives: R 123; R 145.

R 143
R Joshua b Qarḥa Answers a Heathen and Then his Disciples Regarding Israel's Imitation of the Gentiles.
Lev. Rab. 4,6. Soncino, 55-56.

R El'asa said: A certain heathen asked R Joshua b Qarḥa: In your Torah it is written [Exod 23:2]:[1] "It is proper to incline after the many." We are more numerous than you, why then do you not become like us in respect to idolatry?

R Joshua b Qarḥa said to him: Have you children?

He said to him: You have reminded me of my trouble.

He said to him: Why?

He said to him: I have many children. When they sit at my table, this one blesses one god, the other blesses some other god, and they do not rise from the table before they have cracked each other's skulls.

He said to him: And do you bring about agreement among them?

He said to him: No.

He said to him: Before you make us agree with you, go and bring about agreement among your children. Being pushed aside [like this], he [the heathen] went away.

After he had gone, his disciples said to him: Rabbi, you pushed him away with a broken reed; but what answer do you give us?

He said to them: In the case of Esau, six souls are mentioned by Scripture, and yet the word used of them in Scripture is "souls," in the plural, as it is written [Gen 36:4]: "And Esau took his wives, and his sons, and his daughters, and all the souls of his house," etc. Of Jacob, on the other hand, there were seventy souls, and yet the word used of them in Scripture is "soul," as it is written [Exod 1:5]: "And all the *nepesh* [soul] that came out of the loins of Jacob," etc. The reason is that in the case of Esau who worshipped many deities, the word used by Scripture is "souls" in the plural, but in the case of Jacob who worshipped one God, the word used by Scripture is "soul," in the singular: "And all the *nepesh*," etc.

¹ This represents a particular Rabbinic reading of this text. See *m. Sanh.* 1,6; *m. 'Ed.* 1,5.

R 144
R Judah b Ilai Explains Why His Face is Shining.
Qoh. Rab. 8,1. Soncino, 215.

> [This story is found within the discussion of Qoh 8:1: "Who is like the wise man, and who knows the interpretation of a thing? A man's wisdom makes his face to shine, and the hardness of his countenance is changed."]

A gentile saw R Judah b Ilai. Noticing that his face shone, he said: This man is one of three things: he is either intoxicated, a usurer, or a breeder of pigs.

R Judah b Ilai heard the remark and said: A curse upon you! I am none of these three things. I am not a usurer, for it is written [Deut 23:20]: "You shall not lend on interest to your

brother." Nor am I a breeder of pigs because this is forbidden to
a son of Israel, as we have learnt in the Mishnah: It is not right
to breed pigs in any place whatever. Nor am I intoxicated, for
even the four cups of wine which I drink on the night of Passover give me a headache from Passover to Pentecost.

He said to him: Why, then, is your face so bright?

He said to him: My study of Torah brightens my face, as it is
written, "A man's wisdom makes his face to shine."

R 145
R Meir's Series of Answers Regarding Resurrection.
Qoh. Rab. 5,10. Soncino, 145-47.

A Cuthean [a Samaritan] asked R Meir, saying to him: Do
the dead live again?

He said to him: Yes.

He said to him: [Do they come back to life] secretly or in
public?

He said to him: In public.

He said to him: How can you prove it to me?

He said to him: Not from Scripture nor from the Mishnah,
but from the way things are I will answer you. There was a
trustworthy man in our city, with whom everyone deposited
[money] secretly and he restored it to the owners in public.
Somebody came and deposited it with him in public; so how
should he restore it to him, in secret or publicly? Will he not do
it publicly?

He said to him: Certainly.

[R Meir] said to him: Do not your ears hear what your lips
speak? Men deposit a white drop [in secret] with their wives,
and the Holy One, blessed be he, restores that drop publicly in
the form of a beautiful and perfect creature. How much more
will a dead person who departs [from the world] publicly return
publicly? As he departs with loud cries, so will he return with
loud cries.

> [The dialogue continues after a short baraita by R
> Jonathan of Beth Gubrin, on "the grave and the barren
> womb" (Prov 30:16).]

The Cuthean asked: How will they come [from the grave],
naked or clothed?

He said to him: Clothed.

He said to him: How can you prove it to me?

He said to him: Not from Scripture, nor from the Mishnah,

but from the way things are I will answer you. Have you ever sown beans?

He said to him: Yes.

He said to him: How did they come up, clothed or naked?

He said to him: Clothed.

[R Meir] said to him: Do not your ears hear what your mouth speaks? If beans, when a person sows them naked, come up clothed, how much more will the dead which depart clothed [in shrouds] return clothed!

> Comparable Narratives: R 122; R 123; R 142; 1 Cor 15:35-44.

THE FOURTH GENERATION OF TANNAIM
APPROXIMATELY 160-200 C.E.

A Series of Stories About R Judah the Prince and the Emperor Antoninus

(1) R 146
Rabbi Judah the Prince Answers Antoninus' Problem by an Acted Out Parable.
b. *'Abod. Zar.* 10a. Soncino, 50-51.

Antoninus [once] said to Rabbi: It is my desire that my son Asverus should reign instead of me and that Tiberias should be declared a colony. And though I were to ask these two things, only one would be granted.

Thereupon [Rabbi] brought a man which he made ride on the shoulders of another and gave him a dove [to hold in his hands]. He told the man who was carrying the other man to order him to liberate the dove. The Emperor perceived this to mean that he was advised to ask [of the Senate] to appoint his son Asverus to reign in his stead, and that subsequently he might get Asverus to make Tiberias a free colony.

(2) R 147
Another Acted Out Parable Response.
b. *'Abod. Zar.* 10a. Soncino, 51.

[On another occasion] Antoninus said to him: Some prominent Romans are annoying me.

[Rabbi] therefore took him into the garden and, in his presence, picked some radishes, one at a time.

Said [the Emperor to himself]: His advice to me is: Do away with them one at a time, but do not attack all of them at once.

> [Some later discussion of Rabbi's gesture is inserted here.]
> Comparable Narrative: *Gen. Rab.* 67,6.

(3) R 148
A Cryptic Message Between the Emperor and Rabbi Based on a Play on Words.
b. *'Abod. Zar.* 10b. Soncino, 51.

The Emperor had a daughter named Gilla who committed a sin, so he sent to Rabbi a rocket-herb, and Rabbi in return sent him coriander. The Emperor then sent some leeks, and he sent lettuce in return.[1]

[1] An interpretation of the words used in this story can be found in Soncino, 51. For a slightly different interpretation, see *JE* I, 657a. Generally, the interchange can be interpreted this way: "Gilla has gone astray." "You have the right to reprove or forgive or slay her." "I will cut her off." "I would recommend compassion."

(4) R 149
Antoninus' Gift of Gold and His Irony.
b. 'Abod. Zar. 10b. Soncino, 52.

When Antoninus sent Rabbi gold dust in a leather bag filled with wheat at the top, he said [to his servants]: Carry the wheat to Rabbi!

Rabbi sent word to say: I do not need it; I have quite enough of my own.

Antoninus answered: Leave it then to those who will come after you, so they might give it to those who will come after me. For your descendants and those who will follow them will hand it over to them [who hold Roman power after me].

(5) R 150
A Disciple of Rabbi Raises Antoninus' Slave Through Prayer.
b. 'Abod. Zar. 10b. Soncino, 52-53.

Antoninus had a cave which led from his house to the house of Rabbi. Every time [he visited Rabbi] he brought two slaves, one of whom he slew at the door of Rabbi's house and the other [who had been left behind] was killed at the door of his own house.

Antoninus said to Rabbi: When I come to you, do not let anyone be found with you. One day, he found R Ḥaninah b Ḥama sitting there.

He said to him: Did I not tell you that no man should be found with you at the time when I call?

Rabbi said to him: This is not an [ordinary] human being.

He said to him: Then tell that servant who is sleeping outside the door to rise and come in.

R Ḥaninah b Ḥama thereupon went out, but found that the man had been slain. He thought: How shall I act now? Shall I call and say that the man is dead? But one should not bring a sad report. Shall I leave him and walk away? That would be slighting the king. So he prayed for mercy for the man, and he was restored to life. He then sent him in.

Said Antoninus: I am well aware that the least one among you can bring the dead to life; still when I call, let no one be found with you.

Comparable Narrative: R 157.

(6) R 151
How Antoninus Waited on Rabbi.
b. 'Abod. Zar. 10b. Soncino, 53.

Every time [Antoninus called], he used to attend on Rabbi and wait on him with food or drink. When Rabbi wanted to get on his bed, Antoninus crouched in front of it saying: Get onto your bed by stepping on me.

Rabbi, however, said: Is it proper to disregard the king so much?

Antoninus said: May I serve as a mattress for you in the world to come!

Once he asked him: Shall I enter the world to come?

Rabbi said to him: Yes!

He said to him: But, is it not written [Obad 1:18]: "There will be no remnant to the house of Esau"?

He said: That applies only to those whose evil deeds are like to those of Esau. We have learnt also, "There will be no remnant to the house of Esau," might have been taken to apply to all; therefore Scripture says distinctly, "to the house of Esau," so as to make it apply only to those who act as Esau did.

He said to him: But is it not also written [Ezek 32:29]: "There [in the nether world] is Edom, her kings, and all her princes."

He said to him: There, too, [it says] "her kings;" it does not say "all" her kings; "all her princes," but not all her officers!

This indeed is what has been taught: "her kings" but not "all" her kings; "all her princes," but not all her officers. "Her kings," but not all her kings—excludes Antoninus the son of Asverus. "All her princes," but not all her officers—excludes Keti'ah the son of Shalom.

R 152
Rabbi Explains Judgment to Antoninus by Means of a Parable.
b. Sanh. 91a-b. Soncino, 610-11.

Antoninus said to Rabbi: The body and the soul can both

free themselves from judgment. For the body can say: The soul has sinned, because from the day it left me, I lie like a dumb stone in the grave. And the soul can say: The body has sinned because from the day that I departed from it, I fly about in the air like a bird.

He said to him: I will tell you a parable. To what may this be compared? To a human king who owned a beautiful orchard which contained splendid figs. He appointed two watchmen, one lame and the other blind. [One day] the lame man said to the blind, "I see beautiful figs in the orchard. Come and take me on your shoulder so that we may get and eat them." So the lame one rode on the body of the blind, and they got and ate them. Some time after, the owner of the orchard came and said to them, "Where are those beautiful figs?" The lame man said to him: "Have I feet to walk with?" The blind man said to him: "Have I eyes to see with?" What did he do? He placed the lame one upon the blind and judged them together. So will the Holy One, blessed be he, bring the soul, replace it in the body, and judge them together, as it is written [Ps 50:4]: "He will call to the heavens from above, and to the earth, that he may judge his people." "He shall call to the heavens above"—this refers to the soul; "and to the earth, that he may judge his people"—to the body.[1]

Same Narrative: *Mek.*, Beshallaḥ Ha-sherah, 2 (Horowitz, 125).
Comparable Narrative: *Lev. Rab.* 4,5.

[1] For a discussion of the background of this parable, see M. R. James, "The Apocryphal Ezekiel," *JTS* 15 (1914) 236-39.

R 153
Rabbi and Antoninus Discuss the Sun.
b. Sanh. 91b. Soncino, 611.

Antoninus said to Rabbi: Why does the sun rise in the east and set in the west?

He said to him: Were it reversed, you would have asked me the same question.

He said to him: But this is what I ask, why does it set in the west?

He said to him: In order to salute its maker, as it is written [Neh 9:6]: "The host of heaven worships you."

He said to him: Then it should go only as far as mid-heaven, pay homage, and then re-ascend.

[He said]: Because of the workers and because of the wayfarers, [it continues on its course and marks the divisions of the day].

R 154
Rabbi Learns From Antoninus About Animation.
b. Sanh. 91b. Soncino, 611-12.

Antoninus also said to Rabbi: When is the soul placed in man; as soon as it is decreed, or when [the embryo] is actually formed?

He said to him: From the moment of formation.

He said to him: Can a piece of meat stand unsalted for three days without becoming spoiled? But it must be from the moment that [God] decrees [its destiny].

Rabbi said: This thing Antoninus taught me, and Scripture supports him, for it is written [Job 10:12]: "And your decree has preserved my spirit."

R 155
Rabbi Learns From Antoninus About Original Sin.
b. Sanh. 91b. Soncino, 612.

Antoninus also said to Rabbi: From what time does the evil tempter rule over man: from its formation [of the embryo], or from its coming forth [into the world]?

He said to him: From the formation.

He said to him: If it were this way, it would rebel in its mother's womb and go forth. But it is from when it comes forth.

Rabbi said: This thing Antoninus taught me, and Scripture supports him, for it is said [Gen 4:7]: "At the door [*i.e.*, where the babe emerges], sin lies in wait."

R 156
Rabbi Heals Two Dumb Men by Prayer.
b. Ḥag. 3a. Soncino, 6.

For it is written [Deut 31:12]: "That they may hear, and that they may learn." It is taught: "That they may hear;" this excludes one that can speak but not hear. "And that they may learn;" this excludes one that can hear but not speak. Does this then mean to say that one that cannot talk cannot learn? But there were two dumb men in the neighborhood of Rabbi, sons of the daughter of R Yoḥanan b Gudgada, and according to others, sons of the sister of R Yoḥanan, who, whenever Rabbi entered the College, went in and sat down [before him], and nodded their heads and moved their lips. And Rabbi prayed for them and they were cured; and it was found that they were versed in Halakah, Sifra, Sifre, and the whole Talmud!

R 157
The Raising of Antoninus' Servant.
Lev. Rab. 10,4. Soncino, 125.

Another interpretation of Lev 8:1: "Take Aaron and his sons with him:" This [illustrates] what Scripture says [Prov 24:11]: "Will you forbear from delivering them that are being taken unto death, and them that are ready to be slain?" Antoninus went to Rabbi and found him sitting with his disciples before him.

He said to him: Are these they of whom you boast?

He said: Yes, the least of them can revive the dying. After some time, a servant of Antoninus was on the point of dying, and the latter sent to Rabbi, saying: Send me one of your disciples that he may revive this dying man. He sent to him one of his disciples—some say it was R Simeon b Ḥalafta—who went and found the man lying down.

He said to him: How is it that you are lying down while your master is standing on his feet? Immediately, the man shook violently and rose.

Comparable Narrative: R 150.

R 158
The Healing of Rabbi's Tooth.
Gen. Rab. 33,3. Soncino, 262.

At the end of the thirty days [the punishment Rabbi had imposed upon R Ḥiyya the Elder], Elijah of blessed memory came before Rabbi in the form of R Ḥiyya the Elder, laid his hand upon his teeth and cured him. When R Ḥiyya subsequently went to Rabbi, he asked him: How is your tooth?

He said to him: Since you laid your hand upon it, it is cured.

He said to him: I know nothing about it. On hearing this, Rabbi showed him honor and set him on the inner [bench].

Same Narrative: *y. Kil.* 9; 32b.

A Catena of Stories Concerning R Pinḥas

(1) R 159
R Pinḥas' Observant Donkey.
y. Dem. 1; 21d-22a.

[The context is set by a story concerning care in tithing which ends with the saying of R Mana.]

R Mana said: At that time, he said: I do not even resemble the she-ass of R Pinḥas b Yair.

Robbers stole the she-ass of R Pinḥas b Yair at night and she was hidden with them for three days and did not eat anything. After three days, they decided to return her to her master.

They said: Let us send her back to her master, so that she does not die with us and smell up the cave. They let her go and she went; arriving at the gate of her master, she set to braying.

He said to them: Open up for that poor wayfarer for it is three days now that she has not eaten anything. They opened up for her and she came in.

He said to them: Give her something to eat. They put barley before her but she did not want to eat.

They said to him: Rabbi, she does not want to eat.

He said to them: Have you made it fit?

They said to him: Yes.

He said to them: Have you paid the demai [the tax in doubtful matters]?

They said to him: But did not rabbi teach that he who purchases grain for beasts, flour for [tanning] hides, oil for light, or oil for pouring on vessels is exempted from the demai?

He said to them: But what can we do with this poor beast when she is so very strict with herself? They paid the demai and she ate.

> Same Narrative: *Gen. Rab.* 60,8.
> Comparable Narratives: R 88; *b. Šabb.* 112b; *y. Šeqal.*
> 5,1; 48c-d.

(2) R 160
R Pinḥas' Honesty and Generosity With the Poor Man's Barley.
y. Dem. 1; 22a.

Two poor men deposited two seahs of barley with R Pinḥas b

Yair. He planted them and harvested them. They came back, wishing to recover their barley.

He said to them: Bring up the camels and donkeys and recover your barley.

> Same Narrative: *Deut. Rab.* 3,3. In *Deut. Rab.*, this story is one of a series illustrating the principle that "from the faithfulness of man, you can learn the faithfulness of God." Another story in this series is that told of Simeon b Sheṭaḥ (R 59).

(3) R 161
R Pinḥas Gets a Town to Pay its Tithes and Frees it From Mice.
y. Dem. 1; 22a.

R Pinḥas b Yair went to a certain town. They came to him, and said to him: Mice eat our grain.

He commanded them [the mice] and gathered them together, and they set to squeaking.

He said to them [the townsfolk]: Do you know what they are saying?

They said to him: No.

He said to them: They are saying that you do not tithe.

They said to him: Our grain [will be tithed]; and they promised; and they [the mice] were no more.

> Same Narrative: *Deut. Rab.* 3,3.

(4) R 162
Pinḥas Recovers the Saracen's Pearl Which a Mouse had Swallowed.
y. Dem. 1; 22a.

A pearl belonging to a king of the Saracens fell, and a mouse swallowed it. He went to R Pinḥas b Yair.

He [Pinḥas] said to him: Who am I, friend?

He said to him: Because of your good name, I come to you.

He commanded them [the mice] and gathered them together. He saw one come in waddling. He said: It is with that one; and he commanded the mouse and it coughed it up.

(5) R 163
R Pinhas Shows a Town Why its Water Supply is Insufficient.
y. Dem. 1; 22a.

R Pinhas b Yair went to a certain town. They came to him, and they said to him: Our spring is not sufficient.

He said to them: Perhaps you do not pay your tithes.

They said to him: Our grain [will be tithed], and they promised; and it [the spring] was sufficient for them.

(6) R 164
R Pinhas Crosses the River Ginnai.
y. Dem. 1; 22a. Safrai, 216.

R Pinhas b Yair was on his way to the meeting place of the sages. Ginnai had risen.

He said to it: Ginnai, Ginnai, how do you restrain me from the meeting place? It divided before him and he crossed.

His disciples said to him: Can we cross?

He said to them: Whoever knows of himself that he has never slighted anyone of Israel all his lifetime, let him cross and no harm will befall him.

> Same Narrative: *y. Ta'an.* 3; 66b.
> Comparable Narratives: *b. Hul.* 7a; OT 11-OT 16; H 177-H 181.

(7) R 165
R Pinhas Confronts R Judah the Prince.
y. Dem. 1; 22a. Safrai, 216.

Rabbi [Judah the Patriarch] sought to abrogate the Sabbatical year. R Pinhas went up to him.

He [Rabbi] said to him: How grows the grain?

He said to him: The endives fare well.

[He said to him]: How is the grain growing?

[He said to him]: The endives fare well.

Rabbi realized that he did not concur with him. Would the master mind eating a small bite with us today?

He said to him: Yes.

When he [Pinhas] came down, he saw R Judah's mules and he said: Do Jews feed all these? Perhaps I will not see his face again. They went and told Rabbi [Judah]. Rabbi [Judah] sent messengers to placate him. They arrived in his city.

He said: Let the men of my city come near me. The men came and surrounded him.

They said to him: Rabbi [Judah] wants to placate him. They left him and went away.

He said: Let my own children come near me. A fire descended from heaven and surrounded him. They went and told Rabbi [Judah].

He said: Since we have not achieved the merit of being satiated with his presence in this world, may we have the merit of being satiated with his presence in the world to come.

> Same Narrative: *y. Ta'an.* 3,1; 66c.
> Comparable Narrative: *b. Ḥul.* 7a.

(8) R 166
R Pinḥas Saves a Girl From Drowning.
y. Dem. 1; 22a.

R Haggai said in the name of R Samuel b Naḥman: It is told of a certain hasid that he used to dig cisterns, ditches and caves for the benefit of wayfarers. Once his daughter was on her way to be married and a river swept her away; and all the people went to him wishing to console him, and their consolation was not acceptable to him. And R Pinḥas b Yair went up to him, wishing to console him, and his consolation was not acceptable to him.

He said to them: Is this your hasid?

They said to him: Rabbi, this is what he used to do, and this is what happened to him.

He said to them: Is it possible that he honored his Creator through water and he [the Creator] brought disaster upon him through water? Just then there was a commotion in the city: the man's daughter had come in. There are those who say that she had clung to a plank and was saved. There are others who say that an angel came down in the form of R Pinḥas b Yair and drew her out.

> [The above story is followed immediately by the account of how R Ḥanina b Dosa was prevented from eating untithed spices (R 89) and then by a similar story about R Tarphon.]
> Same Narrative: *y. Šeqal.* 5,1; 48d.
> Comparable Narratives: R 78-R 79.

MISCELLANEOUS

An Instance of a Three-Fold Application of the Same Story

(1) R 167
The Healing of R Ḥiyya b Abba.
b. Ber. 5b. Soncino, 21.

R Ḥiyya b Abba fell sick.
Visiting him, R Yoḥanan said to him: Are the chastenings precious to you?
He said to him: Neither they nor their reward.
He [Yoḥanan] said to him: Give me your hand. He gave him his hand, and he raised him up.[1]

> [1] Motif: Matt 9:25/Mark 5:41-42/Luke 8:41/also Mark 1:31; 9:27.

(2) R 168
The Healing of Rabbi Yoḥanan.
b. Ber. 5b. Soncino, 21.

R Yoḥanan fell sick. Visiting him, R Ḥanina said to him: Are the chastenings precious to you?
He said to him: Neither they nor their reward.
He said to him: Give me your hand. He gave him his hand and he raised him.
Why could not R Yoḥanan raise himself? They replied: The prisoner cannot free himself from jail.

(3) R 169
The Healing of R Eliezer.
b. Ber. 5b. Soncino, 21-22.

Rabbi Eliezer fell sick. Visiting him, R Yoḥanan saw that he was lying in a dark room. He then bared his arm and light emanated from it; thereupon he saw that R Eliezer was weeping.
He said to him: Why do you weep? Is it because you did not study enough Torah? Surely we learnt: "The one who sacrifices much and the one who sacrifices little have the same merit, provided that the heart is directed to heaven." Is it perhaps lack of sustenance? Not everybody has the privilege to enjoy two tables. Is it perhaps because of [the lack of] children? This is the bone of my tenth son!
He said to him: I am weeping that dust should destroy this beauty [of his body].

He said to him: On that account you surely have a reason to weep; and they both wept.

Then he said to him: Are the chastenings precious to you? He said: Neither they nor their reward.

He said to him: Give me your hand. And he gave him his hand and he raised him.

R 170

A Demon Exorcized by a Ring Bearing Solomon's Name. Josephus, *Jewish Antiquities* 8,2,5. Loeb 5,595-97.

[While discussing King Solomon, Josephus interjects a short description of Eleazar, a contemporary of Josephus.]

There was no form of nature with which he [Solomon] was not acquainted or which he passed over without examining, but he studied them all philosophically and revealed the most complete knowledge of their several properties. And God granted him knowledge of the art used against demons for the benefit and healing of men. He also composed incantations by which illnesses are relieved, and left behind forms of exorcisms with which those possessed by demons drive them out, never to return. And this kind of cure is of very great power among us to this day, for I have seen a certain Eleazar, a countryman of mine, in the presence of Vespasian, his sons, tribunes and a number of other soldiers, free men possessed by demons, and this was the manner of the cure: he put to the nose of the possessed man a ring which had under its seal one of the roots prescribed by Solomon,[1] and then, as the man smelled it, drew out the demon through his nostrils, and, when the man at once fell down, adjured the demon never to come back into him, speaking Solomon's name and reciting the incantations which he had composed. Then, wishing to convince the bystanders and prove to them that he had this power, Eleazar placed a cup or footbasin full of water a little way off and commanded the demon, as it went out of the man, to overturn it and make known to the spectators that he had left the man.[2] And when this was done, the understanding and wisdom of Solomon were clearly revealed, on account of which we have been induced to speak of these things, in order that all men may know the greatness of his nature and how God favoured him, and that no one under the sun may be ignorant of the king's surpassing virtue of every kind.

Comparable Narratives: H 214; H 229.

[1] Josephus is referring to a root found in the region of Baaras whose properties he describes in *J. W.* 7,6,3.
[2] Motif: Mark 1:26/Luke 4:35.

R 171
An Arabian Traveler Kills a Camel, and Then Revives it.
b. Sanh. 67b. Soncino, 460.

Rab said to R Ḥiyya: I myself saw an Arabian traveler take a sword and cut up a camel. Then he rang a bell at which the camel arose.

He said: After that was there any blood or dung? Then it was merely an optical illusion.[1]

[1] For a discussion of this "holding of the eyes" (*'hyzt 'nym*) and its distinction from magic, see E. Urbach, *The Sages. Their Concepts and Beliefs* (Jerusalem: Hebrew University, 1975) 100-02. This expression, from a linguistic point of view, bears comparison with Luke 24:16. For other possible traces of a Judaic background to the Lucan story, see R 98.

R 172
The Jewel Found in a Fish's Mouth.
b. Šabb. 119a. Soncino, 586.

Joseph who-honors-the-Sabbath had in his vicinity a certain gentile who owned much property. Some Chaldeans said to him: Joseph who-honors-the-Sabbath will consume all your property. He [the gentile] went and sold all his property and bought a precious stone with the proceeds, which he set in his turban. As he was crossing a bridge, the wind blew it off and cast it into the water; a fish swallowed it. The fish was hauled up and brought [to the marketplace] on the Sabbath eve towards sunset. They said: Who will buy at this hour?

They said to them: Go and take it to Joseph who-honors-the-Sabbath, as he is in the habit of buying [to stop commerce before the Sabbath]. So they took it to him. He bought it, opened it, and found the jewel[1] therein, and sold it for 13 roomfuls of gold denarii. A certain old man met him and said: He who lends to the Sabbath, the Sabbath repays him.

[1] Motif: Matt 17:27.

R 173
The Prayer of a Jewish Child Saves a Ship.[1]
y. Ber. 9,1; 13b.

R Tanḥuma said: There is a story about a ship of gentiles making its way on the great sea, and there was on board a Jewish boy. And there arose a great storm on the sea, and each one of them stood up and prayed, taking his god in his hand and calling out; but it did not succeed at all. When they saw that they were not succeeding at all, they said to the Jew: My boy, rise up, call to your God[2] for we have heard that he answers you when you cry out to him, and he is powerful. Right away the boy stood up and cried out with all his heart; and the Holy One, blessed be he, accepted his prayer, and the sea was calm.

When they reached land, they all got out to buy what they needed.

They said to the boy: Don't you want to bargain [and get] something for yourself? He said to them: What do you want from this poor stranger?

They said to him: You a poor stranger? They are the poor strangers: they are here and their idols are in Babylon, they are here and their idols are in Rome, they are here and their idols are with them, and they gain nothing thereby. But you, wherever you go, your God is with you, as it is written [Deut 4:7]: "[What great nation has its gods so close to it] as Yhwh our God whenever we call upon him?"

---

1 Story: Matt 8:23-27/Mark 4:35-41/Luke 8:22-25; R 101;
Homeric Hymns 33, *Hymn to the Dioscuri*, Allen, 91-92.
2 Motif: Jonah 1:5-6.

PART III

HELLENISTIC STORIES

WONDER STORIES TOLD IN CONNECTION WITH EMPERORS AND NOTABLES

H 174
How Athena Gave Pericles Advice for Healing a Workman.
Plutarch, *Life of Pericles* 13,7-8. Loeb 3,43-45.

The Propylaea of the acropolis were brought to completion in the space of five years, Mnesicles being their architect. A wonderful thing happened in the course of their building, which indicated that the goddess was not holding herself aloof, but was a helper both in the inception and in the completion of the work. One of its artificers, the most active and zealous of them all, lost his footing and fell from a great height, and lay in a sorry plight, despaired of by the physicians. Pericles was much cast down at this, but the goddess appeared to him in a dream and prescribed a course of treatment for him to use, so that he speedily and easily healed the man. It was in commemoration of this that he set up the bronze statue of Athena Hygieia on the acropolis near the altar of that goddess, which was there before, as they say.

H 175
Alexander's Interest in Healing and Medicine.
Plutarch, *Life of Alexander* 8,1. Loeb 7,243.

Moreover, in my opinion, Alexander's love of the art of healing was inculcated in him by Aristotle preeminently. For he was not only fond of the theory of medicine, but actually came to the aid of his friends when they were sick, and prescribed for them certain treatments and regimens, as one can gather from his letters.

R 176
How Alexander Learned in a Dream the Way to Cure the
Wounded Ptolemy.
Diodorus of Sicily, *Library of History* 17,103,6-8. Loeb 8,417-
19.

> [Diodorus has been describing the awful and fatal effects
> of the poison with which the citizens of Harmatelia
> smeared their weapons.]

So the wounded were dying in this fashion, and for the rest
Alexander was not so much concerned, but he was deeply distressed for Ptolemy, the future king, who was much beloved by
him. An interesting and quite extraordinary event occurred in
the case of Ptolemy, which some attributed to divine Providence. He was loved by all because of his character and his
kindnesses to all, and he obtained a succour appropriate to his
good deeds. The king saw a vision in his sleep. It seemed to him
that a snake appeared carrying a plant in its mouth, and showed
him its nature and efficacy and the place where it grew. When
Alexander awoke, he sought out the plant, and grinding it up
plastered it on Ptolemy's body. He also prepared an infusion of
the plant and gave Ptolemy a drink of it. This restored him to
health.

Comparable Narrative: Strabo, *Geography* 15,2,7.

*Various Accounts of How Alexander Crossed the Inlet of the
Pamphylian Sea*

A) H 177
How the Wind Favored Alexander's March.
Arrian, *The Anabasis of Alexander* 26,1. Loeb 1,109.

Leaving Phaselis, Alexander sent part of his force through
the mountain passes towards Perga, where the Thracians had
made him a road, the approach being otherwise difficult and
long. He himself led his men by the sea along the shore, a route
practicable only with north winds blowing; south winds make
the passage along the shore impossible. There had been
southerlies but a north wind had set in, not without divine inter-
position, as Alexander and his followers interpreted it, and made
the passage easy and swift.

B) H 178
Plutarch Endeavors to Refute the Allegation of a Miraculous
Crossing of the Sea of Pamphylia.
Plutarch, *Life of Alexander* 17,3. Loeb 7,271-73.

Encouraged by this prophecy [the miraculous appearance of
a bronze tablet foretelling a Greek victory over Persia], Alexander hastened to clear up the sea-coast as far as Cilicia and Phoenicia. His rapid passage along the coasts of Pamphylia has
afforded many historians material for bombastic and terrifying
description. They imply that by some great and heaven-sent
good fortune, the sea retired to make way for Alexander,
although at other times it always came rolling in with violence
from the main, and scarcely ever revealed to sight the small
rocks which lie close up under the precipitous and riven sides of
the mountain. And Menander, in one of his comedies, evidently
refers jestingly to this marvel:

> "How Alexander-like, indeed, this is; and if I seek
> someone,
> Spontaneous he'll present himself; and if I clearly must
> Pass through some place by sea, this will lie open to my
> steps."

Alexander himself, however, made no such prodigy out of it
in his letters, but says that he marched by way of the so-called
Ladder, and passed through it, setting out from Phaselis.

C) H 179
Strabo's Description of Alexander's March Through the
Pamphylian Sea.
Strabo, *Geography* 14,3,9. Loeb 6,321.

Then one comes to Phaselis, with three harbours, a city of
note, and to a lake. Above it lies Solyma, a mountain, and also
Termessus, a Pisidian city situated near the defiles, through
which there is a pass over the mountain to Milyas. Alexander
destroyed Milyas for the reason that he wished to open the defiles. Near Phaselis, by the sea, there are defiles, through which
Alexander led his army. And here there is a mountain called
Climax, which lies near the Pamphylian Sea and leaves a narrow
pass on the shore; and in calm weather this pass is free from
water, so that it is passable for travellers, but when the sea is at
flood-tide it is to a considerable extent hidden by the waves.
Now the pass that leads over through the mountain is circuitous
and steep, but in fair weather people use the pass along the

shore. Alexander, meeting with a stormy season, and being a man who in general trusted to luck [*tyche*], set out before the waves had receded; and the result was that all day long his soldiers marched in water submerged to their navels. Now this city too is Lycian, being situated on the borders towards Pamphylia, but it has no part in the common League and is a separate organisation to itself.

D) H 180
How Alexander was Aided by a Wonder in Pamphylia.
Ps.-Callisthenes, *Life of Alexander* 1,28. Bergson, 42-43.

. . . He entered Phrygia and Lycia and then Pamphylia, and here a wonder [*paradoxon*] occurred. Since Alexander did not have a boat with him, a part of the sea withdrew so that the infantry could pass through.

> Comparable Narrative: Translated from the Armenian version of Ps.-Callisthenes' work, #184. See: A. M. Wolohojian (tr.), *The Romance of Alexander the Great by Pseudo-Callisthenes* (New York: Columbia University Press, 1969) 97.

E) H 181
Josephus' Reference to Alexander's Crossing of the Inlet of the Pamphylian Sea.
Josephus, *Jewish Antiquities* 2,16,5.1 Loeb 4,317.

For my part, I have recounted each detail here told just as I found it in the sacred books. Nor let anyone marvel at the astonishing nature of the narrative or doubt that it was given to men of old, innocent of crime, to find a road of salvation through the sea itself, whether by the will of God or maybe by accident, seeing that the hosts of Alexander king of Macedon, men born but the other day, beheld the Pamphylian Sea retire before them and, when other road there was none, offer a passage through itself, what time it pleased God to overthrow the Persian empire; and on that all are agreed who have recorded Alexander's exploits. However on these matters, everyone is welcome to his own opinion.[1]

> For the complete text of which this is the conclusion, see:
> OT 16.

1 This type of disclaimer probably comes to Josephus from Dionysius of Halicarnassus. See: *Roman Ant.* 1,48.

H 182
The Healing Power of Pyrrhus' Right Foot.
Plutarch, *Life of Pyrrhus* 3,4-5. Loeb 9,353.

In the aspect of his countenance, Pyrrhus had more of the terror than of the majesty of kingly power. He had not many teeth, but his upper jaw was one continuous bone, on which the usual intervals between the teeth were indicated by slight depressions. People of a splenetic habit believed that he cured their ailment; he would sacrifice a white cock and, while the patient lay flat upon his back, would press gently with his right foot against the spleen.

Nor was anyone so obscure or poor as not to get this healing service from him if he asked it. The king would also accept the cock after he had sacrificed it, and this honorarium was most pleasing to him.

It is said, further, that the great toe of his right foot had a divine virtue, so that after the rest of his body had been consumed, this was found to be untouched and unharmed by the fire. These things, however, belong to a later period.

H 183
How Cleomenes' Body was Protected by a Serpent.
Plutarch, *Agis and Cleomenes* 39,1-3. Loeb 10,141.

[Cleomenes, king of Sparta, went to Egypt with the hope of fomenting a rebellion. He was disappointed, and then betrayed and killed. His body was exposed to indignity and his family and followers were also killed.]

And a few days afterwards, those who were keeping watch upon the body of Cleomenes where it hung, saw a serpent of great size coiling itself about the head and hiding the face so that no ravening bird of prey could light upon it. In consequence of this, the king was seized with superstitious fear, and thus gave the women occasion for various rites of purification, since they felt that a man had been taken off who was of a superior nature and beloved of the gods.

And the Alexandrians actually worshipped him, coming frequently to the spot and addressing Cleomenes as a hero and a child of the gods; but at last the wiser men among them put a stop to this by explaining that, as putrefying oxen breed bees, and horses wasps, and as beetles are generated in asses which are in the like condition of decay, so human bodies, when the juices about the marrow collect together and coagulate, produce serpents.

And it was because they observed this that the ancients associated the serpent more than any other animal with heroes.

H 184
Augustus: Portents Surrounding His Birth.
Suetonius, *Augustus* 94. Loeb 1,263-69.

Having reached this point, it will not be out of place to add an account of the omens which occurred before he was born, on the very day of his birth, and afterwards, from which it was possible to anticipate and perceive his future greatness and uninterrupted good fortune.

In ancient days, when a part of the wall of Velitrae had been struck by lightning, the prediction was made that a citizen of that town would one day rule the world. Through their confidence in this, the people of Velitrae had at once made war on the Roman people and fought with them many times after that almost to their utter destruction; but at last long afterward the event proved that the omen had foretold the rule of Augustus.

According to Julius Marathus, a few months before Augustus was born, a portent was generally observed at Rome, which gave warning that nature was pregnant with a king for the Roman people; thereupon the senate in consternation decreed that no male child born that year should be reared;[1] but those whose wives were with child saw to it that the decree was not filed in the treasury, since each one appropriated the prediction to his own family.

I have read the following story in the books of Asclepias of Mendes entitled *Theologumena*. When Atia had come in the middle of the night to the solemn service of Apollo, she had her litter set down in the temple and fell asleep, while the rest of the matrons also slept. On a sudden, a serpent glided up to her and shortly went away. When she awoke, she purified herself, as if after the embraces of her husband, and at once there appeared on her body a mark in colours like a serpent, and she could never get rid of it; so that presently she ceased ever to go to the public baths. In the tenth month after that, Augustus was born and was therefore regarded as the son of Apollo. Atia, too, before she gave him birth, dreamed that her vitals were borne up to the stars and spread over the whole extent of land and sea, while Octavius dreamed that the sun rose from Atia's womb.

The day he was born, the conspiracy of Catiline was before the House, and Octavius came late because of his wife's confinement; then Publius Nigidius, as everyone knows, learning the reason for his tardiness and being informed also of the hour of the birth, declared that the ruler of the world had been born. Later, when Octavius was leading an army through remote parts of Thrace, and in the grove of Father Liber consulted the priests about his son with barbarian rites, they made the same prediction; since such a pillar of flame sprang forth from the wine that was poured over the altar, that it rose above the temple roof and mounted to the very sky, and such an omen had befallen no one save Alexander the Great, when he offered sacrifice at the same altar. Moreover, the very next night, he dreamt that his son appeared to him in a guise more majestic than that of mortal man, with the thunderbolt, sceptre, and insignia of Jupiter Optimus Maximus, wearing a crown begirt with rays and mounted upon a laurel-wreathed chariot drawn by twelve horses of surpassing whiteness. When Augustus was still an infant, as is recorded by the hand of Gaius Drusus, he was placed by his nurse at evening in his cradle on the ground floor and the next morning had disappeared; but after long search, he was at last found lying on a lofty tower with his face towards the rising sun.

As soon as he began to talk, it chanced that the frogs were making a great noise at his grandfather's country place; he bade them be silent, and they say that since then no frog has ever croaked there. As he was breakfasting in a grove at the fourth milestone on the Campanian road, an eagle surprised him by snatching his bread from his hand, and after flying to a great height, equally to his surprise dropped gently down again and gave it back to him.

After Quintus Catulus had dedicated the Capitol, he had dreams on two nights in succession: first, that Jupiter Optimus Maximus called aside one of a number of boys of good family, who were playing around his altar, and put in the lap of his toga an image of Roma, which he was carrying in his hand; the next night he dreamt that he saw this same boy in the lap of Jupiter of the Capitol, and that when he had ordered that he be removed, the god warned him to desist, declaring that the boy was being reared to be the saviour of his country [ad tutelam reipublicae]. When Catulus next day met Augustus, whom he had never seen before, he looked at him in great surprise and said that he was very like the boy of whom he had dreamed.

[There follow other portents concerning his destiny, especially the confidence he had in his horoscopic sign of Capricorn.]

1 Motif: Exod 1:16.22; Matt 2:16.

H 185
Augustus: Portents Surrounding his Death.
Suetonius, *Augustus* 97,99. Loeb 1,275-77,281.

His death, too, of which I shall speak next, and his deification after death, were known in advance by unmistakable signs. As he was bringing the lustrum to an end in the Campus Martius before a great throng of people, an eagle flew several times about him and then going across to the temple hard by, perched above the first letter of Agrippa's name. On noticing this, Augustus bade his colleague Tiberius recite the vows which it is usual to offer for the next five years; for although he had them prepared and written out on a tablet, he declared that he would not be responsible for vows which he should never pay. At about the same time, the first letter of his name was melted from the inscription on one of his statues by a flash of lightning; this was interpreted to mean that he would live only a hundred days from that time, the number indicated by the letter C, and that he would be numbered with the gods, since *aesar* (that is, the part of the name Caesar which was left) is the word for god in the Etruscan tongue.

Then, too, when he was on the point of sending Tiberius to Illyricum and was proposing to escort him as far as Beneventum, and litigants detained him on the judgment seat by bringing forward case after case, he cried out that he would stay no longer in Rome, even if everything conspired to delay him—and this, too, was afterwards looked upon as one of the omens of his death. When he had begun the journey, he went on as far as Astura and from there, contrary to his custom, took ship by night since it chanced that there was a favourable breeze, and thus contracted an illness beginning with a diarrhoea . . . .

On the last day of his life, he asked every now and then whether there was any disturbance without on his account; then calling for a mirror, he had his hair combed and his falling jaws set straight. After that, calling in his friends and asking whether it seemed to them that he had played the comedy of life fitly, he added the tag:

"Since well I've played my part, all clap your hands
And from the stage dismiss me with applause."

Then he sent them all off, and while he was asking some
newcomers from the city about the daughter of Drusus, who
was ill, he suddenly passed away as he was kissing Livia, uttering
these last words: "Live mindful of our wedlock, Livia, and fare-
well," thus blessed with an easy death and such a one as he had
always longed for. For almost always on hearing that anyone
had died swiftly and painlessly, he prayed that he and his might
have a like *euthanasia*, for that was the term he was wont to use.
He gave but one single sign of wandering before he breathed his
last, calling out in sudden terror that forty young men were carrying him off. And even this was rather a premonition than a
delusion, since it was that very number of soldiers of the preto-
rian guard that carried him forth to lie in state.

H 186

Augustus: Other Portents and His Regard for Them.
Suetonius, *Augustus* 90-93,95-96. Loeb 1,259-63,273-75.

This is what we are told of his attitude towards matters of
religion. He was somewhat weak in his fear of thunder and
lightning, for he always carried a seal-skin about with him everywhere as a protection, and at any sign of a violent storm took
refuge in an underground vaulted room; for as I have said, he
was once badly frightened by a narrow escape from lightning
during a journey by night.
He was not indifferent to his own dreams or to those which
others dreamed about him. At the battle of Philippi, though he
had made up his mind not to leave his tent because of illness, he
did so after all when warned by a friend's dream; fortunately, as
it turned out, for his camp was taken and when the enemy
rushed in, his litter was stabbed through and through and torn
to pieces, in the belief that he was still lying there ill. All
through the spring his own dreams were very numerous and
fearful, but idle and unfulfilled; during the rest of the year, they
were less frequent and more reliable. Being in the habit of making constant visits to the temple of Jupiter the Thunderer,
which he had founded on the Capitol, he dreamed that Jupiter
Capitolinus complained that his worshippers were being taken
from him, and that he answered that he had placed the Thunderer hard by to be his doorkeeper; and accordingly he presently festooned the gable of the temple with bells, because these
commonly hung at house-doors. It was likewise because of a

dream that every year on an appointed day, he begged alms of
the people, holding out his open hand to have pennies dropped
in it.

Certain auspices and omens he regarded as infallible. If his
shoes were put on in the wrong way in the morning, the left
instead of the right, he considered it a bad sign. If there
chanced to be a drizzle of rain when he was starting on a long
journey by land or sea, he thought it a good omen, betokening a
speedy and prosperous return.

But he was especially affected by prodigies. When a palm
tree sprang up between the crevices of the pavement before his
house, he transplanted it to the inner court beside his household
gods and took great pains to make it grow. He was so pleased
that the branches of an old oak, which had already drooped to
the ground and were withering, became vigorous again on his
arrival in the island of Capreae, that he arranged with the city of
Naples to give him the island in exchange for Aenaria. He also
had regard to certain days, refusing ever to begin a journey on
the day after a market day, or to take up any important business
on the Nones; though in the latter case, as he writes Tiberius, he
merely dreaded the unlucky sound of the name.

He treated with great respect such foreign rites as were ancient and well established, but held the rest in contempt. For
example, having been initiated at Athens and afterwards sitting
in judgment of a case at Rome involving the privileges of the
priests of Attic Ceres, in which certain matters of secrecy were
brought up, he dismissed his councillors and the throng of bystanders and heard the disputants in private. But on the other
hand, he not only omitted to make a slight detour to visit Apis,
when he was travelling through Egypt, but highly commended
his grandson Gaius for not offering prayers at Jerusalem as he
passed by Judaea . . . .

As he was entering the city on his return from Apollonia after Caesar's death, though the heaven was clear and cloudless, a
circle like a rainbow suddenly formed around the sun's disc, and
straightway the tomb of Caesar's daughter Julia was struck by
lightning. Again, as he was taking the auspices in his first consul-
ship, twelve vultures appeared to him, as to Romulus, and when
he slew the victims, the livers within all of them were found to
be doubled inward at the lower end, which all those who were
skilled in such matters unanimously declared to be an omen of a
great and happy future.

He even divined beforehand the outcome of all his wars.
When the forces of the triumvirs were assembled at Bononia, an

eagle that had perched upon his tent made a dash at two ravens, which attacked it on either side, and struck them to the ground. From this, the whole army inferred that there would one day be discord among the colleagues, as actually came to pass, and divined its result. As he was on his way to Philippi, a Thessalian gave him notice of his coming victory on the authority of the deified Caesar, whose shade had met him on a lonely road. When he was sacrificing at Perusia without getting a favourable omen, and so had ordered more victims to be brought, the enemy made a sudden sally and carried off all the equipment of the sacrifice; whereupon the soothsayers agreed that all the dangers and disasters with which the sacrificer had been threatened would recoil on the heads of those who were in possession of the entrails; and so it turned out. As he was walking on the shore the day before the sea-fight off Sicily, a fish sprang from the sea and fell at his feet. At Actium, as he was going down to begin the battle, he met an ass with his driver, the man having the name Eutychus and the beast that of Nicon; and after the victory, he set up bronze images of the two in the sacred enclosure into which he converted the site of his camp.

Three Accounts of Vespasian's Healing of Two Men in Alexandria

A) H 187
Vespasian Heals a Blind Man and a Lame Man in Alexandria. Suetonius, *Vespasian* 8,7. Loeb 2,299.

Vespasian as yet lacked prestige and a certain divinity, so to speak, since he was an unexpected and still new-made emperor; but these were also given to him. A man of the people who was blind, and another who was lame, came to him together as he sat on the tribunal, begging for the help for their disorders which Serapis had promised in a dream; for the god declared that Vespasian would restore the eyes, if he would spit upon them,[1] and give strength to the leg, if he would deign to touch it with his heel.

Though he had hardly any faith [*fides*] that this could possibly succeed, and therefore shrank even from making the attempt, he was at last prevailed upon by his friends and tried both things in public before a large crowd; and with success.

[1] Motif: Mark 7:33.

B) H 188
Vespasian Heals a Blind Man and a Maimed Man in
Alexandria.
Dio Cassius, *Roman Hist.* 65,8. Loeb 8,271.

Following Vespasian's entry into Alexandria, the Nile over-
flowed, having in one day risen a palm higher than usual; such
an occurrence, it was said, had taken place only once before.

Vespasian himself healed two persons, one having a withered
hand, the other being blind, who had come to him because of a
vision seen in dreams; he cured the one by stepping on his hand
and the other by spitting upon his eyes.

Yet, though heaven was thus magnifying him, the Alexandrians, far from delighting in his presence, detested him so heartily
that they were forever mocking and reviling him, not only in
private but also in public. For they had expected to receive
from him some great reward because they had been the first to
make him emperor, but instead of securing anything, they had
additional contributions levied upon them.

C) H 189
Vespasian Heals a Blind Man and a Maimed Man in
Alexandria.
Tacitus, *History* 4,81. Loeb 2,159-61.

During the months while Vespasian was waiting at Alexandria for the regular season of the summer winds and a settled
sea, many marvels occurred to mark the favour of heaven and a
certain partiality of the gods toward him. One of the common
people of Alexandria, well known for his loss of sight, threw himself before Vespasian's knees, praying him with groans to cure
his blindness, being so directed by the god Serapis, whom this
most superstitious of nations worships before all others; and he
besought the Emperor to deign to moisten his cheeks and eyes
with his spittle.

Another, whose hand was useless, prompted by the same
god, begged Caesar to step and trample on it. Vespasian at first
ridiculed these appeals and treated them with scorn; then,
when the men persisted, he began at one moment to fear the
discredit of failure, at another to be inspired with hopes of success by the appeals of the suppliants and the flattery of his court-
iers: finally, he directed the physicians to give their opinion as
to whether such blindness and infirmity could be overcome by
human aid [*ope humana*]. Their reply treated the two cases dif-
ferently: they said that in the first, the power of sight had not

been completely eaten away and it would return if the obstacles were removed; in the other, the joints had slipped and become displaced, but they could be restored if a healing pressure were applied to them. Such perhaps was the wish of the gods, and it might be that the Emperor had been chosen for this divine service [*id fortasse cordi deis et divino ministerio principem electum*]; in any case, if a cure were obtained, the glory would be Caesar's, but in the event of failure, ridicule would fall only on the poor suppliants. So Vespasian, believing that his good fortune was capable of anything and that nothing was any longer incredible, with a smiling countenance, and amid intense excitement on the part of the bystanders, did as he was asked to do. The hand was instantly restored to use, and the day again shone for the blind man.

Both facts are told by eye-witnesses even now when falsehood brings no reward.

H 190
Toward the End of His Life, Hadrian is Responsible for the Healing of Two Blind People.
Aelius of Sparta, *Life of Hadrian* 25,1-4. Loeb (*Scriptores Historiae Augustae*) 1,77.

About this time, there came a certain woman, who said that she had been warned in a dream to coax Hadrian to refrain from killing himself, for he was destined to recover entirely, but that she had failed to do this and had become blind; she had nevertheless been ordered a second time to give the same message to Hadrian and to kiss his knees, and was assured of the recovery of her sight if she did so.

The woman then carried out the command of the dream, and received her sight after she had bathed her eyes with the water in the temple from which she had come.[1]

Also a blind man from Pannonia came to Hadrian when he was ill with fever, and he touched him, whereupon the man received his sight, and the fever left Hadrian.

All these things, however, Marius Maximus declares were done as a hoax.

[1] Motif: John 9:7.

ANECDOTES TOLD IN CONNECTION WITH
EMPERORS AND NOTABLES

H 191
Alexander's Reply to His Wounded Father.
Plutarch, *The Fortune of Alexander* 1,9. Loeb, *Moralia* 4,409.

When the thigh of his father Philip had been pierced by a spear in battle with the Triballians, and Philip, although he escaped with his life, was vexed with his lameness, Alexander said, "Be of good cheer, father, and go on your way rejoicing, that at each step you may recall your valour." Are not these the words of a truly philosophic spirit which, because of its rapture for noble things, already revolts against mere physical encumbrances? How, then, think you, did he glory in his own wounds, remembering by each part of his body affected a nation overcome, a victory won, the capture of cities, the surrender of kings? He did not cover over nor hide his scars, but bore them with him openly as symbolic representations, graven on his body, of virtue and manly courage.

H 192
A Series of Anecdotes Revealing Alexander's Character.
Plutarch, *The Fortune of Alexander* 1,11. Loeb, *Moralia* 4,417.

It occurs to me to introduce here an incident touching Porus. For when Porus was brought as a captive before Alexander, the conqueror asked how he should treat him. "Like a king, Alexander," said Porus. When Alexander asked again if there were nothing else, "No," said he, "for everything is included in that word." And it naturally occurs to me also to exclaim over each of Alexander's deeds, "Like a philosopher!" For in this is included everything.

He became enamoured of Roxanê, the daughter of Oxyartes, as she danced among the captive maidens; yet he did not offer any violence to her, but made her his wife. "Like a philosopher!"

When he saw Darius pierced through by javelins, he did not offer sacrifice nor raise the paean of victory to indicate that the long war had come to an end; but he took off his own cloak and threw it over the corpse as though to conceal the divine retribution that waits upon the lot of kings. "Like a philosopher!"

Once when he was reading a confidential letter from his

mother, and Hephaestion who, as it happened, was sitting beside him, was quite openly reading it, too, Alexander did not stop him, but merely placed his own signet-ring on Hephaestion's lips, sealing them to silence with a friend's confidence. "Like a philosopher!"

For if these actions be not those of a philosopher, what others are?

H 193
Examples of Augustus' Jurisprudence.
Suetonius, *Life* 33. Loeb 1,177.

He himself administered justice regularly and sometimes up to nightfall, having a litter placed upon the tribunal, if he was indisposed, or even lying down at home.

In his administration of justice he was both highly conscientious and very lenient; for to save a man clearly guilty of parricide from being sewn up in the sack, a punishment which was inflicted only on those who pleaded guilty, he is said to have put the question to him in this form: "You surely did not kill your father, did you?"

Again, in a case touching a forged will, in which all the signers were liable to punishment by the Cornelian Law, he distributed to the jury not merely the two tablets for condemnation or acquittal, but a third as well, for the pardon of those who were shown to have been induced to sign by misrepresentation or misunderstanding.

H 194
Hadrian's Remark to a Man who Tried the Same Plea Twice.
Aelius of Sparta, *Life of Hadrian* 20. Loeb (*Scriptores Historiae Augustae*) 1,63.

He [Hadrian] was also very witty, and of his jests many still survive. The following one has even become famous: When he had refused a request to a certain gray-haired man, and the man repeated the request but this time with dyed hair, Hadrian replied: "I have already refused this to your father."

H 195
How Hadrian Treated an Insolent Slave.
Aelius of Sparta, *Life of Hadrian* 21. Loeb (*Scriptores Historiae Augustae*) 1,65.

With regard to his treatment of his slaves, the following incident, stern but almost humorous, is still related. Once when he saw one of his slaves walk away from his presence between two senators, he sent someone to give him a box on the ear and say to him: "Do not walk between those whose slave you may some day be."

H 196
Antoninus' Remarks About Polemo's Putting Him Out of His House.
Philostratus, *Lives of the Sophists* 1,25. Loeb, 115.

This is the sort of jest he would make. When Polemo came to Rome, Antoninus embraced him, and then said: "Give Polemo a lodging and do not let anyone turn him out of it."

And once when a tragic actor who had performed at the Olympic games in Asia, over which Polemo presided, declared that he would prosecute him, because Polemo had expelled him at the beginning of the play, the Emperor asked the actor what time it was when he was expelled from the theatre, and when he replied that it happened to be at noon, the Emperor made this witty comment: "But it was midnight when he expelled *me* from his house, and I did not prosecute him."

H 197
How Antoninus Answered the Sophist Alexander.
Philostratus, *Lives of the Sophists* 2,5. Loeb, 191-93.

After Alexander had reached manhood, he went on an embassy to Antoninus on behalf of Seleucia, and malicious gossip became current about him, that to make himself look younger he used artificial means. Now the Emperor seemed to be paying too little attention to him, whereupon Alexander raised his voice and said: "Pay attention to me, Caesar."

The Emperor, who was much irritated with him for using so unceremonious a form of address, retorted: "I am paying attention, and I know you well. You are the fellow who is always arranging his hair, cleaning his teeth, and polishing his nails, and always smells of perfume."

WONDER STORIES ABOUT PHILOSOPHERS AND OTHER WISE MEN

H 198
A Story Regarding Socrates' *Daimon*.[1]
Plutarch, *On Socrates' Daimon* 10. Loeb, *Moralia* 7,405-07.

Very well, said Theocritus; but what, my dear sir, do we call Socrates' daimon? An imposture? For my part, nothing reported of Pythagoras' skill in divination has struck me as so great or so divine; for exactly as Homer has represented Athena as "standing at" Odysseus' "side in all his labours," so heaven seems to have attached to Socrates from his earliest years as his guide in life a vision of this kind, which alone,

"Showed him the way, illumining his path,"

in matters dark and inscrutable to human wisdom, through the frequent concordance of the daimon with his own decisions, to which it lent a divine sanction.

For further and greater instances, you must ask Simmias and Socrates' other friends; but I was myself present (I had come to visit Euthyphron the soothsayer) when Socrates—you recall the incident, Simmias—happened to be making the ascent toward the Symbolon and the house of Andocides, putting some question to Euthyphron the while and sounding him out playfully. Suddenly he stopped short and fell silent, lost for a good time in thought; at last he turned back, taking the way through the street of the cabinetmakers, and called out to the friends who had already gone onward to return, saying that the daimon had come to him. Most turned back with him, I with the rest, clinging close to Euthyphron; but certain young fellows went straight ahead, imagining that they would discredit Socrates' daimon, and drew along Charillus the flute-player, who had also come to Athens with me to visit Cebes.

As they were walking along the street of the statuaries past the law-courts, they were met by a drove of swine, covered with mud and so numerous that they pressed against one another; and as there was nowhere to step aside, the swine ran into some and knocked them down, and befouled the rest. Charillus came home like the others, his legs and clothes covered with mud; so that we always mentioned Socrates' daimon with laughter, at the same time marveling that heaven [*to theion*] never deserted or neglected him.

¹ I have retained the term *daimon* despite the fact that the Loeb translators use "sign." The notion that a *daimon* was a mysterious force existing somewhere between the realm of the human and that of the divine was too firmly rooted in both popular religion and philosophy to have been understood merely as a "sign" in this context. For a discussion of a Hellenistic outlook on *daimones*, one may consult the article by Foerster in *TDNT* 2, 1-20, esp. pp. 1-8.

Three Collections of Wonderful Things Reported of Pythagoras

A) H 199
A Summary of Some of the Wonders Connected with the Life of Pythagoras.
Apollonius the Paradoxographer, *Wonderful Tales* 6. Tiede, 315-16.

Although Pythagoras the son of Mnesarchus came after these and at first labored diligently at mathematics and numbers, subsequently he did not refrain from the wonderworking of Pherecydes.

a) For once in Metapontus when a boat entered bearing a cargo and those who were present were praying that it might be safe on account of the cargo, as he stood there he said this, "It shall now be evident to you that this ship is bearing a dead body."

b) And (this happened) again in Kaulonia as Aristotle reports . . . who in writing about him says many and various things and reports that in Tyrrhenia he himself bit a deadly biting serpent and killed it.[1]

c) And he also predicted the division which took place among the Pythagoreans.

d) And consequently he departed from Metapontus without being observed by anyone, and as he passed over the Cosa river with others, he heard a great supra-human voice say, "Hail Pythagoras!" And those who were with him were in great fear.

e) And once he appeared both in the Croton and Metapontus on the same day and hour.

f) Once while he was seated in the theater, he stood up, as Aristotle reports, and he showed his thigh to be golden to those who were seated.

And some other miraculous things are told about him. But

since we do not wish to produce a work of the transcribers, we will end the report.

1 Motif: Mark 16:18; R 80.

B) H 200
An Enumeration of Some of the Wonders Wrought by Pythagoras.
Iamblichus, *Life* 28. Taylor, 71-72.

That which follows after this, we shall no longer discuss generally, but direct our attention particularly to the works resulting from the virtues of Pythagoras. And we shall begin in the first place from the gods, as it is usual to do, and endeavour to exhibit his piety, and the admirable works which he performed.

a) Let this, therefore, be one specimen of his piety, which also we have mentioned, that he knew what his soul was, and whence it came into the body, and also its former lives, and that of these things he gave most evident indications.

b) After this also, let the following be another specimen; that once passing over the river Nessus with many of his associates, he spoke to it, and the river in a distinct and clear voice, in the hearing of all his followers, answered, Hail Pythagoras!

c) Farther still, nearly all historians of his life confidently assert, that in one and the same day, he was present at Metapontum in Italy, and Tauromenium in Sicily, and discoursed in common with his disciples in both places, though these cities are separated from each other by many stadia both by land and sea, and cannot be passed through in a great number of days.

d) The report, also, is very much disseminated that he showed his golden thigh to the Hyperborean Abaris, who said that he resembled the Apollo among the Hyperboreans, and of whom Abaris was the priest; and that he did this in order that Abaris might apprehend this to be true, and that he was not deceived in his opinion.

Ten thousand other more divine and more admirable particulars likewise are uniformly and unanimously related of the man:[1] such as infallible predictions of earthquakes, rapid expulsions of pestilence and violent winds, instantaneous cessations of the effusion of hail, and a tranquillization of the waves of rivers and seas, in order that his disciples might easily pass over them.

1 Motif: John 21:25.

H 201

An Enumeration of Wonders Connected with Pythagoras.
Porphyry, *Life* 27-29. Nauck, 31-32. Hadas-Smith, 116.

a) It is reported that once when Pythagoras with many of his companions was crossing the river Caucasus, he spoke to it and the river, loud and clear, in the hearing of all, uttered, "Greetings, Pythagoras."

b) Almost all authorities assert that on one and the same day he was present and talked together with his companions both in Metapontum of Italy and in Tauromenium of Sicily, although the distance between these two cities is one of a great many stadia, both by land and by sea, and not to be traversed in many days.

c) It is commonly told that when Abaris, of the Hyperboreans, guessed him to be the Hyperborean Apollo, of whom Abaris was a priest, Pythagoras showed him that his thigh was of gold, thus confirming that the guess was right.

d) Equally common is the story that when a ship was putting in to land and his friends were praying that they might have the cargo, Pythagoras said, "So you'll get a corpse." And the ship sailed into port with a corpse on board.

Ten thousand other things yet more marvellous and more divine are told about the man, and told uniformly in stories that agree with each other. To put it bluntly, about no one else have greater and more extraordinary things been believed.

For he is reported to have uttered proclamations which earthquakes would not transgress, spells which rapidly drove off plagues and checked violent winds and hailstorms and calmed the waters of rivers and seas, so that his companions could easily cross them.

It is said, moreover, that these were handed down to Empedocles and Epimenides and Abaris, who thus in many places performed similar miracles, as their poems clearly evidence.

H 202

Pythagoras' Control Over Animals.
Porphyry, *Life* 23-25. Nauck, 29-30. Hadas-Smith, 114-15.

Moreover, if the ancient and reputable authors who wrote accounts of his life are to be credited, his admonitions extended even to irrational animals.

For catching the Daunian bear, that is said to have wounded many of those who lived in its country, he stroked it for a long time and fed it with barley cake and acorns, and having sworn it never again to touch living creatures, let it go. Thereupon it went off into the mountains and thickets, and was never again seen attacking any animal at all.

Again, when he saw an ox in Tarentum eating green beans in a pasture that contained many sorts of food, he went up to the oxherd and advised him to tell the ox to abstain from beans. The oxherd answered him with ridicule and said that, himself, he didn't speak ox language. So Pythagoras went near and whispered in the ear of the ox. It not only left the beanfield at that moment but never again touched beans. It lived to an extreme old age in Tarentum, staying near the temple of Hera, and was called the sacred ox and ate such food as the passers-by offered it.

Yet again, at Olympia, when he chanced to speak to his acquaintances concerning auguries from the flights of birds and omens and signs from the sky, saying that these too are messages of a sort from the gods to those among men who are truly dear to them, it is reported that he drew to earth an eagle that was flying over, stroked it, and again, let it go.

> [The account continues with other examples of Pythagoras' preternatural knowledge.]

H 203
The Knowledge of the Cosmos and the Perceptivity Possessed by Pythagoras.
Porphyry, *Life* 30. Nauck, 33. Hadas-Smith, 117.

Pythagoras also charmed away both psychic and somatic sufferings and passions, by rhythms and tunes and incantations he adapted to the needs of his followers. But he himself listened to the harmony of all things, understanding the universal harmony of the spheres and of the stars that move according to them—a harmony we do not hear because of the pettiness of our nature.

H 204
Empedocles Speaks of Having Power Over the Forces of Nature.
On Nature, Fragment. *Vorsokr.* 1,353 (fr. 111).

You will learn about medicines, as many as there are, and helps against evils and old age, because for you alone I will accomplish all this.

You will halt the power of untiring winds which move over

the earth, and by their blowing destroy the seedland; and again, if you have the will, you will summon the winds to return.

You will make from dark rain, dryness for men in its season; you will make summer drought into streams that nourish trees, pouring down from the sky.

You will lead out from Hades the power of a dead man.

H 205
A Discussion of Empedocles' Resuscitation of a Woman Kept in a Trance.
Diogenes Laertius, *Lives of Eminent Philosophers* 8,58-61,72.
Loeb 2,373-77,387.

[Only some of Diogenes' remarks are listed here.]

Satyrus in his *Lives* says that he was also a physician and an excellent orator: at all events Gorgias of Leontini, a man pre-eminent in oratory and the author of a treatise on the art, had been his pupil. Of Gorgias Apollodorus says in his *Chronology* that he lived to be one hundred and nine. Satyrus quotes this same Gorgias as saying that he himself was present when Empedocles performed magical feats . . . . [Diogenes then quotes what we have given in H 204.]

Heraclides in his book *On Diseases* says that he furnished Pausanias with the facts about the woman in a trance. This Pausanias, according to Aristippus and Satyrus, was his bosom friend, to whom he dedicated his poem *On Nature* thus:

"Give ear, Pausanias, son of Anchitus the wise!"
Moreover he wrote an epigram upon him:

"The physician Pausanias, rightly so named, son of Anchitus, descendant of Asclepius, was born and bred at Gela. Many a wight pining in fell torments did he bring back from Persephone's inmost shrine."

At all events Heraclides testifies that the case of the woman in a trance was such that for thirty days he kept her body without pulsation though she never breathed; and for that reason Heraclides called him not merely a physician [*iētros*] but a diviner [*mantis*] as well . . . .

After urging some such arguments, Timaeus goes on to say, "But Heraclides is everywhere just such a collector of wonderful tales [*paradoxologos*], telling us, for instance, that a man dropped down to earth from the moon."

H 206
Epimenides' Wonderful Sleep.
Apollonius the Paradoxographer, *Wonderful Tales* 1. Tiede,
313.

According to Bolus, Epimenides the Cretan was reported to
have been sent by his father and brothers into the country in
order to bring back a sheep into the city. When night overtook
him, he deviated from the path and went to sleep for 57 years,
exactly as many others have said. And even Theopompus
touches on the marvels at places in his history. Then, in the
mean time, Epimenides' relatives died; but when he woke up
from his sleep, he continued to seek the sheep for which he had
been sent. And although he did not find it, he proceeded to the
farm. (And he supposed that he had awakened on the same day
in which he believed he had fallen asleep.) And when he arrived at the farm and found it sold and the style of dress
changed, he departed for the city. And when he had arrived
home, thence he knew everything, even including the things
that had happened around the time when he had disappeared.
And the Cretans say, as Theopompus reports, that when he had
lived 157 years, he died. And not a few other amazing things
are told about this man.

Comparable Narrative: R 74.

H 207
Epimenides' Visit to Athens.
Plutarch, *Life of Solon* 1,12,4-6. Loeb 1,433-35.

[Plutarch has been describing various calamities that beset
Athens.]
Under these circumstances, they summoned to their aid
from Crete Epimenides of Phaestus, who is reckoned as the sev-
enth Wise Man by some of those who refuse Periander a place in
the list. He was reputed to be a man beloved of the gods, and
endowed with a mystical and heaven-sent wisdom in religious
matters. Therefore the men of his time said that he was the son
of a nymph named Balte, and called him a new Cures. On coming to Athens, he made Solon his friend, assisted him in many
ways, and paved the way for his legislation. For he made the
Athenians decorous and careful in their religious services, and
milder in their rites of mourning, by attaching certain sacrifices
immediately to their funeral ceremonies, and by taking away

the harsh and barbaric practices in which their women had usually indulged up to that time.

Most important of all, by sundry rites of propitiation and purification, and by sacred foundations, he hallowed and consecrated the city, and brought it to be observant of justice and more easily inclined to unanimity.

It is said that when he had seen Munychia [the acropolis of the Peiraeus] and considered it for some time, he remarked to the bystanders that man was indeed blind to the future; for if the Athenians only knew what mischiefs the place would bring upon their city, they would devour it with their own teeth. A similar insight into futurity is ascribed to Thales.

They say that he gave directions for his burial in an obscure and neglected quarter of the city's territory, predicting that it would one day be the market-place of Miletus.

Well, then, Epimenides was vastly admired by the Athenians, who offered him much money and large honours; but he asked for nothing more than a branch of the sacred olive-tree, with which he returned home.

Comparable Narrative: Diogenes Laertius, *Lives of Eminent Philosophers. Epimenides* 1,10.

Four Accounts of Asclepiades' Medical Skill

A) H 208
A List of the Wonderful Accomplishments of Asclepiades.
Pliny, *Natural History* 7,37. Loeb 2,589.

But the highest reputation belongs to Asclepiades of Prusa, for having founded a new school, despised the envoys and overtures of King Mithridates, discovered a method of preparing medicated wine for the sick, brought back a man from burial and saved his life, but most of all for having made a wager with fortune that he should not be deemed a physician if he were ever in any way ill himself: and he won his bet, as he lost his life in extreme old age by falling downstairs.

B) H 209
Pliny's Reference to Asclepiades' Saving of a Man on the Way to Burial.
Pliny, *Natural History* 26,8. Loeb 7,277.

His fame was no less great when, on meeting the funeral cortège[1] of a man unknown to him, he had him removed from the

pyre and saved his life. This incident I give lest any should think
that it was on slight grounds that so violent a change took place.
One thing alone moves me to anger: that one man, of a very
superficial race, beginning with no resources, in order to increase his income suddenly gave to the human race rules for
health, which however have subsequently been generally
discarded.

[1] Motif: Luke 7:12. R. Bultmann, in *The History of the
Synoptic Tradition* (New York: Harper and Row, 1963)
221, follows Reitzenstein (p. 3, n. 2) and Weinrich (p. 173)
in considering a common feature of "revivifying the
dead" to be that "the healer meet the funeral procession." They cite some of the four accounts given here in
H 208-H 211, and usually add H 214 and then adduce H
228 and H 289. As can be seen, H 208-H 211 are four
narratives of the same story of a healing. H 214 is alluding to this well known incident and H 228 and H 289 are
not applicable. This, as far as I know, constitutes all that
can be alleged to establish this "common feature."

C) H 210
A Mention of Asclepiades' Skill as a Doctor.
Celsus, *On Medicine* 2,6. Loeb 1,115.

[The discussion is about interpreting the signs of death in
a patient.]

In answer to these I shall not even assert that some signs,
stated as approximately certain, often deceive inexperienced
practitioners, but not good ones; for instance, Asclepiades, when
he met the funeral procession, recognized that a man who was
being carried out to burial was alive; and it is not primarily a
fault of the art if there is a fault on the part of its professor.

D) H 211
A Long Narrative Account of How Asclepiades Raised a Man
Considered Dead.
Apuleius, *Florida* 19.

The famous Asclepiades, among the foremost medical men,
if you except Hippocrates the prince of them all, was the first to
hit upon wine for aid of the sick, provided, of course, it be given
at the right time. In this regard, he had remarkable powers of
observation, applying most diligent care to noticing exceptional
or irregular pulse in the veins.

Once, when he was coming back into the city from his country place, he saw on the outskirts of the city a great funeral procession accompanied by a large crowd of people who had come for the obsequies, all very sad and dressed in shabby clothes.

He approached, either because of some natural curiosity regarding the identity of the dead man (no one would answer his questions), or so that he himself might learn something useful for his art. Certainly for the man lying there and just about to be dispatched it was fate who brought him. The poor fellow was already sprinkled with spices, his face was smeared with ointments, the perfumes were prepared, in fact he was nearly ready.

Asclepiades gazed at him intently, having noted most carefully certain signs; he even felt the body of the man; and he found life still latent in him. Immediately he shouted out that the man was alive: let them withdraw the torches, let them remove the fires, let them take down the pyre, let them change their funeral banquet into a celebration. A murmur began in the crowd, some said the doctor should be believed, others made fun of all medicine. Eventually, even though the man's near relations were opposed, either because they had already taken possession of the inheritance or because they still did not believe him, Asclepiades finally and with great difficulty obtained a brief respite for the dead man. Thus, like some prey snatched from the hands of the undertakers, as it were from the underworld, he brought him back to his house and quickly restored his spirit. Quickly with certain medicines, he stirred up the soul hidden in some recesses of the body.

Comparable Narrative: H 215

H 212
How Apollonius Gives a Young Man Good Advice That Leads to His Being Healed.
Philostratus, *Life of Apollonius* 1,9. Loeb 1,21-23.[1]

> [Philostratus has just been telling us of the ascetic life led
> by Apollonius in the temple of Asclepius at Aegae.]

Now it is well that I should not pass over, in my narrative, the life led in the Temple by my hero, who was held in esteem even by the gods.

For an Assyrian stripling came to Asclepius, and though he was sick, yet he lived the life of luxury, and being continually drunk, I will not say he lived, rather he was ever dying. He suffered then from dropsy, and finding his pleasure in drunkenness took no care to dry up his malady. On this account then Asclepius took no care of him, and did not visit him even in a dream. The youth grumbled at this, and thereupon the god, standing over him, said, "If you were to consult Apollonius you would be easier."

He therefore went to Apollonius, and said: "What is there in your wisdom that I can profit by? for Asclepius bids me consult you." And he replied: "I can advise you of what, under the circumstances, will be most valuable to you; for I suppose you want to get well." "Yes, by Zeus," answered the other, "I want the health which Asclepius promises, but never gives."

"Hush," said the other, "for he gives to those who desire it, but you do things that irritate and aggravate your disease, for you give yourself up to luxury, and you accumulate heavy meals upon your water-logged and worn-out stomach, and as it were, choke water with a flood of mud."

This was a clearer response, in my opinion, than Heraclitus, in his wisdom, gave. For he said when he was visited by this affliction that what he needed was someone to substitute a drought for his rainy weather, a very unintelligible remark, it appears to me, and by no means clear; but the sage restored the youth to health by a clear interpretation of the wise saw.

> [1] Philostratus' *Life* contains many stories of wonders worked by Apollonius. The narratives included here are those which, from a stylistic point of view, bear some resemblance to Gospel narratives. A complete list would include: 1,9; 3,38.39.40; 4,10.20.25.45; 5,18.24.42; 6,27.39 .40.41.43; 7,38; 8,5.8.26-27. Also 1,4.5.6; 8,31.

H 213
Iarchus and His Associates Work Three Cures and Give Advice Which is Meant to Lead to a Fourth.
Philostratus, *Life of Apollonius* 3,39. Loeb 1,317-19.

> [Apollonius is in India conversing with the sage Iarchus and his disciples. "This discussion was interrupted by the appearance among the sages of the messenger bringing in certain Indians who were in want of succour" (3,38). To the first, a woman whose son was attacked by the ghost of a disgruntled man, Iarchus gives a letter to the ghost [*eidōlon*] which he says will have the desired effect: we are not told the result.]

There also arrived a man who was lame. He, already thirty years old, was a keen hunter of lions; but a lion had sprung upon him and dislocated his hip so that he limped with one leg. However when they massaged with their hands the hip, the youth immediately recovered his upright gait.

And another man had had his eyes put out, and he went away having recovered the sight of both of them.

Yet another man had his hand paralysed, but left their presence in full possession of the limb.

And a certain woman had suffered in labour already seven times, but was healed in the following way through the intercession of her husband. He bade the man, whenever his wife should be about to bring forth her next child, to enter her chamber carrying in his bosom a live hare; then he was to walk once round her and at the same moment to release the hare; for that the womb would be expelled together with the fetus, unless the hare was at once driven out.

H 214

Apollonius Expels a Demon from a Boy in Athens.
Philostratus, *Life of Apollonius* 4,20. Loeb 1,389-93.

Now while he was discussing the question of libations, there chanced to be present in his audience a young dandy who bore so evil a reputation for licentiousness, that his conduct had once been the subject of coarse street-corner songs. His home was Corcyra, and he traced his pedigree to Alcinous the Phaeacian who entertained Odysseus.

Apollonius then was talking about libations, and was urging them not to drink out of a particular cup, but to reserve it for the gods, without ever touching it or drinking out of it. But when he also urged them to have handles on the cup, and to pour the libation over the handle, because that is the part of the cup at which men are least likely to drink, the youth burst out into loud and coarse laughter, and quite drowned his voice. Then Apollonius looked up at him and said: "It is not yourself that perpetrates this insult, but the demon [*daimōn*], who drives you on without your knowing it."

And in fact the youth was, without knowing it, possessed by a demon; for he would laugh at things that no one else laughed at, and then he would fall to weeping for no reason at all, and he would talk and sing to himself. Now most people thought that it was the boisterous humour of youth which led him into such excesses; but he was really the mouth-piece of a demon, though it only seemed a drunken frolic in which on that occasion he was indulging.

Now when Apollonius gazed on him, the ghost [*eidōlon*] in him began to utter cries of fear and rage, such as one hears from people who are being branded or racked; and the ghost swore that he would leave the young man alone and never take possession of any man again.

But Apollonius addressed him with anger, as a master might a shifty, rascally, and shameless slave and so on, and he ordered him to quit the young man and show by a visible sign that he had done so. "I will throw down yonder statue," he said, and pointed to one of the images which was in the king's portico, for there it was that the scene took place.

But when the statue began by moving gently, and then fell down,[1] it would defy anyone to describe the hubbub which arose thereat and the way they clapped their hands with wonder.

But the young man rubbed his eyes as if he had just woke up, and he looked towards the rays of the sun, and won the consideration of all who now had turned their attention to him; for he no longer showed himself licentious, nor did he stare madly about, but he had returned to his own self, as thoroughly as if he had been treated with drugs; and he gave up his dainty dress and summery garments and the rest of his sybaritic way of life, and he fell in love with the austerity of philosophers, and donned their cloak, and stripping off his old self[2] modelled his life in future upon that of Apollonius.

Comparable Narrative: *Life of Apollonius* 4,10.

[1] Motif: Mark 1:26/Luke 4:35; R 170; H 229.
[2] The translator makes the NT resonances closer than Philostratus' vocabulary would warrant at this point.

H 215
Apollonius Raises a Girl, Apparently Dead.
Philostratus, *Life of Apollonius* 4,45.[1] Loeb 1,457-59.

Here too is a miracle which Apollonius worked: A girl seemed to have died just in the hour of her marriage, and the bridegroom was following her bier lamenting as was natural, his marriage left unfulfilled, and the whole of Rome was mourning with him, for the maiden belonged to a consular family.

Apollonius then witnessing their grief, said: "Put down the

bier, for I will stay the tears that you are shedding for this maiden." And withal he asked what was her name. The crowd accordingly thought that he was about to deliver such an oration as is commonly delivered as much to grace the funeral as to stir up lamentation; but he did nothing of the kind, but merely touching her and whispering in secret some spell over her, at once woke up the maiden from her seeming death; and the girl spoke out loud, and returned to her father's house, just as Alcestis did when she was brought back to life by Hercules. And the relations of the maiden wanted to present him with the sum of 150,000 sesterces, but he said that he would freely present the money to the young lady by way of a dowry.

Now whether he detected some spark of life in her, which those who were nursing her had not noticed—for it is said that although it was raining at the time, a vapour went up from her face—or whether life was really extinct, and he restored it by the warmth of his touch, is a mysterious problem which neither I myself nor those who were present could decide.

> Comparable Narrative: H 211.

> [1] This story is often invoked as comparable to Luke 7:11-17. A more pointed allusion is to be found in the gesture recorded in Luke 7:15 (see 1 Kgs 17:23).

H 216
How Apollonius Knew That a Ship was Going to Sink.
Philostratus, *Life of Apollonius* 5,18. Loeb 1,503.

He stayed in Sicily and taught philosophy there as long as he had sufficient interest in doing so, and then repaired to Greece about the rising of Arcturus. After a pleasant sail he arrived at Leucas, where he said: "Let us get out of this ship, for it is better not to continue in it our voyage to Achaea."

No one took any notice of the utterance except those who knew the sage well, but he himself together with those who desired to make the voyage with him embarked on a Leucadian ship, and reached the port of Lechaeum; meanwhile the Syracusan ship sank as it entered the Crisaean Gulf.

> Comparable Narratives: H 199 and H 200. This story may be another attempt to make Apollonius a second Pythagoras. There is an explicit comparison established in *Life of Apollonius* 4,10 between Apollonius' miraculous

journey from Smyrna to Ephesus and Pythagoras' biloca-
tion: see H 199-H 201.

H 217
Apollonius' Prophecy Concerning Vespasian's Future.
Philostratus, *Life of Apollonius* 5,28. Loeb 1,525-27.

[With 5,27, we enter upon the story of Vespasian. Philostratus tells us about the meeting between Apollonius and
Vespasian in the temple of Alexandria, and explains that
this is how the story grew that while Vespasian was be-
sieging Jerusalem, he first thought of becoming emperor
and sent for Apollonius who refused to enter a polluted
country: thus Vespasian went to Alexandria to see him.]

For after Vespasian had sacrificed, and before he gave official
audiences to the cities, he addressed himself to Apollonius, and,
as if making prayer he said to him: "Make me king."

And he answered: "I have done so already, for I have already offered a prayer for a king who should be just and noble
and temperate, endowed with the wisdom of grey hairs, and the
father of legitimate sons; and surely in my prayer I was asking
from the gods for none other but yourself." The Emperor was
delighted with this answer, for the crowd too in the temple
shouted their agreement with it. "What then," said the Emperor, "did you think of the reign of Nero?" And Apollonius
answered: "Nero perhaps understood how to tune a lyre, but he
disgraced the empire both by letting the strings go too slack and
by drawing them too tight." "Then," said the other, "you would
like a ruler to observe the mean?" "Not I," said Apollonius, "but
God himself, who has defined equality as consisting in the mean.
And these gentlemen here, they too are good advisers in this
matter," he added, pointing to Dion and Euphrates, for the latter had not yet quarrelled with him.

Thereupon the king held up his hand and said: "O Zeus,
may I hold sway over wise men, and wise men hold sway over
me." And turning himself round towards the Egyptians he said:
"You shall draw as liberally upon me as you do upon the Nile."

Comparable Narrative: R 96. This account and the portion of the text immediately preceding are an obvious po-
lemic against other claimants to the honor of having
predicted Vespasian's reign. See the note at R 96.

H 218

How Apollonius Discerned the Soul of Amasis in the Body of a
Lion.
Philostratus, *Life of Apollonius* 5,42. Loeb 1,569-71.

The following incident also of Apollonius' stay in Egypt was
thought remarkable. There was a man who led a tame lion
about by a string, as if it had been a dog; and the animal not only
fawned upon him, but on anyone who approached it. It went
collecting alms all round the towns, and was admitted even in
the temples, being a pure animal; for it never licked up the
blood of the victims, nor pounced on them when they were being flayed and cut up, but lived upon honeycakes and bread and
dried fruits and cooked meat; and you also came on it drinking
wine without changing its character.

One day it came up to Apollonius when he was sitting in the
temple, and whined and fawned at his knees, and begged of him
more earnestly than it had ever done of anybody. The bystanders imagined it wanted some solid reward, but Apollonius exclaimed: "This lion is begging me to make you understand that
a human soul is within him, the soul namely of Amasis, the king
of Egypt in the province of Sais." And when the lion heard that,
he gave a piteous and plaintive roar, and crouching down began
to lament, shedding tears. Thereupon Apollonius stroked him,
and said: "I think the lion ought to be sent to Leontopolis and
dedicated to the temple there, for I consider it wrong that a
king who has been changed into the most kingly of beasts should
go about begging, like any human mendicant."

In consequence, the priests met and offered sacrifice to
Amasis; and having decorated the animal with a collar and rib-
bons, they conveyed him up country into Egypt with pipings,
hymns and songs composed in his honour.

H 219

Apollonius, by Knowing the Causes and Appropriate
Propitiation for Divine Wrath, Saves Some Cities.
Philostratus, *Life of Apollonius* 6,41. Loeb 2,139.

At one time the cities on the left side of the Hellespont were
visited by earthquakes, and Egyptians and Chaldeans went begging about through them to collect money, pretending that they
wanted ten talents with which to offer sacrifices to earth and to
Poseidon. And the cities began to contribute under the stress of
fear, partly out of their common funds and partly out of private.

But the imposters refused to offer the sacrifices in behalf of their dupes unless the money was deposited in the banks.

Now the sage determined not to allow the peoples of the Hellespont to be imposed upon; so he visited their cities, and drove out the quacks who were making money out of the misfortunes of others, and then he divined the causes of the supernatural wrath, and by making such offerings as suited each case averted the visitation at small cost, and the land was at rest.

H 220
How Apollonius Heals a Boy Gone Mad From the Bite of a Mad Dog; and Then Heals the Dog.
Philostratus, *Life of Apollonius* 6,43. Loeb 2,141-43.

Here too is a story which they tell of him in Tarsus. A mad dog had attacked a lad, and as a result of the bite the lad behaved exactly like a dog, for he barked and howled and went on all four feet using his hands as such, and ran about in that manner. And he had been ill in this way for thirty days, when Apollonius, who had recently come to Tarsus, met him and ordered a search to be made for the dog which had done the harm. But they said that the dog had not been found, because the youth had been attacked outside the wall when he was practising with javelins, nor could they learn from the patient what the dog was like, for he did not even know himself any more.

Then Apollonius reflected a moment and said: "O Damis, the dog is a white shaggy sheep-dog, as big as an Amphilochian hound, and he is standing at a certain fountain trembling all over, for he is longing to drink the water, but at the same time is afraid of it. Bring him to me to the bank of the river, where there are the wrestling grounds, merely telling him that it is I who call him."

So Damis dragged the dog along, and it crouched at the feet of Apollonius, crying out as a suppliant might do before an altar.

But he quite tamed it by stroking it with his hand, and then he stood the lad close by, holding him with his hand; and in order that the multitude might be cognisant of so great a mystery, he said: "The soul of Telephus of Mysia has been transferred into this boy, and the Fates impose the same things upon him as upon Telephus."

And with these words he bade the dog lick the wound all round where he had bitten the boy, so that the agent of the wound might in turn be its physician and healer.

After that, the boy returned to his father and recognised his mother, and saluted his comrades as before, and drank of the waters of the Cydnus.

Nor did the sage neglect the dog either, but after offering a prayer to the river he sent the dog across it; and when the dog had crossed the river, he took his stand on the opposite bank, and began to bark, a thing which mad dogs rarely do, and he folded back his ears and wagged his tail, because he knew that he was all right again, for a draught of water cures a mad dog, if he has only the courage to take it.

Such were the exploits of our sage in behalf of both temples and cities; such were the discourses he delivered to the public or in behalf of different communities, and in behalf of those who were dead or who were sick; and such were the harangues he delivered to wise and unwise alike, and to the sovereigns who consulted him about moral virtue.

H 221
Apollonius Shows Damis How Little He is Bound by Fetters.
Philostratus, *Life of Apollonius* 7,38. Loeb 2,255-57.

> [Apollonius and Damis are in prison by order of Domi-
> tian, and the situation is growing constantly worse,
> though Apollonius continues to discourse to the
> prisoners.]

Damis says then that though Apollonius uttered many more discourses of the same kind, he was himself in despair of the situation, because he saw no way out of it except such as the gods have vouchsafed to some in answer to prayer, when they were in even worse straits. But a little before mid-day, he tells us that he said:

"O man of Tyana,"—for he took a special pleasure, it ap-pears, in being called by that name—"what is to become of us?" "Why what has become of us already," said Apollonius, "and nothing more, for no one is going to kill us." "And who," said Damis, "is so invulnerable as that? But will you ever be liber-ated?" "So far as it rests with the verdict of the court," said Apollonius, "I shall be set at liberty this day, but so far as de-pends upon my own will, now and here." And with these words he took his leg out of the fetters and remarked to Damis: "Here is proof positive to you of my freedom, so cheer up."

Damis says that it was then for the first time that he really and truly understood the nature of Apollonius, to wit that it was divine and superhuman [*theia kai kreittōn anthrōpou*], for without any sacrifice—and how in prison could he have offered any?—and without a single prayer, without even a word, he quietly laughed at the fetters, and then inserted his leg in them afresh, and behaved like a prisoner once more.

Portents Surrounding the Birth and Death of Apollonius

(1) H 222
Apollonius is Really Proteus.
Philostratus, *Life of Apollonius* 1,4. Loeb 1,11-13.

Apollonius' home, then, was Tyana, a Greek city amidst a population of Cappadocians. His father was of the same name, and the family was ancient and directly descended from the first settlers. It excelled in wealth the surrounding families, though the district is a rich one. To his mother, just before he was born, there came an apparition of Proteus, who changes his form so much in Homer, in the guise of an Egyptian demon. She was in no way frightened, but asked him what sort of child she would bear. And he answered: "Myself." "And who are you?" she asked. "Proteus," answered he, "the god of Egypt." Well, I need hardly explain to readers of the poets the quality of Proteus and his reputation as regards wisdom; how versatile he was, and forever changing his form, and defying capture, and how he had the reputation of knowing both past and future.

And we must bear Proteus in mind all the more, when my advancing story shews its hero to have been more of a prophet than Proteus, and to have triumphed over many difficulties and dangers in the moment when they beset him most closely.

(2) H 223
The Circumstances of Apollonius' Birth.
Philostratus, *Life of Apollonius* 1,5. Loeb 1,13-15.

Now he is said to have been born in a meadow, hard by which there has been now erected a sumptuous temple to him; and let us not pass by the manner of his birth. For just as the hour of his birth was approaching, his mother was warned in a dream to walk out into the meadow and pluck the flowers; and in due course she came there and her maids attended to the flowers, scattering themselves over the meadow, while she fell asleep lying on the grass. Thereupon the swans who fed in the meadow set up a dance around her as she slept, and lifting their wings, as they are wont to do, cried out aloud all at once, for there was somewhat of a breeze blowing in the meadow. She then leaped up at the sound of their song and bore her child, for any sudden fright is apt to bring on a premature delivery.[1]

But the people of the country say that just at the moment of the birth, a thunderbolt seemed about to fall to earth and then rose up into the air and disappeared aloft; and the gods thereby indicated, I think, the great distinction to which the sage was to attain, and hinted in advance how he should transcend all things upon earth and approach the gods, and signified all the things that he would achieve.

[1] Motif: H 213.

H 224
How Apollonius Established the Immortality of the Soul by Appearing to a Young Man After His Death.
Philostratus, *Life of Apollonius* 8,31. Loeb 2,403-05.

And even after his death he continued to preach that the soul is immortal; but although he taught this account of it to be correct, yet he discouraged men from meddling in such high subjects. For there came to Tyana a youth who did not shrink from acrimonious discussions, and would not accept truth in argument. Now Apollonius had already passed away from among men, but people still wondered at his passing, and no one ventured to dispute that he was immortal. This being so, the discussions were mainly about the soul, for a band of youths were there passionately addicted to wisdom. The young man in question, however, would on no account allow the tenet of the immortality of the soul, and said: "I myself, gentlemen, have done nothing now for over nine months but pray to Apollonius that he would reveal to me the truth about the soul; but he is so utterly dead that he will not appear to me in response to my entreaties, nor give me any reason to consider him immortal."

Such were the young man's words on that occasion, but on the fifth day following, after discussing the same subject, he fell asleep where he was talking with them, and of the young men who were studying with him, some were reading books, and others were industriously drawing geometrical figures on the ground, when on a sudden, like one possessed, he leapt up from an uneasy sleep, streaming with perspiration, and cried out: "I believe you." And when those who were present asked him what was the matter: "Do you not see," said he, "Apollonius the sage, how that he is present with us and is listening to our discussion, and is reciting wondrous verses about the soul?" "But where is he?" they asked, "for we cannot see him anywhere, although we would rather do so than possess all the blessings of mankind." And the youth replied: "It would seem that he is come to converse with myself alone concerning the tenets which I would not believe. Listen therefore to the inspired argument which he is delivering."

> [The youth then goes on to recite some of the verse he has heard, and Philostratus concludes his work by commenting on them.]

Examples of Summary Examples in Philostratus' Life of Apollonius

(1) H 225
A Summary of Apollonius' Visit to Iarchus.[1]
Philostratus, *Life of Apollonius* 3,40. Loeb 1,319-21.

With such lore as this then they surfeited themselves, and they were astonished at the many-sided wisdom of the company, and day after day they asked all sorts of questions, and were themselves asked many in turn.

> [1] For a discussion of the summaries in the *Life of Apollonius*, see: G. Petzke, *Die Traditionen über Apollonius von Tyana und das Neue Testament* (StCorpHellNT, 1; Leiden: E. J. Brill, 1970) 76-79 *et passim*. Petzke, however, does not mention 3,40 in this context. Summaries include: 3,40; 4,1.11.41; 6,35.43; 8,24.

(2) H 226
A Summary of Apollonius' Activity in Pergamum and Ilium.
Philostratus, *Life of Apollonius* 4,11. Loeb 1,367.

Having made his way then to Pergamum, and being pleased with the temple of Asclepius, he gave hints to the supplicants of the god, what to do in order to obtain favourable dreams; and having healed many of them he came to the land of Ilium. And as his mind was stored with all the traditions of their past, he went to visit the tombs of the Achaeans, and he delivered himself of many speeches over them, and he offered many sacrifices of a bloodless and pure kind; and then he bade his companions go on board ship, for he himself, he said, must spend a night on the mound of Achilles.

(3) H 227
A "Report Type" Summary of Apollonius' Activity in Rome.
Philostratus, *Life of Apollonius* 4,41. Loeb 1,449.

The result of his discourses about religion was that the gods were worshipped with more zeal, and that men flocked to the temples where he was, in the belief that by doing so they would obtain an increase of divine blessings. And our sage's conversations were so far not objected to, because he held them in public and addressed himself to all men alike; for he did not hover about rich men's doors, nor hang about the mighty, though he welcomed them if they resorted to him, and he talked with them just as much as he did to the common people.

H 228
How a Chaldean Cured a Man Dying of a Snake Bite.
Lucian, *The Lover of Lies* 11. Loeb 3,335-37.

> [We are assisting at a conversation in which the topic is men's love for lying and believing strange tales. Some of the party are trying to justify the existence of the marvelous things of which these tales tell.]

"Never mind him," said Ion, "and I will tell you a wonderful story. I was still a young lad, about fourteen years old, when someone came and told my father that Midas the vine-dresser, ordinarily a strong and industrious servant, had been bitten by a viper toward midday and was lying down, with his leg already in a state of mortification. While he was tying up the runners and twining them about the poles, the creature had crawled up and bitten him on the great toe; then it had quickly gone down again into its hole, and he was groaning in mortal anguish.

"As this report was being made, we saw Midas himself being brought up on a litter by his fellow-slaves, all swollen and livid, with a clammy skin and but little breath left in him. Naturally my father was distressed, but a friend who was there said to him: 'Cheer up: I will at once go and get you a Babylonian, one of the so-called Chaldeans, who will cure the fellow.' Not to make a long story of it, the Babylonian came and brought Midas back to life, driving the poison out of his body by a spell, and also binding upon his foot a fragment which he broke from the tombstone of a dead maiden.

"Perhaps this is nothing out of the common: although Midas himself picked up the litter on which he had been carried and went off to the farm,[1] so potent was the spell and the fragment of the tombstone."

[The story continues to recount further wonders wrought by the Babylonians.]

[1] Motif: Matt 9:7/Mark 2:12/Luke 5:25; John 5:9; H 284. Some sort of "proof" of cure can also be found in *Aesclepius*, Edelstein 423,12.13.14.15.(25).30.(41).

H 229
The Story of an Exorcism.
Lucian, *The Lover of Lies* 16. Loeb 3,345.

"You act ridiculously," said Ion, "to doubt everything. For my part, I should like to ask you what you say to those who free possessed men [*daimonōntas*] from their terrors by exorcising the spirits [*phasmata*] so manifestly. I need not discuss this: everyone knows about the Syrian from Palestine, the adept in it, how many he takes in hand who fall down in the light of the moon and roll their eyes and fill their mouths with foam; nevertheless, he restores them to health and sends them away normal in mind, delivering them from their straits for a large fee. When he stands beside them as they lie there and asks: 'How did you come in his body?' the patient himself is silent, but the spirit answers in Greek or in the language of whatever foreign country he comes from telling how and whence he entered into the man; whereupon, by adjuring the spirit and if he does not obey, threatening him, he drives him out. Indeed, I actually saw one coming out, black and smoky in colour." "It is nothing much," I remarked, "for you, Ion, to see that kind of sight, when even the 'forms' [*ideai*] that the father of your school, Plato, points out are plain to you, a hazy object of vision to the rest of us, whose eyes are weak."

[The conversation continues with Eucrates discussing the fact that demons are common. Later on (#30-31), Arignotus tells how he freed a haunted house from a *daimon*.]
Comparable Narrative: H 214. See the motif given there.

H 230
Lucian's Account of How Alexander Established Himself as a
Seer.
Lucian, *Alexander the False Prophet* 13-14,16-17. Loeb 4,193-
99.

[Lucian begins by describing Alexander's return to his na-
tive town of Abonoteichus, mentioning some of the de-
vices by which Alexander made himself out to be
"inspired." Then he describes a mechanical serpent
which Alexander and Cocconas, his aide, had fashioned
for use in a ruse to gain fame and money.]

When at length it was time to begin, he contrived an ingenious ruse. Going at night to the foundations of the temple
which were just being excavated, where a pool of water had
gathered which either issued from springs somewhere in the
foundations themselves or had fallen from the sky, he secreted
there a goose-egg, previously blown, which contained a snake
just born; and after burying it deep in the mud, he went back
again.

In the morning he ran out into the market-place naked,
wearing a loin-cloth (this too was gilded), carrying his falchion,
and tossing his unconfined mane like a devotee of the Great
Mother in the frenzy. Addressing the people from a high altar
upon which he had climbed, he congratulated the city because
it was at once to receive the god in visible presence. The assembly—for almost the whole city, including women, old men, and
boys, had come running—marvelled, prayed and made obei-
sance. Uttering a few meaningless words like Hebrew or Phoe-
nician, he dazed the creatures, who did not know what he was
saying save only that he everywhere brought in Apollo and Asclepius. Then he ran at full speed to the future temple, went to
the excavation and the previously improvised fountain-head of
the oracle, entered the water, sang hymns in honour of Asclepius and Apollo at the top of his voice, and besought the god,
under the blessing of heaven, to come to the city.

Then he asked for a libation-saucer, and when somebody
handed him one, deftly slipped it underneath and brought up,
along with water and mud, that egg in which he had immured
the god; the joint about the plug had been closed with wax and
white lead. Taking it in his hands, he asserted that at that moment he held Asclepius! They gazed unwaveringly to see what
in the world was going to happen; indeed, they had already

marvelled at the discovery of the egg in the water. But when he broke it and received the tiny snake into his hollowed hand, and the crowd saw it moving and twisting about his fingers, they at once raised a shout, welcomed the god, congratulated their city, and began each of them to sate himself greedily with prayers, craving treasures, riches, health, and every other blessing from him.

But Alexander went home again at full speed, taking with him the new-born Asclepius, "born twice, when other men are born but once," whose mother was not Coronis, by Zeus, nor yet a crow, but a goose! And the whole population followed, all full of religious fervour and crazed with expectations . . . .

Now then, please imagine a little room, not very bright and not admitting any too much daylight; also, a crowd of heterogeneous humanity, excited, wonder-struck in advance, agog with hopes. When they went in, the thing, of course, seemed to them a miracle, that the formerly tiny snake within a few days had turned into so great a serpent [the one Alexander and Cocconas had made], with a human face, moreover, and tame! They were immediately crowded towards the exit, and before they could look closely were forced out by those who kept coming in, for another door had been opened on the opposite side as an exit. That was the way the Macedonians did, they say, in Babylon during Alexander's illness, when he was in a bad way and they surrounded the palace, craving to see him and say good-bye. This exhibition the scoundrel gave not merely once, they say, but again and again, above all if any rich men were newly arrived.

H 231
How Chloe is Saved by Pan From her Kidnappers.
Longus, *Daphnis and Chloe* 2,26-29. Loeb, 105-09.

> [Chloe has been taken captive, and Daphnis prays before the statue of Pan and vows to sacrifice a he-goat if Pan will rescue Chloe. Then the Methymnaeans, resting in their boats offshore, begin to see fearful things and other wonders followed.]

Yet those things which then happened might very well be understood by such as were wise, namely that those spectres, phantasms, and sounds proceeded from Pan, shewing himself angry at the voyagers.

Yet the cause they could not conjecture (for nothing sacred

to Pan was robbed), until about high noon, their grand captain
not without the impulse of some deity fallen into a sleep, Pan
himself appeared to him and rated him thus: "O most unholy
and wickedest of mortals! What made you so bold as madly to
attempt and do such outrages as these? You have not only filled
with war these fields that are so dear to me, but also you have
driven away herds of cattle, flocks of sheep and goats that were
my care. Besides, you have taken sacrilegiously from the altars
of the Nymphs a maid of whom Love himself will write a story.
Nor did you at all revere the Nymphs that looked upon you
when you did it, nor yet me whom very well you knew to be
Pan. Therefore you shall never see Methymna, sailing away
with those spoils, nor shall you escape that terrible pipe from
the promontore, but I will drown you every man and make you
food for the fish, unless you speedily restore to the Nymphs as
well Chloe as Chloe's herds and flocks. Rise therefore and send
the maid ashore, send her with all that I command you; and I
shall be as well to you a convey in your voyage home as to her a
conduct on her way to the fields."

Bryaxis, being astonished at this, started up, and calling together the captains of the ships, commanded that Chloe should
be quickly sought for among the captives. They found her presently and brought her before him; for she sat crowned with the
pine. The general, remembering that the pine was the mark
and signal distinction which he had in his dream, carried the
maid ashore in the flagship with no small observance and cere-
monious fear.

Now as soon as Chloe was set on shore, the sound of the pipe
from the promontore began to be heard again, not martial and
terrible as before, but perfectly pastoral such as is used to lead
the cattle to feed in the fields. The sheep ran down the scale of
the ship, slipping and sliding on their horny hooves; the goats
more boldly, for they were used to climb the crags and steeps of
the hills. The whole flock encircled Chloe, moving as in a dance
about her, and with their skipping and their bleating shewed a
kind of joyfulness and exultation. But the goats of other
goatherds, as also the sheep and the herds, stirred not a foot, but
remained still in the holds of the ships as if the music of that
pipe did not at all call for them.

When therefore they were all struck with admiration at
these things and celebrated the praises of Pan, there were yet
seen in both the elements things more wonderful than those
before. For the ships of the Methymnaeans before they had
weighed their anchors ran amain, and a huge dolphin bouncing

still out of the sea went before and led their admiral. On the land a most sweet melodious pipe led to the goats and the sheep, and yet nobody saw the piper; only all the cattle went along together and fed rejoicing at his music.

H 232
How the God/River Nile Protected Habrocomes From Perils.
Xenophon of Ephesus, *Habrocomes and Anthia* 4,2,3-10.
Dalmeyda, 50-51.

[Habrocomes is condemned unjustly by the Prefect of Egypt to be suspended on a cross as a murderer.][1]

Having set up the cross, they tied Habrocomes to it hand and foot (such is the manner of crucifixion in that place). Then leaving, they thought him securely fastened whom they left behind. He, however, turning his eyes toward the sun and then toward the Nile, began to pray: O you, of all the gods the most benevolent, you who reign over Egypt, through whom earth and sea have appeared for all men, if it is true that Habrocomes is guilty, then let him perish miserably and, if possible, undergo an even worse punishment. However, if it be that I have been betrayed by an evil woman, then may the waters of the Nile never be stained by the touch of my body unjustly destroyed, and may you never see an innocent man put to death on sacred ground.

He prayed and the god took pity. A sudden storm wind came up and beat against the cross, causing the ground which covered the rock in which the cross was planted to give way. Habrocomes fell into the river which carried him along without the waters swallowing him, nor his bonds impeding him, nor the beasts molesting him. Borne along by the current, he reached the mouth of the Nile where the guards seized him and brought him, as a condemned man who was seeking to escape punishment, to the governor of Egypt. The governor was more angry than ever, and judging him to be a knavish fellow, gave the order that they prepare a pyre and setting Habrocomes upon it, do away with him. Everything was ready: the wood had been prepared on the bank of the Nile near its mouth, Habrocomes was placed on it and the fire had been lit. Already the flames were about to reach his body, when, once again, he uttered a short prayer with the strength left to him, that he be saved from these besetting evils.

Just then the Nile rose, the river fell upon the fire and extinguished the flame. This was a miracle [*thauma*] for those who stood by, and taking Habrocomes along, they brought him to the Prefect of Egypt, telling him what happened, and recounting how the Nile came to the rescue. He was astonished when he heard these things and he ordered that Habrocomes be kept in prison with great care "until," he said, "we learn what kind of man this is and why the gods concern themselves with him."

[1] This same situation is related of Chariton's hero Chaereas who, however, is rescued but not miraculously: *Chaereas and Callirhoe* 4,2,6 (Blake, pp. 56-59).

ANECDOTES RECOUNTING SAYINGS OF
PHILOSOPHERS AND WISE MEN

H 233
A Series of Anecdotes About Socrates.
Xenophon, *Memorabilia* 3,13. Loeb 4,253-57.

a) On a man who was angry because his greeting was not returned: "Ridiculous!" he exclaimed; "you would not have been angry if you had met a man in worse health; and yet you are annoyed because you have come across someone with ruder manners!"

b) On another who declared that he found no pleasure in eating: "Acumenus," he said, "has a good prescription for that ailment." And when asked "What?" he answered, "Stop eating; and you will then find life pleasanter, cheaper, and healthier."

c) On yet another who complained that the drinking water at home was warm: "Consequently," he said, "when you want warm water to wash in, you will have it at hand."

"But it's too cold for washing," objected the other.

"Then do your servants complain when they use it both for drinking and washing?"

"Oh no: indeed I have often felt surprised that they are content with it for both these purposes."

"Which is the warmer to drink, the water in your house or Epidaurus water?"

"Epidaurus water."

"And which is the colder to wash in, yours or Oropus water?"

"Oropus water."

"Then reflect that you are apparently harder to please than servants and invalids."

d) When someone punished his footman severely, he asked why he was angry with his man.

"Because he's a glutton and he's a fool," said the other: "he's rapacious and he's lazy."

"Have you ever considered, then, which deserves the more stripes, the master or the man?"

e) When someone was afraid of the journey to Olympia, he said: "Why do you fear the distance? When you are at home, don't you spend most of the day in walking about? On your way there, you will take a walk before lunch, and another before dinner, and then take a rest. Don't you know that if you put together the walks you take in five or six days, you can easily cover the distance from Athens to Olympia? It is more comfortable, too, to start a day early rather than a day late, since to be forced to make the stages of the journey unduly long is unpleasant; but to take a day extra on the way makes easy going. So it is better to hurry over the start than on the road."

f) When another said that he was worn out after a long journey, he asked him whether he had carried a load.

"Oh no," said the man; "only my cloak."

"Were you alone, or had you a footman with you?"

"I had."

"Empty-handed or carrying anything?"

"He carried the rugs and the rest of the baggage, of course."

"And how has he come out of the journey?"

"Better than I, so far as I can tell."

"Well then, if you had been forced to carry his load, how would you have felt, do you suppose?"

"Bad, of course, or rather, I couldn't have done it."

"Indeed! Do you think a trained man ought to be so much less capable of work than his slave?"

H 234

A Series of Anecdotes Told of Diogenes.
Diogenes Laertius, *Lives* 6,25-28. Loeb 2,27-31.

a) Observing Plato one day at a costly banquet taking olives, "How is it," he said, "that you the philosopher who sailed to Sicily for the sake of these dishes, now when they are before you do not enjoy them?"

"Nay, by the gods, Diogenes," replied Plato, "there also for the most part I lived upon olives and such like."

"Why then," said Diogenes, "did you need to go to Syracuse? Was it that Attica at that time did not grow olives?"

But Favorinus in his *Miscellaneous History* attributes this to Aristippus.

b) Again, another time he was eating dried figs when he encountered Plato and offered him a share of them. When Plato took them and ate them, he said, "I said you might share them, not that you might eat them all up."

c) And one day when Plato had invited to his house friends coming from Dionysius, Diogenes trampled upon his carpets and said, "I trample upon Plato's vainglory." Plato's reply was, "How much pride you expose to view, Diogenes, by seeming not to be proud." Others tell us that what Diogenes said was, "I trample upon the pride of Plato," who retorted, "Yes, Diogenes, with pride of another sort."

Sotion, however, in his fourth book makes the Cynic address this remark to Plato himself.

d) Diogenes once asked him [Plato] for wine, and after that also for some dried figs; and Plato sent him a whole jar full. Then the other said, "If someone asks you how many two and two are, will you answer twenty? So, it seems, you neither give as you are asked nor answer as you are questioned."

Thus he scoffed at him as one who talked without end.

e) Being asked where in Greece he saw good men, he replied, "Good men nowhere, but good boys at Lacedaemon."

f) When one day he was gravely discoursing and nobody attended to him, he began whistling, and as people clustered about him, he reproached them with coming in all seriousness to hear nonsense, but slowly and contemptuously when the theme was serious.

g) He would say that men strive in digging and kicking to outdo one another, but no one strives to become a good man and true.

h) And he would wonder that the grammarians should investigate the ills of Odysseus, while they were ignorant of their own. Or that the musicians should tune the strings of the lyre, while leaving the dispositions of their own souls discordant; that the mathematicians should gaze at the sun and the moon, but overlook matters close at hand; that the orators should make a fuss about justice in their speeches, but never practise it; or that the avaricious should cry out against money, while inordinately fond of it . . . .

H 235
Another Series of Anecdotes Related of Diogenes.
Diogenes Laertius, *Lives* 6,32-35. Loeb 2,35-37.

a) One day he shouted out for men, and when people collected, hit out at them with his stick, saying, "It was men I called for, not scoundrels."

This is told by Hecato in the first book of his *Anecdotes* (*Tōn Chreiōn*).

b) Alexander is reported to have said, "Had I not been Alexander, I should have liked to be Diogenes."

c) The word "disabled" (*anapērous*), Diogenes held, ought to be applied not to the deaf or blind, but to those who have no wallet (*pēra*).

d) One day he made his way with head half-shaven into a party of young revellers, as Metrocles relates in his *Anecdotes* [*tais Chreiais*], and was roughly handled by them.

Afterwards he entered on a tablet the names of those who had struck him and went about with the tablet hung round his neck, till he had covered them with ridicule and brought universal blame and discredit upon them.

e) He described himself as a hound [*kuna*] of the sort which all men praise, but no one, he added, of his admirers dared go out hunting along with him.

f) When someone boasted that at the Pythian games he had vanquished men, Diogenes replied, "Nay, I defeat men, you defeat slaves."

g) To those who said to him, "You are an old man; take a rest," "What?" he replied, "if I were running in the stadium, ought I to slacken my pace when approaching the goal? ought I not rather to put on speed?"[1]

h) Having been invited to a dinner, he declared that he wouldn't go; for, the last time he went, his host had not expressed a proper gratitude.

i) He would walk upon snow barefoot and do the other things mentioned above.

Not only so, he even attempted to eat meat raw, but could not manage to digest it.

j) He once found Demosthenes the orator lunching at an inn, and when he retired within, Diogenes said, "All the more you will be inside the tavern."

k) When some strangers expressed a wish to see Demosthenes, he stretched out his middle finger and said, "There goes the demagogue of Athens."

l) Someone dropped a loaf of bread and was ashamed to pick it up; whereupon Diogenes, wishing to read him a lesson, tied a rope to the neck of a wine-jar and proceeded to drag it across the Ceramicus.

> [1] Motif: Phil 3:13-14. The Greek text reads literally, "Should I stop and not rather increase intensity even more?"

Examples of Apollonius' Wisdom

(1) H 236
Apollonius Describes How a Wise Man Should Teach.
Philostratus, *Life of Apollonius* 1,17. Loeb 1,49.

And his sentences were short and crisp, and his words were telling and closely fitted to the things he spoke of, and his words had a ring about them as of the dooms delivered by a sceptred king. And when a certain quibbler asked him why he asked no questions of him, he replied: "Because I asked questions when I was a stripling; and it is not my business to ask questions now, but to teach people what I have discovered." "How then," the other asked him afresh, "O Apollonius, should the sage converse?" "Like a law-giver," he replied, "for it is the duty of the law-giver to deliver to the many the instructions of whose truth he has persuaded himself."

This was the line he pursued during his stay in Antioch, and he converted to himself the most unrefined people.[1]

> [1] In this small collection of *chreiai* from the *Life of Apollonius*, only some examples are given. A complete list would include: 1,17.20.27; 4,9; 5,22.23.25; 6,42; 7,5.6.7 .23.24.27.36.

(2) H 237
Apollonius Describes His Journey With the Virtues.
Philostratus, *Life of Apollonius* 1,20. Loeb 1,55.

As they fared on into Mesopotamia, the tax-gatherer who presided over the Bridge (*Zeugma*) led them into the registry and asked them what they were taking out of the country with them.

And Apollonius replied: "I am taking with me temperance, justice, virtue, continence, valour, discipline." And in this way, he strung together a number of feminine nouns or names.

The other, already scenting his own perquisites, said: "You must then write down in the register these female slaves."

Apollonius answered: "Impossible, for they are not female slaves that I am taking out with me, but ladies of quality."

(3) H 238
Apollonius' Parable About the Ship of State.
Philostratus, *Life of Apollonius* 4,9. Loeb 1,363.

And as he was thus discoursing, he saw a ship with three sails leaving the harbour, of which the sailors were each discharging their particular duties in working it out to sea. Accordingly, by way of reforming his audience he said: "Now look at that ship's crew, how some of them being rowers have embarked in the tugboats, while others are winding up and making fast the anchors, and others again are spreading the sails to the wind, and others are keeping an outlook at bow and stern. Now if a single member of this community abandoned any one of his particular tasks or went about his naval duties in an inexperienced manner, they would have a bad voyage and would themselves impersonate the storm; but if they vie with one another and are rivals only with the object of one showing himself as good a man as the other, then their ship will make the best of all havens, and all their voyage be one of fair weather and fair sailing, and the precaution they exercise about themselves will prove to be as valuable as if Poseidon our lord of safety were watching over them."

(4) H 239
How Apollonius Rebukes a Dissolute Young Man.
Philostratus, *Life of Apollonius* 5,23. Loeb 1,515.

And meeting a young man who was young and fat and who prided himself upon eating more than anybody else, and on drinking more wine than others, he remarked: "Then you, it seems, are the glutton."

"Yes, and I sacrifice to the gods out of gratitude for the same."

"And what pleasure," said Apollonius, "do you get by gorging yourself in this way?"

"Why, everyone admires me and stares at me; for you have probably heard of Hercules, how people took as much pains to celebrate what he ate as what labours he performed."

"Yes, for he was Hercules," said Apollonius; "but as for yourself, you scum, what good points are there about you? There is nothing left for you but to burst, if you want to be stared at."

(5) H 240
One of Apollonius' Witticisms at Domitian's Expense.
Philostratus, *Life of Apollonius* 6,42. Loeb 2,139-41.

The Emperor Domitian about the same time passed a law against making men eunuchs, and against planting fresh vineyards, and also in favour of cutting down vineyards already planted, whereon Apollonius, who was visiting the Ionians, remarked: "These rescripts do not concern me, for I, alone perhaps of mankind, require neither to beget my kind nor to drink wine; but our egregious sovereign seems not aware that he is sparing mankind, while he eunuchises the earth."

This witticism emboldened the Ionians to send a deputation to the Emperor in behalf of their vines, and ask for a repeal of the law which ordered the earth to be laid waste and not planted.

(6) H 241
How Apollonius Challenged a Local Governor Who was Made
Nervous by Apollonius' Opposition to the Emperor.
Philostratus, *Life of Apollonius* 7,5. Loeb 2,157.

And on an occasion when a tragic actor visited Ephesus and
came forward in the play called the *Ino*, and when the governor
of Asia was one of the audience, a man who though still young
and of distinguished rank among the consuls, was nevertheless
very nervous about such matters, just as the actor finished the
speech in which Euripides describes in his Iambics how tyrants
after long growth of their power are destroyed by little causes,
Apollonius leapt up and said: "But yonder coward understands
neither Euripides nor myself."

(7) H 242
An Example of the Way in Which Apollonius Criticized
Domitian.
Philostratus, *Life of Apollonius* 7,24. Loeb 2,217.

[Apollonius is in prison awaiting trial and the prisoners
are discussing how they came to be there.]

Another man came and said that he was being prosecuted
because at a public sacrifice in Tarentum, where he held office,
he had omitted to mention in the public prayers that Domitian
was the son of Athene. Said Apollonius: "You imagined that
Athene could not possibly have a son, because she is a virgin for
ever and ever; but you forgot, methinks, that this goddess once
on a time bore a dragon to the Athenians."

H 243
How Gorgias answered Chaerophon.
Philostratus, *Lives of the Sophists* 1. Loeb, 11.

There was at Athens a certain Chaerophon, not the one who
used to be nicknamed "Boxwood" in Comedy, because he suffered from anaemia due to hard study, but the one I now speak
of had insolent manners and made scurrilous jokes; he rallied
Gorgias for his ambitious efforts, and said: "Gorgias, why is it
that beans blow out my stomach, but do not blow up the fire [aid
the intelligence]?"
But he was not at all disconcerted by the question and replied: "This I leave for you to investigate; but here is a fact
which I have long known, that the earth grows canes [for steal-
ing fire like Prometheus, and for beating] for such as you."

H 244
The Remarks of Leon of Byzantium.
Philostratus, *Lives of the Sophists* 1,2. Loeb, 13-15.

Leon of Byzantium was in his youth a pupil of Plato, but when he reached man's estate he was called a sophist because he employed so many different styles of oratory, and also because his repartees were so convincing.

a) For example, when Philip brought an army against Byzantium, Leon went out to meet him and said: "Tell me, Philip, what moved you to begin war on us?"

And when he replied: "Your birthplace, the fairest of cities, lured me on to love her, and that is why I have come to my charmer's door," Leon retorted: "They come not with swords to the beloved's door who are worthy of requited love. For lovers need not the instruments of war but of music."

And Byzantium was freed, after Demosthenes had delivered many speeches to the Athenians on her behalf, while Leon had said but these few words to Philip himself.

b) When this Leon came on an embassy to Athens, the city had long been disturbed by factions and was being governed in defiance of established customs. When he came before the assembly, he excited universal laughter since he was fat and had a prominent paunch, but he was not at all embarrassed by the laughter. "Why," said he, "do you laugh, Athenians? Is it because I am so stout and so big? I have a wife at home who is much stouter than I, and when we agree, the bed is large enough for us both, but when we quarrel not even the house is large enough."

Thereupon the citizens of Athens came to a friendly agreement, thus reconciled by Leon, who had so cleverly improvised to meet the occasion.[1]

> [1] The Loeb translator, W. Wright, notes that the same story is told about Python by Leon himself (Athenaeus 12,550). (His reference to a similar story in Diogenes Laertius' *Life of Arcesilaus* is not apposite. *Lives* 4,37.) This is a good illustration of a "floating anecdote." There is an example of such an anecdote in R 167-R 169. See as well the discussion in the Introduction.

H 245
Some of Nicetes of Smyrna's Expressions.
Philostratus, *Lives of the Sophists* 1,19. Loeb, 65.

a) Though he was deemed worthy of the highest honour in

Smyrna, which left nothing unsaid in its loud praise of him as a marvellous man and a great orator, he seldom came forward to speak in the public assembly; and when the crowd accused him of being afraid: "I am more afraid," said he, "of the public when they praise than when they abuse me."

b) And once when a tax-collector behaved insolently to him in the law court, and said: "Stop barking at me," Nicetes replied with ready wit: "I will, by Zeus, if you too will stop biting me."

H 246
Some Remarks of Isaeus the Assyrian.
Philostratus, *Lives of the Sophists* 1,20. Loeb, 69.

a) When Dionysius of Miletus, who had been his pupil, delivered his declamations in a sing-song, Isaeus rebuked him, saying: "Young man from Ionia, I did not train you to sing."

b) And when a youth from Ionia admired in his presence the grandiloquent saying of Nicetes in his *Xerxes*, "Let us fasten Aegina to the king's ship," Isaeus burst into a loud laugh and said: "Madman, how will you put to sea?"

H 247
Polemo's Insolent Remark to Asclepius.
Philostratus, *Lives of the Sophists* 1,25. Loeb, 117.

Again, when he came to Pergamon suffering from a disease of the joints, he slept in the temple, and when Asclepius appeared to him and told him to abstain from drinking anything cold, "My good sir," said Polemo, "but what if you were doctoring a cow?"

H 248
The Emperor Nerva's Replies to Atticus Who Reported Finding a Treasure.
Philostratus, *Lives of the Sophists* 2,1. Loeb, 141-43.

His [Hipparchus'] son Atticus, however, the father of Herodes, was not overlooked by Fortune after he had lost his wealth and became poor, but she revealed to him a prodigious treasure in one of the houses which he had acquired near the theatre. And since, on account of its vastness, it made him cautious rather than overjoyed, he wrote the following letter to the Emperor:
"O Emperor, I have found a treasure in my own house. What commands do you give about it?"

To which the Emperor (Nerva at that time was on the throne) replied: "Use what you have found."

But Atticus did not abandon his caution and wrote that the extent of the treasure was beyond his station.

"Then misuse your windfall," replied the Emperor, "for yours it is."

H 249
Some Stories about Antiochus of Aegae.
Philostratus, *Lives of the Sophists* 2,4. Loeb, 185-89.

a) When Antiochus was accused of cowardice in not appearing to speak before the assembly and taking no part in public business, he said: "It is not you but myself that I fear." No doubt that was because he knew that he had a bitter and violent temper, and that he could not control it . . . .

b) He used to spend very many nights in the temple of Asclepius, both on account of the dreams that he had there, and also on account of all the intercourse there is between those who are awake and converse with one another, for in his case the god used to converse with him while awake, and held it to be a triumph of his healing art to ward off disease from Antiochus . . . .

c) The other theme is as follows. A tyrant abdicates on condition of immunity for himself. He is slain by one whom he has caused to be made a eunuch, and the latter is on his defence for the murder. In this case Antiochus refuted the strongest point made by the prosecution when they quoted the compact between the people and the tyrant; and threw in an ingenious argument while he set forth the eunuch's personal grievance: "With whom, pray," cried he, "did he make this agreement? With children, weak women, boys, old men, and men. But there is no description of me in that contract."

H 250
How Philostratus of Lemnos Rebuked Aelian.
Philostratus, *Lives of the Sophists* 2,31. Loeb, 305.

Philostratus of Lemnos once met him when he was holding a book in his hands and reading it aloud in an indignant and emphatic voice, and he asked him what he was studying. He replied: "I have composed an indictment of Gynnis ["womanish man" = Heliogabalus], for by that name I call the tyrant who has just been put to death, because by every sort of wanton wickedness he disgraced the Roman Empire." On which Philostratus retorted: "I should admire you for it, if you had indicted him while he was alive." For he said that while it takes a real man to try to curb a living tyrant, anyone can trample on him when he is down.

H 251
Some Examples of the Wit of Demonax.
Lucian, *Demonax* 12,14,16,20,27,28,31,39,48,55,62. Loeb 1,151-71.

a) I should like to cite a few of his well-directed and witty remarks, and may as well begin with Favorinus and what he said to him.

When Favorinus was told by someone that Demonax was making fun of his lectures and particularly of the laxity of their rhythm, saying that it was vulgar and effeminate and not by any means appropriate to philosophy, he went to Demonax and asked him: "Who are you to scoff at my compositions?"

"A man with an ear that is not easy to cheat," said he.

The sophist kept at him and asked: "What qualifications had you, Demonax, to leave school and commence philosophy?"

"Those you lack," he retorted . . . .

b) When the Sidonian sophist was once showing his powers at Athens, and was voicing his own praise to the effect that he was acquainted with all philosophy—but I may as well cite his very words: "If Aristotle calls me to the Lyceum, I shall go with him; if Plato calls me to the Academy, I shall come; if Zeno calls, I shall spend my time in the Stoa; if Pythagoras calls, I shall hold my tongue." Well, Demonax arose in the midst of the audience and said: "Ho (addressing him by name), Pythagoras is calling you!" . . . .

c) When an athlete, whom he had ridiculed for letting himself be seen in gay clothes although he was an Olympic champion, struck him on the head with a stone and drew blood, each of the bystanders was as angry as if he himself had been struck, and they shouted, "Go to the proconsul!"

But Demonax said, "No! not to the proconsul—for the doctor!" . . . .

d) When a man asked him what he thought was the definition of happiness, he replied that none but a free man is happy; and when the other said that free men were numerous, he rejoined: "But I have in mind the man who neither hopes nor fears anything."

"But how can one achieve this? For the most part, we are all slaves of hope and fear."

"Why, if you observe human affairs you will find that they do not afford justification either for hope or for fear since, whatever you may say, pains and pleasures are alike destined to end." . . . .

e) When one of his friends said: "Demonax, let's go to the Aesculapium and pray for my son," he replied: "You must think Aesculapius very deaf, that he can't hear our prayers from where we are."

f) On seeing two philosophers very ignorantly debating a given subject, one asking silly questions and the other giving answers that were not at all to the point, he said: "Doesn't it seem to you, friends, that one of these fellows is milking a he-goat and the other is holding a sieve for him!" . . . .

g) When he saw Apollonius the philosopher leaving the city with a multitude of disciples (he was called away to be tutor to the emperor), Demonax remarked: "There goes Apollonius and his Argonauts!" . . . .

h) Moreover, when questions were unanswerable, he always had an apt retort ready. When a man asked him banteringly: "If I should burn a thousand pounds of wood, Demonax, how many pounds of smoke would it make?" he replied: "Weigh the ashes: all the rest will be smoke." . . . .

i) Above all, he made war on those who cultivate philosophy in the spirit of vainglory and not in the spirit of truth. For example, on seeing a Cynic with cloak and wallet, but with a bar (*hyperon*) for a staff, who was making an uproar and saying that he was the follower of Antisthenes, Crates, and Diogenes, Demonax said: "Don't lie! You are really a disciple of Barson (Hyperides)!" . . . .

j) When Epictetus rebuked him and advised him to get married and have children, saying that a philosopher ought to leave nature a substitute when he is gone, his answer was very much to the point: "Then give me one of your daughters, Epictetus!" [Epictetus was not married.] . . . .

k) When he was once asked which of the philosophers he liked, he said: "They are all admirable, but for my part I revere Socrates, I wonder at Diogenes, and I love Aristippus."

STORIES ABOUT WONDERS WORKED BY GODS AND HEROES

H 252
Serapis Restores a Horse's Eye.
Aelian, *On Animals* 11,31. Loeb 2,397-99.

A cavalry officer of the name of Lenaeus owned a horse of fine appearance, very fleet of foot and of dauntless spirit; in displays it was good at running the course it had been taught; in war itself it was capable of endurance; and was quite excellent both in pursuit, when occasion arose, and in retreat, where necessity called for it. And in consequence of all this, the horse was a valued possession, and the owner was accounted most fortunate by his fellow cavalrymen. Now the horse, with the excellent qualities I have described, in consequence of a blow which it received in its right eye was incapacitated for seeing. Accordingly Lenaeus seeing all his hopes anchored upon the condition of his noble horse (the cavalry shield covered the left eye which alone could see), went to the temple of Serapis bringing a patient of a most unusual kind—his horse, and as though he were pleading for a brother or a son, implored the god for the horse's sake to have compassion on his suppliant, especially as it had done no wrong. For men, he said, may bring misfortune upon themselves either by some impious act or some blasphemous speech. "But what sacrilege," he exclaimed, "or what murder has a horse committed, and how and by what means has it blasphemed?" And he called the god to witness that he himself had never wronged any man, and for this reason he implored the god to relieve his comrade-in-arms and friend of its blindness.

And the god, although so mighty, did not neglect or scorn to heal the dumb beast, and therefore took pity both on the sick animal and on the man who besought him on its behalf, and prescribed a cure, not by fomenting the eye but by warming it with vapour baths at midday in the temple precinct.

So this was done and the eye of the horse was restored. And Lenaeus sacrificed thank-offerings and donations for its recovery, while the horse pranced and snorted and seemed larger and more beautiful and was full of joy, and speeding to the altar moved so proudly, and as it rolled in front of the steps was seen to be giving thanks with all its might to the god who had healed it.

H 253
Serapis Heals a Farmer Who Had Fallen into a State of
Madness Because He Had Cut a Sacred Asp in Half.
Aelian, *On Animals* 11,32. Loeb 2,401.

A husbandman was digging a trench in a vineyard in order to plant some fine, choice cutting, when he brought down his mattock upon a sacred Asp that had its lair below the soil and was far from hostile to men, and without knowing it cut the snake in half. And as he was breaking up the soil he caught sight of the tail involved in the sand, while the severed portion from the belly upwards to the neck was still crawling and covered with gore from the cut.

He was horror-struck, went out of his mind, and passed into a state of real madness of the most acute description. By day, he lost control of himself and of his reason; moreover, at night, he was in a state of frenzy, and would leap out of bed saying that the Asp was pursuing him, and as though he was on the point of being bitten would utter the most horrifying cries and shout for help. He would even say that he saw the form of the snake which he had slain, angrily threatening him; at times he avowed that he had been bitten, and it was evident from his groans that he was in pain.

So when his affliction had lasted for some time, his relations took him as a suppliant to the temple of Serapis and implored the god to remove and abolish the phantom of the aforesaid Asp.

Well, the god took pity on the man and cured him. But I have described how the Asp had not to wait for its revenge, and a very sufficient revenge, too.

H 254
Stories Relating How Serapis Used Animals to Cure Men.
Aelian, *On Animals* 11,34-35. Loeb 2,405-07.

a) One Cissus by name, a devoted servant of Serapis, was the victim of a plot on the part of a woman whom he had once loved and later married: he ate some eggs of a snake, which caused him pain; he was in a grievous state and in danger of death. But he prayed to the god, who bade him buy a live Moray and thrust his hand into the creature's tank. Cissus obeyed and thrust in his hand. And the Moray fastened on and clung to him, but when it was pulled off, it pulled away the sickness from the young man at the same time. It was because this Moray was a minister of the god's healing power that the tale reached my hearing.

b) And this same god in the days of Nero cured Chrysermus who was vomiting blood and already beginning to waste away, by means of a draught of bull's blood.

And I mention these facts because animals are so dearly beloved by the gods that their lives are saved by them, and when the gods desire, they save others.

c) It was this god (Serapis) who when Basilis the Cretan fell into a wasting disease, rid him of this terrible complaint by causing him to eat the flesh of an ass. And the result was in accordance with the name of the beast, for the god said that this treatment and remedy would be of ass-istance to him. On these topics enough has been said.

H 255
Serapis: Strabo Recounts the Wonders Worked at Canopus.
Strabo, *Geography* 17,1,17. Loeb 8,63-65.

Canobus is a city situated at a distance of one hundred and twenty stadia from Alexandria, if one goes on foot, and was named after Canobus, the pilot of Menelaus, who died there. It contains the temple of Serapis, which is honoured with great reverence and effects such cures that even the most reputable men believe in it and sleep in it—themselves on their own behalf or others for them. Some writers go on to record the cures, and others the virtues, of the oracles there.[1]

But to balance all this is the crowd of revelers who go down from Alexandria by the canal to the public festivals; for every day and every night is crowded with people on the boats who play the flute and dance without restraint and with extreme licentiousness, both men and women, and also with the people of Canobus itself, who have resorts situated close to the canal and adapted to relaxation and merry-making of this kind.

[1] Among the interesting variants at this point, we have *aretalogion*.

H 256
Isis: A Summary of her Benefactions.
Diodorus of Sicily, *The Library of History* 1,25. Loeb 1,81.

As for Isis, the Egyptians say that she was the discoverer of many health-giving drugs and was greatly versed in the science of healing; consequently, now that she has attained immortality, she finds her greatest delight in the healing of mankind and gives aid in their sleep to those who call upon her, plainly manifesting both her very presence and her beneficence towards men who ask her help. In proof of this, as they say, they advance not legends, as the Greeks do, but manifest facts; for practically the entire inhabited world is their witness, in that it eagerly contributes to the honours of Isis because she manifests herself in healings. For standing above the sick in their sleep, she gives them aid for their diseases and works remarkable cures upon such as submit themselves to her; and many who have been despaired of by their physicians because of the difficult nature of their malady are restored to health by her, while numbers who have altogether lost the use of their eyes or of some other part of their body, whenever they turn for help to this goddess, are restored to their previous condition.

H 257
Story of Alcestis Who Dies for Her Husband Admetus, But is Brought Back to Her Husband from Hades by Hercules.
Apollodorus, *The Library* 1,9,15. Loeb 1,91-93.

When Admetus reigned over Pherae, Apollo served him as his thrall, while Admetus wooed Alcestis, daughter of Pelias. Now Pelias had promised to give his daughter to him who should yoke a lion and a boar to a car, and Apollo yoked and gave them to Admetus, who brought them to Pelias and so obtained Alcestis. But in offering a sacrifice at his marriage, he forgot to sacrifice to Artemis; therefore when he opened the marriage chamber, he found it full of coiled snakes. Apollo bade him appease the goddess and obtained as a favour of the Fates that, when Admetus should be about to die, he might be released from death if someone should choose voluntarily to die for him. And when the day of his death came, neither his father nor his mother would die for him, but Alcestis died in his stead.

But the Maiden [Persephone] sent her up again, or, as some say, Hercules fought with Hades and brought her up to him.[1]

---

[1] There is an allusion to this incident in H 215.

H 258
The Bacchanals Imprisoned by Pentheus, King of Thebes, are
Miraculously Freed by Dionysus.
Euripides, *Bacchanals* 443-50. Loeb 3,37.

[Pentheus' servant reports the event.]

The captured Bacchanals you did put in ward,
And in the common prison bind with chains,
Fled to the meadows are they; loosed from bonds,
And dance and call on Bromius the God.
The fetters from their feet self-sundered fell;
Doors, without mortal hand, unbarred themselves.
Yes, fraught with many marvels this man came
To Thebes! To you the rest does appertain.

H 259
A Report of How Wine is Obtained on the Festival of
Dionysus.
Pausanias, *Description of Greece* 6,26,1.[1] Loeb 3,157-59.

Between the market-place and the Menius is an old theatre
and a shrine of Dionysus. The image is the work of Praxiteles.
Of the gods the Eleans worship Dionysus with the greatest reverence, and they assert that the god attends their festival, the
Thyia.

The place where they hold the festival they name the Thyia
is about eight stades from the city. Three pots are brought into
the building by the priests and set down empty in the presence
of the citizens and of any strangers who may chance to be in the
country. The doors of the building are sealed by the priests
themselves and by any others who may be so inclined. On the
morrow, they are allowed to examine the pots filled with wine.

I did not myself arrive at the time of the festival, but the
most respected Elean citizens, and with them strangers also,
swore that what I have said is the truth. The Andrians too assert
that every other year at their feast of Dionysus wine flows of its
own accord from the sanctuary.

If the Greeks are to be believed in these matters, one might
with equal reason accept what the Aethiopians above Syene say
about the table of the sun.

[1] It was common to adduce this story as a parallel to John
2:1-11.

H 260
A Summary of the Benefactions of Hemithea.
Diodorus of Sicily, *The Library of History* 5,63. Loeb 3,267-69.

[Diodorus is explaining the reason why the temple of Hemithea is held in such great honor.]

And the reason which men advance for its continued development is the benefactions which the goddess confers upon all mankind alike; for she appears in visible shape in their sleep to those who are in suffering and gives them healing, and many who are in the grip of diseases for which no remedy is known are restored to health; furthermore, to women who are suffering in childbirth the goddess gives relief from the agony and perils of travail.

Consequently, since many have been saved in these ways from most ancient times, the sacred precinct is filled with votive offerings, nor are these protected by guards or by a strong wall, but by the habitual reverence of the people.

H 261
The Mother of the Gods Provides for the Healing of a Lame Man.
Aristophanes, *Metragyrtes* fr. 154 (Kock, *Comicorum Att. Frag.* 2,74).

. . . [She] commanded the girl to take ointment [*aleimmata*] from the goddess and to anoint first the feet and then the knees. As soon as the girl touched his feet and rubbed them, he got up on his feet.

H 262
Titus Latinius is Punished by Jupiter for not Having Delivered His Message, and is Then Healed.
Livy, *From the Founding of the City* 2,36. Loeb 1,337-39.

It so happened that at Rome preparations were making to repeat the Great Games. The reason of the repetition was as follows: at an early hour of the day appointed for the games, before the show had begun, a certain householder had driven his slave, bearing a yoke, through the midst of the circus, scourging the culprit as he went. The games had then begun, as though this circumstance had in no way affected their sanctity.

Not long after, Titus Latinius, a plebeian, had a dream. He dreamt that Jupiter said that the leading dancer at the games had not been to his liking; that unless there were a sumptuous repetition of the festival the City would be in danger; that Latinius was to go and announce this to the consuls.

Though the man's conscience was by no means at ease, nevertheless the awe he felt at the majesty of the magistrates was too great; he was afraid of becoming a laughing-stock. Heavy was the price he paid for his hesitation, for a few days later he lost his son.

Lest this sudden calamity should leave any uncertainty as to its cause in the mind of the wretched man, the same phantom appeared again before him in his dreams, and asked him, as he thought, whether he had been sufficiently repaid for spurning the gods; for a greater recompense was at hand unless he went quickly and informed the consuls. This brought the matter nearer home.

Yet he still delayed and put off going, till a violent attack of illness suddenly laid him low. Then at last the anger of the gods taught him wisdom. And so, worn out with his sufferings, past and present, he called a council of his kinsmen and explained to them what he had seen and heard, how Jupiter had so often confronted him in his sleep, and how the threats and anger of the god had been instantly fulfilled in his own misfortunes.

Then, with the unhesitating approval of all who were present, he was carried on a litter to the consuls in the Forum; and thence, by their command, to the Curia, where he had no sooner told the same story to the Fathers, greatly to the wonder of them all, when—lo, another miracle! For it is related that he who had been carried into the senate-house afflicted in all his members, returned home, after discharging his duty, on his own feet.

H 263
How Hector was Restored by Apollo.
Homer, *The Iliad* 15,240-62. Loeb 2,125-27.

> [Hector is wounded by the stone of Aias; Zeus sends Apollo to help him.]

And Apollo, who works from afar, came near him, and said: "Hector, son of Priam, why is it that you, apart from the rest, abide here fainting? Is it haply that some trouble has come upon you?"

Then, his strength all spent, Hector of the flashing helm spoke to him: "Who of the gods are you, mightiest one, that questions me face to face? Do you not know that at the sterns of the Achaeans' ships, as I made havoc of his comrades, Aias, good at the war-cry, smote me on the breast with a stone, and made me cease from my furious might? Yes, and I deemed that on this day I should behold the dead and the house of Hades, when I had gasped forth my life."

Then the lord Apollo, who works from afar, spoke to him again: "Be now of good cheer, so mighty a helper has the son of Cronos sent forth from Ida to stand by your side and succour you, even me, Phoebus Apollo of the golden sword, who of old ever protects you, yourself as well as the steep citadel. But come now, bid your many charioteers drive against the hollow ships their swift horses, and I will go before and make smooth all the way for the chariots, and will turn in flight the Achaean warriors."

So saying, he breathed great might into the shepherd of the host.

H 264
How Machaon, Son of Asclepius, Heals Menelaus.
Homer, *The Iliad* 4,193-219. Loeb 1,167-69.

[The two sons of Asclepius have already been described to us as warriors (2,731-32); now Agamemnon sends the messenger to get Machaon to tend to Menelaus who has been wounded in the thigh by an arrow.]

Therewith he [Agamemnon] spoke to Talthybius, the godlike herald: "Talthybius, make haste to call hither Machaon, son of Asclepius, the peerless leech [*iētēros*], to see warlike Menelaus, son of Atreus, whom some man well skilled in archery has smitten with an arrow, some Trojan or Lycian, compassing glory for himself but for us sorrow."

So spake he, and the herald failed not to hearken, as he heard, but went his way throughout the host of the brazen-coated Achaeans, glancing this way and that for the warrior Machaon; and he marked him as he stood, and round about him were the stalwart ranks of the shield-bearing hosts that followed him from Trica, the pastureland of horses. And he came up to him, and spoke winged words, saying: "Rouse yourself, son of Asclepius; lord Agamemnon calls you to see warlike Menelaus, captain of the Achaeans, whom some man, well skilled in archery, has smitten with an arrow, some Trojan or Lycian, compassing glory for himself but for us sorrow."

So spoke he, and roused the heart in his breast, and they went their way in the throng throughout the broad host of the Achaeans.

And when they were come where was fair-haired Menelaus, wounded, and around him were gathered in a circle all they that were chieftains, the godlike hero came and stood in their midst, and straightway drew forth the arrow from the clasped belt; and as it was drawn forth the sharp barbs were broken backwards. And he loosed the flashing belt and the kilt beneath and the taslet that the coppersmiths fashioned. But when he saw the wound where the bitter arrow had lighted, he sucked out the blood, and with sure knowledge spread thereon soothing simples, which of old Cheiron had given to his father with kindly thought.

Various Testimonies to the Healing Power of Asclepius

A) H 265
Testimony of Asclepius' Healing Activity in Epidaurus, Cos and Tricca.
Strabo, *Geography* 8,6,15. Edelstein, #382.

And this city [Epidaurus] is not without distinction, and particularly because of the epiphany of Asclepius, who is believed to cure diseases of every kind and always has his temple full of the sick, and also of the votive tablets on which the treatments are recorded, just as at Cos and Tricca.

B) H 266
Testimony to Asclepius' Healing Activity Recorded on Votive Tablets.
Pausanias, *Description of Greece* 2,27,3. Edelstein, #384.

Tablets stood within the enclosure. Of old, there were more of them: in my time six were left. On these tablets are engraved the names of men and women who were healed by Asclepius, together with the disease from which each suffered, and how he was cured. The inscriptions are in the Doric dialect.

C) H 267
A Summary of Asclepius' Benefactions.
Aristides, *Speech on Asclepius, Orat.* 42,4.10-11. Edelstein, #317.

Asclepius has great and many powers, or rather he has every power, and not alone that which concerns human life. And it is not by chance that the people here [Pergamum] have built a temple of Zeus Asclepius . . . .

Now I have heard some people saying that, when they were at sea and in the midst of a storm, the god appeared to them and stretched forth his hand; others again will tell how they settled their affairs following the advice of the god. Even these things we know not from hearsay, but we can talk about them from our own experience; and whichever of these incidents are worth re-membering, these, too, are contained in the *Sacred Speeches*. But it is said that the god revealed even boxing tricks to one of our contemporary boxers while he was asleep, by the use of which it is no wonder that he knocked out one of his outstand-ing competitors. To us, however, he has revealed knowledge and melodies and the subjects of speeches and in addition the ideas themselves and even the wording, just like those who teach children to read and write. Having reached, then, the cli-max, as it were, of the god's benefits, I shall conclude the dis-course here.

D) H 268
A Summary Account of the Healing Career of Asclepius and His Punishment for Excessive Success.
Diodorus of Sicily, *The Library of History* 4,71. Loeb 3,43-45.

Now that we have examined these matters we shall endeavor to set forth the facts concerning Asclepius and his descendants. This, then, is what the myths relate:

Asclepius was the son of Apollo and Coronis, and since he excelled in natural ability and sagacity of mind, he devoted him-self to the science of healing and made many discoveries which contribute to the health of mankind. And so far did he advance along the road of fame that, to the amazement of all, he healed many sick whose lives had been despaired of, and for this reason it was believed that he had brought back to life many who had died.

Consequently, the myth goes on to say, Hades brought accu-sation against Asclepius, charging him before Zeus of acting to the detriment of his own province, for, he said, the number of the dead was steadily diminishing, now that men were being healed by Asclepius. So Zeus, in indignation, slew Asclepius with his thunderbolt, but Apollo, indignant at the slaying of As-clepius, murdered the Cyclopes who had forged the thunder-bolt for Zeus; but at the death of the Cyclopes Zeus was again indignant and laid a command upon Apollo that he should serve as a labourer for a human being and that this should be the punishment he should receive from him for his crimes.

To Asclepius, we are told further, sons were born, Machaon and Podaleirius, who also developed the healing art and accompanied Agamemnon in the expedition against Troy. Throughout the course of the war they were of great service to the Greeks, healing most skilfully the wounded, and because of these benefactions they attained to great fame among the Greeks; furthermore, they were granted exemption from the perils of battles and from the other obligations of citizenship, because of the very great service which they offered by their healing.

Now as regards Asclepius and his sons we shall be satisfied with what has been said.

H 269
Asclepius Heals Phalysius of His Blindness.
Pausanias, *Description of Greece* 10,38,13. Edelstein, #444.

The sanctuary of Asclepius [at Naupactus] was . . . originally built by a private person called Phalysius. For he had a complaint of the eyes, and when he was almost blind the god at Epidaurus sent to him the poetess Anyte [ca. 300 B.C.], who brought with her a sealed tablet. This appeared to the woman as the vision of a dream, but it proved at once to be a waking reality. For she found in her own hands a sealed tablet; so sailing to Naupactus she bade Phalysius take away the seal and read what was written.

He did not think it possible under other circumstances to read the writing with his eyes in such a condition, but hoping to get some benefit from Asclepius he took away the seal, and when he looked at the wax he was sound, and gave to Anyte what was written on the tablet, two thousand staters of gold.

H 270
How Asclepius Renders Neocleides Blind and Cures Wealth.
Aristophanes, *Plutus*, lines 707-47. Loeb 3,429-31.

[Cario tells his wife what he saw when he and "Wealth" went to spend the night in the Asclepion.]

Cario — So then, alarmed, I muffled up my head,
    While *he* went round, with calm and quiet tread,
    To every patient, scanning each disease.
    Then by his side a servant placed a stone
    Pestle and mortar, and a medicine chest.
Wife — A stone one?
Cario — Hang it, not the medicine chest.
Wife — How saw you this, you villain, when your head,
    You said just now, was muffled?
Cario — Through my cloak.
    Full many a peep-hole has that cloak, I trow.
    Well, first he set himself to mix a plaster
    For Neocleides, throwing in three cloves
    Of Tenian garlic; and with these he mingled
    Verjuice and squills; and brayed them up together
    Then drenched the mass with Sphettian vinegar,
    And turning up the eyelids of the man
    Plastered their inner sides, to make the smart
    More painful. Up he springs with yells and roars
    In act to flee; then laughed the God, and said,
    "Nay, sit there, beplastered; I'll restrain you,
    You reckless swearer, from the Assembly now."
Wife — O what a clever, patriotic god [*daimon*]!
Cario — Then, after this, he sat him down by Wealth,
    And first he felt the patient's head, and next
    Taking a linen napkin, clean and white
    Wiped both his lids, and all around them, dry.
    Then Panacea with a scarlet cloth
    Covered his face and head; then the god clucked,
    And out there issued from the holy shrine
    Two great enormous serpents.
Wife — O good heavens!
Cario — And underneath the scarlet cloth they crept
    And licked his eyelids, as it seemed to me;
    And, mistress dear, before you could have drunk
    Of wine ten goblets, Wealth arose and saw.
    O then for joy I clapped my hands together
    And woke my master, and, hey presto! both
    The god and serpents vanished in the shrine.
    And those who lay by Wealth, imagine how
    They blessed and greeted him, nor closed their eyes
    Whole night long till daylight did appear.

And I could never praise the god enough
For both his deeds, enabling Wealth to see,
And making Neocleides still more blind.
Wife   —   O lord and king, what mighty power is thine!

Four Healings from an Inscription in the Tiber

(1) H 271
Gaius is Cured of His Blindness.
Inscription from the island in the Tiber. *IG* 14,966. Edelstein,
#438.

In those days he [the god] revealed to Gaius, a blind man,
that he should go to the holy base [of the statue] [*bēma*] and
there should prostrate himself; then go from the right to the left
and place his five fingers on the base and raise his hand and lay
it on his own eyes. And he could see again clearly [*orthon
aneblepse*] while the people stood by and rejoiced that glorious
deeds [*aretai*] lived again under our Emperor Antoninus.[1]

[1] Motif: Acclamation. Mark 1:27/Luke 4:36; Mark 2:12/
Luke 5:26, etc.

(2) H 272
Lucius Suffering From Pleurisy.
Inscription from the island in the Tiber. *IG* 14,966. Edelstein,
#438.

To Lucius who suffered from pleurisy and had been despaired of by all men the god revealed that he should go and
from the threefold altar lift ashes and mix them thoroughly with
wine and lay them on his side. And he was saved and publicly
offered thanks to the god, and the people rejoiced with him.

(3) H 273
Julian Spitting Blood.
Inscription from the island in the Tiber. *IG* 14,966. Edelstein,
#438.

To Julian who was spitting up blood and had been despaired
of by all men the god revealed that he should go and from the
threefold altar take the seeds of a pine cone and eat them with
honey for three days. And he was saved [*esōthē*] and went and
publicly offered thanks [*eucharistēsen*] before the people.

(4) H 274

Valerius Aper is Cured of His Blindness.
Inscription from the island in the Tiber. *IG* 14,966. Edelstein, #438.

To Valerius Aper, a blind soldier, the god revealed that he should go and take the blood of a white cock along with honey and compound an eye salve [*kollyrion*], and for three days should anoint it upon his eyes [*epichreisai epi tous ophthalmous*].[1]

And he could see again [*aneblepsen*] and went and publicly offered thanks [*ēucharistēsen*] to the god.

[1] Motif: John 9:6; Rev 3:18.

Inscriptions from Lebena

(1) H 275

Asclepius Cures Poplius Granius Rufus of a Bloody Cough.
Inscription from Lebena. *Inscr. Creticae* 1,17,17. Edelstein, #439.

To Asclepius
Poplius Granius Rufus
according to command.

When for two years I had coughed incessantly so that I discharged purulent and bloody pieces of flesh all day long, the god took in hand to cure me . . . .

He gave me rocket to nibble on an empty stomach, then Italian wine flavored with pepper to drink, then again starch with hot water, then powder of the holy ashes and some holy water, then an egg and pine-resin, then again moist pitch, then iris with honey, then a quince and a wild purslane to be boiled together—the fluid to be drunk, while the quince was to be eaten—then to eat a fig with holy ashes taken from the altar where they sacrifice to the god.[1]—

> [1] Though the part of the inscription remaining to us does not speak explicitly of a cure, we may presume that this is the reason for the inscription, especially since it is being erected "according to command." The phrase is typical of this group of inscriptions.

(2) H 276
A Woman is Healed from Pain in her Finger.
Inscription from Lebena. *Inscr. Creticae* 1,17,19. Edelstein,
#441.

. . . [A certain woman] . . . at the head and . . . gives thanks to
Asclepius the Savior; having suffered from a malignant sore on
her little finger she was healed by the god who ordered her to
apply the shell of an oyster, burnt and ground down by her with
rose-ointment, and to anoint [her finger] with mallow, mixed
with olive oil. And thus he cured her. After I had seen many
more glorious deeds of the god in my sleep the god ordered me
to inscribe my visions . . . in my sleep the god ordered . . . .

Inscriptions from Epidaurus

(1) H 277
Cleo is Delivered After a Five-Year Pregnancy.
Epidaurus Inscr. *IG* IV^2,1,121. Edelstein #423,1.

Cleo was with child for five years.
After she had been pregnant for five years she came as a suppliant to the god and slept in the Abaton.
As soon as she left it and got outside the temple precincts she
bore a son who, immediately after birth, washed himself at the
fountain and walked about with his mother.
In return for this favor she inscribed on her offering: "Admirable is not the greatness of the tablet, but the divinity in that
Cleo carried the burden in her womb for five years until she
slept in the Temple and he made her sound."

(2) H 278
Ithmonice is Taught to Pray for a Delivery.
Epidaurus Inscr. *IG* IV^2,1,121. Edelstein #423,2.

A three-years' pregnancy.
Ithmonice of Pellene came to the Temple for offspring.
When she had fallen asleep she saw a vision. It seemed to her
that she asked the god that she might get pregnant with a
daughter and that Asclepius said that she would be pregnant
and that if she asked for something else he would grant her that
too, but that she answered she did not need anything else.
When she had become pregnant she carried in her womb for
three years, until she approached the god as a suppliant concerning the birth. When she had fallen asleep she saw a vision.
It seemed to her that the god asked her if she had not obtained
all she had asked for and was pregnant; about the birth she had

added nothing, and that, although he had asked if she needed anything else, she should say so and he would grant her this too. But since now she had come for this as a suppliant to him, he said he would accord even it to her.

After that, she hastened to leave the Abaton, and when she was outside the sacred precincts she gave birth to a girl.

(3) H 279
Ambrosia is Healed of Her Blindness and Her Unbelief.
Epidaurus Inscr. *IG* IV^2,1,121. Edelstein #423,4.

Ambrosia of Athens, blind of one eye.
She came as a suppliant to the god.
As she walked about in the Temple she laughed at some of the cures [recorded there] as incredible and impossible, that the lame and blind should be healed by merely seeing a dream. In her sleep she had a vision. It seemed to her that the god stood by her and said he would cure her, but that in payment he would ask her to dedicate to the Temple a silver pig as a memorial of her ignorance. After saying this, he cut the diseased eyeball and poured in some drug.
When day came she walked out sound.

(4) H 280
A Voiceless Boy is Cured.
Epidaurus Inscr. *IG* IV^2,1,121. Edelstein #423,5.

A voiceless boy.
He came as a suppliant to the Temple for his voice.
When he had performed the preliminary sacrifices and fulfilled the usual rites, thereupon the temple servant who brings in the fire for the god, looking at the boy's father, demanded he should promise to bring within a year the thank-offering for the cure if he obtained that for which he had come.
But the boy suddenly said, "I promise."
His father was startled at this and asked him to repeat it. The boy repeated the words and after that became well.

(5) H 281
Pandarus is Healed of Marks on His Forehead.
Epidaurus Inscr. *IG* IV^2,1,121. Edelstein #423,6.

Pandarus, a Thessalian, who had marks on his forehead.
He saw a vision as he slept. It seemed to him that the god bound the marks round with a headband and enjoined him to

remove the band when he left the Abaton and dedicate it as an offering to the Temple.

When day came he got up and took off the band and saw his face free of the marks; and he dedicated to the Temple the band with the signs which had been on his forehead.

(6) H 282
Echedorus Receives the Marks of Pandarus for Failing to Offer Pandarus' Money to the God at Epidaurus.
Epidaurus Inscr. *IG* IV^2,1,121. Edelstein #423,7.

Echedorus received the marks of Pandarus in addition to those which he already had. He had received money from Pandarus to offer to the god at Epidaurus in his name, but he failed to deliver it.

In his sleep he saw a vision. It seemed to him that the god stood by him and asked if he had received any money from Pandarus to set up as an offering to Athena in the Temple. He answered that he had received no such thing from him, but if he [the god] would make him well he would have an image painted and offer it to him [the god]. Thereupon the god seemed to fasten the headband of Pandarus round his marks, and ordered him upon leaving the Abaton to take off the band and to wash his face at the fountain and to look at himself in the water. When day came he left the Abaton, took off the headband, on which the signs were no longer visible. But when he looked into the water he saw his face with his own marks and the signs of Pandarus in addition.

(7) H 283
Euphanes, a Boy of Epidaurus, is Healed of Stone.
Epidaurus Insc. *IG* IV^2,1,121. Edelstein #423,8.

Euphanes, a boy from Epidaurus.

Suffering from stone he slept in the Temple. It seemed to him that the god stood by him and asked: "What will you give me if I cure you?"

"Ten dice," he answered.

The god laughed and said to him that he would cure him. When day came he went out sound.

(8) H 284
Hermodicus, a Paralyzed Man, is Healed.
Epidaurus Inscr. *IG* IV^2,1,121. Edelstein #423,15.

Hermodicus of Lampsacus was paralyzed in body.

This one, when he slept in the Temple, the god healed and he ordered him upon coming out to bring to the Temple as large a stone as he could.

The man brought the stone which now lies before the Abaton.

(9) H 285
Alcetas is Healed of His Blindness.
Epidaurus Inscr. *IG* IV^2,1,121. Edelstein #423,18.

Alcetas of Haliesis.

This blind man saw a dream. It seemed to him that the god came up to him and with his fingers opened his eyes, and that he first saw trees in the sanctuary. At daybreak he walked out sound.

(10) H 286
Lyson of Hermione, a Blind Boy, is Healed at Epidaurus.
Epidaurus Inscr. *IG* IV^2,1,121. Edelstein #423,20.

Lyson of Hermione, a blind boy.

While wide-awake he had his eyes cured by one of the dogs in the Temple and went away healed.

(11) H 287
Hermon of Thasos is Cured of His Blindness Twice.
Epidaurus Inscr. *IG* IV^2,1,122. Edelstein #423,22.

Hermon of Thasos.

His blindness was cured by Asclepius.

But, since afterwards he did not bring the thank-offerings, the god made him blind again.

When he came back and slept again in the Temple, he made him well.

(12) H 288
Aristagora of Troezen is Cured of Her Tapeworm by Asclepius After His Sons Failed to Cure Her.
Epidaurus Inscr. *IG* IV^2,1,122 (compare Aelian, *On the Nature of Animals* 9,33). Edelstein #423,23.

Aristagora of Troezen.

She had a tapeworm in her belly, and she slept in the Temple of Asclepius at Troezen and saw a dream. It seemed to her that the sons of the god, while he was not present but away in Epidaurus, cut off her head, but, being unable to put it back again, they sent a messenger to Asclepius asking him to come.

Meanwhile day breaks and the priest clearly sees her head cut off from the body.

When night approached, Aristagora saw a vision. It seemed to her the god had come from Epidaurus and fastened her head onto her neck. Then he cut open her belly, took the tapeworm out, and stitched her up again.

And after that she became well.

(13) H 289
Sostrata, a Woman of Pherae, is Cured of Her Worms.
Epidaurus Inscr. *IG* IV^2,1,122. Edelstein #423,25.

Sostrata, a woman of Pherae, was pregnant with worms.

Being in a very bad way, she was carried into the Temple and slept there. But when she saw no distinct dream she let herself be carried back home. Then, however, near a place called Kornoi, a man of fine appearance seemed to come upon her and her companions. When he had learned from them about their bad luck, he asked them to set down on the ground the litter in which they were carrying Sostrata. Then he cut open her abdomen and took out a great quantity of worms—two washbasins full. After having stitched her belly up again and made the woman well, Asclepius revealed to her his presence and enjoined her to send thank-offerings for her treatment to Epidaurus.

(14) H 290
A Boy with a Growth on the Neck.
Epidaurus Inscr. *IG* IV^2,1,122. Edelstein #423,26.

A dog cured a boy from Aegina.

He had a growth on the neck. When he had come to the god, one of the sacred dogs healed him—while he was awake—with its tongue and made him well.

(15) H 291
A Lame Man is Cured at Epidaurus.
Epidaurus Inscr. *IG* IV^2,1,122. Edelstein #423,35.

. . . of Epidaurus, lame.

He came as a suppliant to the sanctuary on a stretcher. In his sleep he saw a vision. It seemed to him that the god broke his crutch and ordered him to go and get a ladder and to climb as high as possible up to the top of the sanctuary. The man tried it at first, then, however, lost his courage and rested up on the cornice; finally he gave up and climbed down the ladder little by little. Asclepius at first was angry about the deed, then he laughed at him because he was such a coward. He dared to carry it out after it had become daytime and walked out unhurt.

H 292
How a Man was First Punished Then Healed by Imouthes-Asclepius Whose Praises He Then Publishes.
Pap. Oxyr. 11,1381. Grenfell-Hunt 230-31.

> [The author relates how he had set to work to translate into Greek a book relating the marvels wrought by Asclepius, but how his "ardour was restrained by the greatness of the story" so that he delayed the writing three years. During this time, his mother was afflicted by "an ungodly quartan ague," and was finally healed "by simple remedies" as the god came to her in a dream.]

When I too afterwards was suddenly seized with a pain in my right side, I quickly hastened to the helper of the human race, and he, being again disposed to pity, listened to me, and displayed still more effectively his peculiar clemency, which, as I am intending to recount his terrible powers, I will substantiate.

It was night, when every living creature was asleep except those in pain, but divinity showed itself the more effectively; a violent fever burned me, and I was convulsed with loss of breath and coughing, owing to the pain proceeding from my side.

Heavy in the head with my troubles I was lapsing half-conscious into sleep, and my mother, as a mother would for her child (and she is by nature affectionate), being extremely grieved at my agonies was sitting without enjoying even a short period of slumber, when suddenly she perceived—it was no dream or sleep, for her eyes were open immovably, though not seeing clearly, for a divine and terrifying vision came to her, easily preventing her from observing the god himself or his servants, whichever it was. In any case there was someone whose height was more than human, clothed in shining raiment and carrying in his left hand a book, who after merely regarding me two or three times from head to foot disappeared.

When she had recovered herself, she tried, still trembling, to wake me, and finding that the fever had left me and that much sweat was pouring off me, did reverence to the manifestation of the god, and then wiped me and made me more collected.

When I spoke with her, she wished to declare the power of the god, but I anticipating her told her all myself; for everything that she saw in the vision appeared to me in dreams. After these pains in my side had ceased, and the god had given me yet another assuaging cure, I proclaimed his benefits.

But when we had again besought his favors by sacrifices to the best of our ability, he demanded through the priest who serves him in the ceremonies the fulfilment of the promise long ago announced to him, and we, although knowing ourselves to be debtors in neither sacrifices nor votive offering, nevertheless supplicated him again with them. But when he said repeatedly that he cared not for these but for what had been previously promised, I was at a loss, and with difficulty, since I disparaged it, felt the divine obligation of the composition.

> [The author then goes on to address a prayer to Asclepius, and then begins the prologue of his work. Very shortly thereafter the papyrus breaks off.]

H 293
Asclepius Heals a Cock.
Aelian, *Fragmenta* 98. Edelstein, #466.

The champion cock from Tanagra. These are celebrated as highbred animals. The cock, inspired by Asclepius, I think, goes to its lord hopping on one foot, and when the paean for Asclepius is sung at daybreak, it appears as one of the members of the god's chorus, and standing in line, as if taking its position at the command of a chorus-leader, it tried, as far as possible, with its bird's voice, to accompany the singing in harmony and in tune.

The cock, standing on one foot, stretched forth the mutilated and crippled one as if bearing witness to and disclosing what sort of things it suffered. The cock praised the savior with whatever voice it could muster and begged that it be made sound of foot.

And Asclepius accomplished what was demanded. Before evening, walking on both feet, flapping its wings and taking large strides, poking its neck forward and shaking its crest, like a majestic heavy-armed soldier, the bird demonstrated the consideration of the god towards animals.

The man from Aspendus sends it to be a votive offering and plaything for Asclepius, a bird to be, as it were, a servant and attendant, roaming about the temple.

H 294

How the Powerful Prayer of Proclus and Pericles Win Healing
for Asclepigenia from Asclepius.

Marinus, *The Life of Proclus* 29. Edelstein, #582.

When still a young maiden and under the care of her parents, Asclepigenia, the daughter of Archiades and Plutarche, . . .
was stricken with a grievous illness, which the physicians were
unable to cure.

Since Archiades rested all his hopes for his family line upon
her alone, he was grieved and greatly distressed, as was natural.
When the physicians despaired, he went, as his custom in criti-
cal situations, to the last resort, or rather as if to a noble savior,
to the philosopher [Proclus], and begged and entreated that he
too make haste to pray for the daughter.

And Proclus, taking along the great Pericles from Lydia, who
was also a truly wise man, went up to the Asclepieion to pray to
the god for the sick girl. For the city [Athens] still enjoyed the
god's presence at that time and still held the temple of the savior unravaged.

While he prayed in the more ancient fashion, all of a sudden
a change seemed to come over the maiden and all at once she
was eased of pain. For easily did the savior, inasmuch as he was
a god, heal her. When the sacrifices were fulfilled, he went to
Asclepigenia and found her now relieved of the suffering that
had gripped her, and in a healthy state.

SUBJECT INDEX*

* Any numbers not preceded by "OT," "R," or "H" indicate page numbers in the
Introduction.

REFERENCES TO NEW TESTAMENT TEXTS

LUKE

WORKS CITED

'ABOT, RABBI NATHAN
    8..R 88
AELIAN, CLAUDIUS (circa 170-235 A.D.)
    Fragmenta
        98...H 293
    On Animals
        11,31..H 252
        11,32..H 253
        11,34-35.....................................H 254
AELIUS OF SPARTA (circa 100-138 A.D.)
    Life of Hadrian
        20...H 194
        21...H 195
        25,1-4 ....H 190
APOLLODORUS OF ATHENS (b. circa 180 B.C.)
    The Library
        1,9,15 ....H 257
APOLLONIUS THE PARADOXOGRAPHER (2nd century B.C.)
    Wonderful Tales
        1 ....H 206
        6 ....H 199
APULEIUS (b. circa 123 A.D.)
    Florida
        19...H 211
ARISTIDES (approx. 117 or 129-181 A.D.)
    Speech on Asclepius
        Orat. 42,4.10-11 ....H 267
ARISTOPHANES OF ATHENS (circa 450-385 B.C.)
    Metragyrtes
        fr. 154 ....H 261
    Plutus
        707-47 ....H 270
ARRIAN (2nd century A.D.)
    The Anabasis of Alexander
        26,1 ....H 177
BIBLE
        Gen 12:10-20................................ OT 1
        Exod 2:15-22 .... OT 7

Exod 14:21-31 .... OT 11
Exod 15:22-25 .... OT 17
Exod 17:1-7 .... OT 22
Exod 17:8-16 .... OT 28
Exod 32:1-14 .... OT 32
Num 17:6-15 .... OT 40
Num 20:1-13 .... OT 25
Num 21:4-9 .... OT 36
1 Sam 7:5-11 .... OT 43
1 Kgs 17:8-16 .... OT 45
1 Kgs 17:17-24 .... OT 47
1 Kgs 19:21-22 .... OT 49
2 Kgs 2:19-22 .... OT 51
2 Kgs 4:1-7 .... OT 53
Wis 16:5-14 .... OT 38
Wis 18:20-25 .... OT 42

BOOK OF BIBLICAL ANTIQUITIES
10,2-6 .... OT 12
11,15 .... OT 19

CELSUS, AULUS CORNELIUS (fl. 14-37 A.D.)
On Medicine
2,6 .... H 210

DEREK EREȘ. RABBAH
57a .... R 70

DIO CASSIUS (2nd-3rd century A.D.)
Roman History
65,8 .... H 188

DIODORUS OF SICILY (1st century B.C.-1st century A.D.)
The Library of History
1,25 .... H 256
4,71 .... H 268
5,63 .... H 260
17,103,6-8 .... H 176

DIOGENES LAERTIUS (circa 3rd century A.D.)
Lives of Eminent Philosophers
6,25-28 .... H 234
6,32-35 .... H 235
8,58-61,72 .... H 205

EMPEDOCLES (circa 493-circa 433 B.C.)
On Nature, Fragment .... H 204

EURIPIDES (circa 485-circa 406 B.C.)
Bacchanals
443-50 .... H 258

LUCIAN (b. circa 120 A.D.)
   Alexander the False Prophet
      13-14,16-17 .... H 230
   Demonax
      12,14,16,20,27,28,31,39,48,55,62 .... H 251
   The Lover of Lies
      11... H 228
      16... H 229

MARINUS (5th century A.D.)
   Life of Proclus
      29... H 294

MIDRASH ON THE PSALMS
      2,11.. R 142

MIDRASH RABBAH
   Genesis
      25,1 .... R 141
      33,3 .... R 158
   Exodus
      3,12 .... R 136
      30,9 .... R 110
   Leviticus
      4,6 .... R 143
      8,1 .... R 137
      10,4 .... R 157
      34,3 .... R 64, R 65
   Numbers
      3,2 .... R 140
   Deuteronomy
      3,3 .... R 59
   Qoheleth
      1,1 .... R 91
      1,7 .... R 97, R 138
      5,10 .... R 145
      8,1 .... R 144
      9,4 .... R 109

MISHNAH
   Ta'anith
      3,8 .... R 72
   'Aboda Zara
      3,4 .... R 115
      4,7 .... R 111

OXYRHYNCHUS PAPYRI
      11,1381 .... H 292

PAUSANIAS (fl. circa 150 A.D.)
   Description of Greece
      2,27,3 .... H 266
      6,26,1 .... H 259

PROPER NAMES IN STORIES

BIBLIOGRAPHY

On Narrative

R. Alter, *The Art of Biblical Narrative* (New York: Basic Books, 1981). (See *JSOT* 27 (1983).)

H. Frei, *The Eclipse of Biblical Narrative* (New Haven: Yale University Press, 1974).

G. Green (ed.), *Scriptural Authority and Narrative Interpretation* (Philadelphia: Fortress Press, 1987).

F. McConnell (ed.), *The Bible and the Narrative Tradition* (New York: Oxford University Press, 1986).

P. Ricoeur, *The Rule of Metaphor. Multidisciplinary Studies of the Creation of Meaning in Language* (Toronto: University of Toronto Press, 1975).

P. Ricoeur, *Temp et Récit*, Vol. 3 (Paris: Seuil, 1985).

P. Ricoeur, *Time and Narrative*, ET Vols. 1 and 2 (Chicago: University of Chicago Press, 1984/85).

R. Scholes and R. Kellog, *The Nature of Narrative* (New York: Oxford University Press, 1966).

M. Sternberg, *The Poetics of Biblical Narrative: Ideological Literature and the Drama of Reading* (Indiana Literary Biblical Series) (Bloomington: Indiana University Press, 1985).

Old Testament

M.E. Boismard, "Elie dans le Nouveau Testament," in, *Elie le Prophète*, Vol. 1 (Etudes Carmélitaines) (Desclée de Brouwer, 1956) 116-28.

B. Botte, "La vie de Moïse. L'Homme de l'Alliance (Cahiers Sioniens 8 (1954)) 55-62.

G.W. Coats, *Rebellion in the Wilderness* (Nashville: Abingdon Press, 1968).

G. Fohrer, *Elia* (ATANT,31) (Zürich: Zwingli, 1957).

J. Gager, *Moses in Greco-Roman Paganism* (SBL Monograph Series, 16) (Nashville: Abingdon Press, 1972).

L. Ginzberg, *The Legends of the Jews*, 7 vols. (Philadelphia: The Jewish Publication Society of America, 1909-38).

C.H. Holladay, *THEIOS ANER in Hellenistic Judaism: A Critique of the Use of This Category in New Testament Christology* (SBL Dissertation Series, 40) (Missoula: Scholars Press, 1977). [Studies the concept in Josephus, Philo, and Artapanus.]

W.A. Meeks, *The Prophet-King: Moses Traditions and the Johannine Christology* (NT Supp., 14) Leiden: E.J. Brill, 1967).

J. Van Seters, *Abraham in History and Tradition* (New Haven: Yale University Press, 1975).

Rabbinic Literature

D. Ben-Amos, *Narrative Forms in the Haggadah: Structural Analysis* (Unpublished Dissertation, Indiana University, 1967) (Ann Arbor: University Microfilms Inc.).

A. Büchler, *Types of Jewish-Palestine Piety from 70 B.C.E. to 70 C.E.*, Reprint (New York: Ktav, 1968).

P. Fiebig, *Der Erzählungsstil der Evangelien im Lichte der rabbinischen Erzählungsstil* (UNT,11) (Leipzig: Hinrichs, 1925).

H. Fischel, *Rabbinic Literature and Greco-Roman Philosophy. A Study of Epicurea and Rhetoric in Early Midrashic Writings* (Studia Post Biblica,21) (Leiden: E.J. Brill, 1973).

J. Heinemann and D. Noy (eds.), *Studies in Aggadah and Folk-Literature* (Scripta Hierosolymitana,22) (Jerusalem: Magnes Press, Hebrew University, 1971).

M. Hengel, *Judaism and Hellenism* (ET London: SCM, 1974).

G.F. Moore, *Judaism in the First Centuries of the Christian Era*, Reprint (New York: Schocken Books, 1971).

J. Neusner, *Development of a Legend: Studies on the Traditions Concerning Yohann Ben Zakkai* (Studia Post Biblica,16) (Leiden: E.J. Brill, 1970).

J. Neusner, "From Exegesis to Fable in Rabbinic Traditions about the Pharisees," *JJS* 25 (1974) 263-69.

L. Sabourin, "Hellenistic and Rabbinic Miracles," *BTB* 2 (1972) 281-307.

A. Saldarini, " 'Form Criticism' of Rabbinic Literature," *JBL* 96 (1977) 257-74.

G.B. Sarfatti, "Pious Men, Men of Deed and the Early Prophets," (Heb.) *Tarbiz* 26 (1956/57) 126-53.

H. Strack, *Introduction to the Talmud and Midrash*, ET Reprint (New York: Meridian Books, 1963).

H. Strack, P. Billerbeck, *Kommentar zum Neue Testament. AUS Talmud und Midrasch*, 5 vols. (München: Beck, 7th ed., 1978).

G. Vermes, *Post-Biblical Jewish Studies* (Studies in Judaism and Late Antiquity,8) (Leiden: E.J. Brill, 1973).

Hellenistic Literature

L. Bieler, *Theios Aner*, Reprint of 1935/36 ed. (Darmstadt: Wissenschaftliche Buchgesellschaft, 1967).

M. Braun, *History and Romance in Graeco-Oriental Literature* (Oxford: Blackwell, 1938).

P. Cox, *Biography in Late Antiquity: A Quest for the Holy Man* (Berkeley: University of California Press, 1983).

E.R. Dodds, *Pagan and Christian in an Age of Anxiety*, Reprint (New York: Norton, 1970).

M. Hadas, *A History of Greek Literature* (New York: Columbia University, paperback ed., 1965).

A.D. Nock, *Essays on Religion and the Ancient World*, (ed.) Z. Stewart (Oxford: Clarendon, 1972).

R. Rattenbury, "Romance: The Greek Novel," in, J. Powell (ed.), *New Chapters in the History of Greek Literature* (Third Series) (Oxford: Clarendon, 1933) 211-57.

R. Reitzenstein, *Hellenistiche Wundererzählungen*, Reprint of 1906 ed. (Darmstadt: Wissenschaftliche Buchgesellschaft, 1963).

M. Simon, *Hercule et le christianisme* (Strasbourg: Université de Strasbourg, 1955).

R. Tannehill (ed.), *Pronouncement Stories, Semeia* 20 (1981).

V. Tcherikover, *Hellenistic Civilization and the Jews*, Reprint (New York: Atheneum, 1970).

D. Tiede, *The Charismatic Figure as Miracle Worker*, (SBL Dissertation Series,1) (Missoula: Scholars Press, 1972).

S. Tuck, *The Form and Function of Sayings-Material in Hellenistic Biographies of Philosophers* (Unpublished Dissertation, Harvard University, 1985) (Ann Arbor: University Microfilms International).

O. Weinreich, *Antike Heilungswunder* (Religionsgeschichtliche Versuche und Vorarbeiten 8/1) (Giessen: Töpelmann, 1909).

The Lover of Lies. Loeb 3 (tr. A.M. Harmon) (1921).

Pausanias, *Description of Greece.* Loeb 3 (tr. W.H.S. Jones and H.A. Ormerod) (1933).

Philo, *On Abraham.* Loeb 6 (tr. F.H. Colson) (1935).

On the Creation—Allegorical Interpretation of Genesis II and III. Loeb 1 (tr. F.H. Colson and G.H Whitaker) (1929).

Life of Moses. Loeb 6 (tr. F.H. Colson) (1935).

Philostratus, *Life of Apollonius of Tyana.* Loeb 1, 2 (tr. F.C. Conybeare) (1912).

Lives of the Sophists (tr. W.C. Wright) (1921).

Pliny, *Natural History.* Loeb 2 (tr. H. Rackham) (1942); Loeb 7 (tr. W.H.S. Jones) (1956).

Plutarch, *Agis and Cleomenes.* Loeb 10 (tr. B. Perrin) (1921).

The Fortune of Alexander. Loeb, *Moralia* 4 (tr. F.C. Babbitt) (1936).

Life of Alexander. Loeb 7 (tr. B. Perrin) (1919).

Life of Pericles. Loeb 3 (tr. B. Perrin) (1916).

Life of Pyrrhus. Loeb 9 (tr. B. Perrin) (1920).

Life of Solon. Loeb 1 (tr. B. Perrin) (1914).

On Socrates' Daimon. Loeb, *Moralia* 7 (tr. P.H. De Lacy and B. Einarson) (1959).

Strabo, *Geography.* Loeb 6 (tr. H.L. Jones) (1924); Loeb 8 (tr. H.L. Jones) (1932).

Suetonius, *Life of Augustus.* Loeb 1 (tr. J.C. Rolfe) (1914; rev. 1951).

Vespasian. Loeb 2 (tr. J.C. Rolfe) (1914).

Tacitus, *History.* Loeb 2 (tr. C.H. Moore) (1925).

Xenophon, *Memorabilia* (tr. E.C. Marchant) (1923).